ENGLISH GLASS FOR THE COLLECTOR, 1660–1860

By the same Author:
  LIVING CRAFTS

By Bernard and Therle Hughes:
  THREE CENTURIES OF ENGLISH DOMESTIC SILVER
  AFTER THE REGENCY
  ENGLISH PORCELAIN AND BONE CHINA
  THE COLLECTOR'S ENCYCLOPAEDIA OF ENGLISH CERAMICS

By Therle Hughes:
  OLD ENGLISH FURNITURE

FRONTISPIECE

Flute with trumpet-shaped bowl, height 18 inches; covered goblet with domed cover and crown finial, facet-cut knopped stem, height 17 inches; toddy serving rummer, its bucket bowl engraved with rose and thistle motifs around the sign of the Golden Lion, Boston, and with the owner's name C. F. Barber in script.

G. BERNARD HUGHES

ENGLISH GLASS
FOR THE COLLECTOR
1660–1860

LUTTERWORTH PRESS
LONDON

First published 1958
Reprinted 1967
Third impression 1969

7188 0267 5

PRINTED IN GREAT BRITAIN
PHOTOLITHO BY EBENEZER BAYLIS AND SON, LTD.
THE TRINITY PRESS, WORCESTER, AND LONDON

CONTENTS

CONTENTS

LIST OF ILLUSTRATIONS

Flute with trumpet-shaped bowl, covered goblet with domed cover, and toddy serving rummer (*in the collection of Lady Bromet*) *Frontispiece*

7

LIST OF ILLUSTRATIONS

11

LINE ILLUSTRATIONS

Chapter One

THE Syrians were making glass 4,500 years ago and to them the world is indebted for the most significant discovery of all in its development—the art of blowing molten glass into hollow forms with the aid of a metal tube, slightly belled at one end. This occurred during the first century B.C. The glass was blown into moulds incised with elaborate patterns, a single earthenware mould being used with each object blown. Word of the new process soon reached Egypt where luxury glass, almost translucent, was being made. Within a few years the Egyptian glassmen were blowing hollow bulbs on the end of blow-pipes and tooling them into vessels of varying forms.

Glass-blowing soon became a staple industry throughout the Roman Empire. In addition to costly ware the Romans produced vast quantities of inexpensive household glass tinged blue or green, the colour deepening in proportion to the quantity of impurities in the sand. Two centuries of experiment passed before it was learned that iron tints could be cleared by the addition of manganese oxide. It was also discovered that certain proportions of this mineral gave glass a yellow or a wine-coloured tint, and that cobalt made it blue. Furnaces were set up near to natural deposits of sand. In Britain the Romans established a glasshouse at Wilderspool, Warrington, less than ten miles from St. Helens, a centre of the modern industry.

Vessels of a coarse, bluish-green tinted glass for domestic use continued to be made after the Roman withdrawal, the craft eventually establishing itself at Chiddingfold, Surrey. A medieval glasshouse was worked by a single experienced glassman assisted by three or four labourers to do the manual work. It was essential to the glassman that he should work in a suitable sand-bearing area in the neighbourhood of a growing beechwood, which was preferred for preparing charcoal to heat the furnace, and where bracken and glasswort grew in sufficient quantities to supply the essential potash.

The Venetians meanwhile were evolving a lightweight glass from which they blew fragile drinking vessels and ornamental hollow-ware decorated with applied filigree work, colours and gilding. The Grand Council of Venice granted privileges to these glassworkers approaching the rights of nobility. On the other hand, these men were "exiled" to the island of Murano, the better to guard their trade secrets. For the divulgence of these secrets the Council administered a wide range of punishments from a term in the galleys to death by hanging from the gallows by one foot. An extensive trade in this beautiful glass was transacted with England from early in the sixteenth century: distance and breakage in transit, however, made Venetian glass a costly luxury, greatly to be treasured. Henry VIII assembled a collection of about three hundred coloured pieces.

The earliest successful artificer in England of delicate transparent glass was Giacomo Verzelini, a Venetian invited to London in about 1570 for the purpose of establishing a glasshouse to manufacture fine table-ware. Upon the proprietor's death a year later Verzelini acquired the business and within four years was selling glass-ware praised by contemporary records as equalling that of Murano. Elizabeth I then granted him a twenty-one-year monopoly to manufacture Anglo-Venetian glass. The contract stipulated that the drinking-glasses should be as cheap or cheaper than those imported from Murano; that no similar glasses should be blown within the Queen's dominions; that Englishmen should be taught the craft. Soon Verzelini received the newly-created office of "Glass-maker to the Queen", his staff embodying about twenty glass-blowers with their appropriate assistants and labourers, probably one hundred and fifty in all. In 1592 he retired a very rich man.

Shortage of beechwood charcoal to heat the small open melting pots, as yet little more capacious than those used in

Plate 1
Drinking glasses: (*top*) with light baluster and knopped stems; (*centre*) plain, knopped and silesian stems; (*bottom*) plain, air-twist, opaque-white-twist and facet-cut stems.

Plate 2
(*Top*) Drinking glasses including two firing glasses and a mercury twist. (*Centre*) Drinking glasses with air-twist and opaque-white-twist stems. (*Bottom*) Tankards, a taper decanter, a syllabub glass (*front left*), a boot puzzle glass, a tumbler and a jelly glass.

ancient Egypt, was always a major problem with Verzelini. Experiments with coal in 1586 proved that the advantage of higher temperature was outweighed by discoloration in the glass. A quarter of a century later Sir William Slyngsby evolved a coal-burning glass furnace capable of melting the glass in covered pots which protected the molten metal from chemical fumes. Its success was such that in 1615 the use of wood fuel was prohibited in glasshouses.

The entire English glass industry in 1618 became the monopoly of Vice-Admiral Sir Robert Mansell, M.P. for King's Lynn. He operated establishments in twenty centres distributed throughout the country, making Anglo-Venetian wares, coarse drinking-glasses and table-ware, bottles, window-glass and mirror plates. In 1624 the House of Commons was informed that Mansell directly employed four thousand men and women and sold licences to others.

Little if any improvement was made in the production of blown table-glass until 1674, when George Ravenscroft was granted a seven-year patent for "manufacturing a sort of crystaline glass resembling rock crystal" (No. 176, May 16, 1674). Clear transparent black flints, calcined, crushed and sifted, formed the silica. Mansell had made it known in 1620 that the ingredients for his fine table-ware included calcined pebbles of flint imported from Northern Italy. The introduction of flint, then, was not the sole reason for granting Ravenscroft his patent.

Ravenscroft named his new glass "fflint crystalline" and the purchase of such ware is recorded in the Duke of Bedford's bills a few days before the patent was granted. The Glass-sellers' Company undertook to market Ravenscroft's entire output provided he worked to their standard designs. Unfortunately, within a few months of manufacture the glass gradually displayed the defect known to collectors as crizzling. This devitrification caused the glass to lose its transparency.

Lead oxide was then introduced in the autumn of 1675, creating the most practical glass yet evolved. The effect of the lead was to make the metal softer, that is, it was more easy to scratch, more malleable, and its refractive power was increased enormously. At the same time its melting point was considerably reduced. The lead made the metal heavier and gave it a dark hue. If over-leaded the glass was later affected by the atmosphere: this resulted in a greyish dullness on its surface, not infrequent on glass made earlier than the 1730s.

Ravenscroft's glass-of-lead was not his own invention. *L'arte Vetraria* by A. Neri, 1612 (translated into English by Christopher Merret, 1662), informed its readers that "glass-of-lead, known to few, is the finest and noblest glass of all others at this day, made in the furnace". The Glass-sellers' Company certified the new metal as wholly successful with the added "distinction of sound [the resonant ring heard when hollow-ware was flicked with thumb and finger] enabling it to be discerned by any person". To enable his glass-of-lead to be distinguished from his earlier productions Ravenscroft marked each piece with a small glass seal impressed with a raven's head as borne on the Ravenscroft coat of arms.

The *London Gazette*, on October 25, 1677, and on other occasions, contained the following advertisement inserted by Ravenscroft: "In pursuance of a former Advertisement concerning the amendment and durability of Flint Glasses, and for entire assurance of such as shall buy any marked with the Raven's Head either from the Glass-House situate in the Savoy on the Riverside, or from Shop-keepers who shall aver to have had them from the said Glass-House. It is further offered and declared, That in case any of the aforesaid Glasses shall happen to crizel or decay (as once they did) they shall be ready changed by the said Shop-keepers or at the above said Glass-House, or the Money returned to the content of the Party agrieved, with his Charges also, if they shall have been sent into the Country, or beyond seas to any remoter parts of the World."

Ravenscroft died in 1681, a few days after the expiry of his patent, and other glasshouses at once began to issue flint-glass. The glassmen accustomed to blowing each glass from a single gathering of smooth-flowing, quick-cooling soda-glass were confronted with a new technique. In flint-glass four gatherings of metal were required, one on top of the other. This resulted in heavy, thick-sectioned hollow-ware, usually sold to the glass-sellers by weight.

Two qualities of flint-glass are recorded from the early 1680s until early in the nineteenth century; advertisements consistently refer to them. At first they were known as thick and thin; then as double and single flint-glass.

It has long been stated by writers on glass that double and single represented the number of gathers of molten glass taken up by the blowing iron. Descriptions of flint-glass blowing throughout the eighteenth century, however, are consistent in stating that four gathers were lifted from the pot. The real difference between double and single flint-glass was that the double contained almost twice as much lead as the single. The latter could be blown to a section approximately half that of the more durable double flint-glass. It was also harder, lighter in weight, without veins, of greater clarity, but possessed less refractive power.

Calculations from bills and advertisement prices show that a dozen wine-glasses in single flint-glass at fourteen to the dozen weighed less than a dozen of equal shape and capacity in double flint-glass at twelve to the dozen. Cullet, that is, broken flint-glass, was advertised for by glass-makers throughout the eighteenth century and its price at $2\frac{1}{2}d.$ or $3d.$ per lb. at various periods implied double flint-glass: advertisements for single flint-glass cullet were infrequent. An advertisement quoted by Westropp from *Faulkiner's Dublin Journal*, January 1746, ended: "N.B. All double flint-glasses, decanters, water-glasses and saucers at seven pence per lb. weight, the single flint wine-glasses at two shillings and four pence, fourteen to the dozen. . . . In exchange will be allowed for double flint broken glass twopence halfpenny per lb., and for single one penny halfpenny per lb."

An improvement in the preparation of lead oxide was made during the late 1690s, freeing it of some of the impurities which blackened the tint of the glass. The resulting flint-glass was considerably clearer in hue than formerly. *The Flying Post*, January 27, 1700, recorded that "the Lytharge commonly called Gold and Lytharge of Silver, made by the Adventurers in the Mine Adventure, by virtue of a Patent lately granted by His Majesty to one Mr. Robert Lydall, now chief operator to the said Company, is made so clean and pure without mixture; and is of such a soft, oiley nature, that it far exceeds all Foreign Lytharge, and is of singular Use for all Potters in glazing Earthen Ware, and for all Makers of fine Glass, and hath been approved by the most eminent Potters and Glass-makers about London, who now use the same in the place and stead of Lead calcined, Lead Ashes, and Red Lead. These are therefore to give Notice, That any person has occasion for such Lytharge, may be furnished by the Company of the Mine-Adventurers at a reasonable Rate: a sample whereof, with a paper on the Nature and Use of Lytharge, and of the Advantages thereof above Lead calcined, Lead-Ashes and Red Lead, may be had at that office in Lincoln's Inn New Square Number Eleven." Litharge was more costly than red lead and used only in the manufacture of fine table-ware.

Masses of tiny air-bubbles, so minute as to resemble sand specks, disfigured the early flint-glass. This resulted from inability to raise furnace heat high enough to eliminate all the air trapped among the grains of raw materials. Increased furnace heat was required to overcome this problem, and for the next century and a half progressive technical improvements in furnace construction were reflected in the quality of the glass. The first of these improvements was the introduction of Savory's double hand-bellows, first applied experimentally to a London glasshouse furnace in 1705 and improved by D. Papin. These bellows contained an interior fan furnishing greater blast than had formerly been possible, raising the furnace fire to greater heat and enabling higher fusing temperatures to be achieved. The Savory bellows were standard equipment in London glass-houses by 1710, enabling a full-bodied, dark, clear, lustrous glass to be manufactured. This glass, when containing litharge, feels almost greasy to the touch. The intensity of its dark hue was never consistent.

There was no major change in manufacturing technique until 1734. Glass-furnace design was revolutionized in that year when Humphrey Perrott of Bristol was granted a patent for a furnace which provided increased blast and temperature and made possible the use of more capacious melting pots. Considerable capital was required to build such a glasshouse. Each furnace cost about £3,500 to build, seldom lasted as long as three years, and required lengthy refitting every three months. The clay melting pots were liable to burst in the furnace, causing a loss in time and materials of about £250.

Glasshouses now became extensive premises where every process in glass production was performed, the glass-blower, as today, being the most important craftsman. A glasshouse was now divided into ten separate departments providing accommodation for: (1) grinding old melting pots (a horse-mill), these pots being an ingredient used in making new pots; (2) mixing and kneading powdered clays into a workable mass; (3) making the pots; (4) drying the pots; (5) washing, preparing, and storing the potash; (6) washing and drying the sand; (7) mixing together sand, potash and oxides; (8) the glasshouse with its furnaces; (9) the annealing oven (later the tunnel leer and receiving room); (10) cutting and engraving shops.

A glass-blowing team, known as a "chair", usually consisted of four operators, gaffer, servitor, foot-maker and taker-in, each playing an individual part in the making of a single glass vessel. The gaffer had complete control over his "chair", directing operations and carrying out the most important processes.

The method of making Georgian glass is described in *The Universal Dictionary of Arts and Sciences*, 1751 : "In working the glass the workman dips his blowing pipe into the melting pot, and by turning it about, the metal sticks to the iron more firmly than turpentine. This he repeats four times, at each time rolling the end of his instrument with the hot metal thereon, on a piece of iron under which is a vessel of water which helps to cool, and so to consolidate more firmly with what is to be taken next out of the melting pot. But after he has dipped a fourth time, and the workman perceives that there is metal enough on the pipe, he claps his mouth immediately to the other end of it, and blows gently through the iron tube, till the metal lengthens like a bladder, about a foot.

"Then he rolls it on a marble stone a little while to polish it, and blows a second time, by which he brings it to the shape of a globe, of about 18 inches or 20 inches circumference. Every time he blows into the pipe he removes it quickly to his cheek, otherwise he would be in danger, by often blowing, of drawing the flame into his mouth. This globe may be flattened by returning it to the fire, and brought into any form by stamp irons, which are always ready.

"When the glass is blown, it is cut off at the collet or neck, which is the narrow part that is stuck to the iron. To do this the pipe is rested on an iron bar, close by the collet, it will crack about a quarter of an inch, which with a light blow, or cut with the shears, will immediately separate the collet.

"After this is done the operator dips the iron rod or punty iron into the melting pot by which he extracts as much metal as serves to attract the glass he has made, to which he now fixes this rod at the bottom of his work opposite to the opening made by the breaking of the collet.

"In this position the glass is carried to the great bocca, or mouth of the oven to be heated and scalded by which means it is again put into such a soft state, that by the help of an iron instrument it can be pierced, opened, and widened without breaking. But the vessel is not finished till it is returned to the great bocca, where it being again heated thoroughly and turned quickly about with a circular motion, it will open to any size, by means of the heat and motion. By this means we come to learn the cause why the edges of all bowls and glasses are thicker than the other parts of the same glasses. Because, in the turning it about in the heat, the edge thickens, and, the glass being as it were doubled in that part, the circumference appears like a selvage. If there remain any superfluities they were cut off with shears; for, till the glass is cool, it remains in a soft flexible state.

"It is therefore taken from the bocca, and carried to an earthen bench covered with brands, which are [char]coals extinguished, keeping it turning. Because that motion prevents any settling, and preserves an evenness in the face of the glass; where, as it cools, it comes to its consistency,

Plate 3
Sweetmeat glass with domed foot of exceptionally large diameter to ensure stability on the dessert table; heavy baluster stem; bowl blown-moulded with all-over diamond pattern; early eighteenth century.

Plate 4

Wine-glasses: (*Upper left*) Pointed funnel bowl engraved with flowers, tears in centre of three knops, domed foot, height 6⅛ inches. (*Upper centre*) Bell bowl, tears in baluster stem, welted foot; height 6 inches. (*Upper right*) Pointed funnel bowl, heavy ball-knopped stem, welted foot; height 5 inches. (*Lower left*) Conical bowl, baluster stem with tear, domed and welted foot; height 9 inches. (*Lower centre*) Lipped bowl with gilded rim, long tear in knopped stem, domed foot; height 8¼ inches. (*Lower right*) Funnel bowl, tear in heavy baluster stem, domed and welted foot; height 8¼ inches. About 1690s.

being first cleared from the iron rod, by a slight stroke with the hand of the workman.

"Feet or handles are made separate and joined by the help of hot metal, which is taken out of the pot with his iron rod. But the glass is not brought to its true hardness, till it has passed the leer or annealing oven."

Annealing was essential to toughen the glass, but until the end of the eighteenth century this process was imperfectly understood. Vessels were often so shaped that stresses and strains were involved that caused a great amount of breakage in cooling, in stock and in the course of use. These defects were recorded in various petitions against the Excise Act of 1695 now preserved in the British Museum. Without annealing the glass would fly with the slightest change of temperature.

Until the 1740s flint-glass was annealed in a kiln or oven, a unit built apart from the furnace. The glass manufactured during the day's run was placed in this, fire being maintained to keep the glass hot. When filled the ovens were sealed and the mass allowed to cool. Small glasshouses annealed by oven until early in the nineteenth century.

It has been stated frequently and wrongly that the tunnel leer was introduced in 1780 to English glasshouses by George Ensall of Stourbridge, the tale being that he disguised himself as a travelling fiddler and visited German glasshouses, thus discovering the secret of the tunnel leer, and narrowly escaped with his life. This entirely fictional story is disproved by the fact that as early as 1745 the Royal Society discussed the tunnel leer. Their *Transactions* for that year state that the glass was "passed very gradually in the space of some hours, through what is called the leer, from a very intense degree of heat to the temperature of the common air. Such glass is found to acquire such a toughness and tenacity as fitted them for use." The annealing tunnel is here shown to have been already in use, but was obviously a new process to be worthy of discussion by a learned society.

A trade card issued in 1748 by Brent and Lowe, now in the collection of Sir Ambrose Heal, states that: "At ye Old Barge House, opposite the Temple in the County of Surry . . . all glass made at this House is Double Anneal'd; no other has had conveniences for that purpose though the most effectual way to make it durable and fit for exportation." The tunnel leer had for long been in use in German glasshouses—the term "leer" is taken from the German *leer ofen*, meaning empty furnace.

The Universal Dictionary of Arts and Sciences, 1751, recorded that the tunnel leer was in considerable use by English glassmen and described the process: "The tunnel is about five or six yards long . . . the glasses are put in with a fork and set on the floor or bottom, but they are drawn out in iron pans, called fraches, through the leer to cool by degrees, so that they are quite cold by the time they reach the mouth of the leer, which enters the room where the glasses are to be stored." In double annealing the cycle was repeated. The operator judged the temperature only by the appearance of the firebrick walls or the length of time taken for a wad of paper to ignite when thrown in at the hot end.

An improved leer was introduced by George Ensall in about 1780: this secret did not penetrate to the German glasshouses until about 1815. With this leer glass-ware of considerable thickness could be annealed and afterwards withstand cutting in deep relief: the heat of the tunnel at the entrance was much greater than required for annealing thin glass or small pieces. (See Chapter 12.)

The fire was situated beneath one end of the leer and the glass removed at a temperature little warmer than the outside air. The gradual way in which the glass cooled allowed the whole to contract into a uniform and consistent substance. The use of the leer was made compulsory by the Excise Act of 1810 and each leer had to be licensed at a cost of £100.

Many writers on flint-glass have considered the Excise Act of 1745 to have been responsible for an immediate increase in the price of table-glass and a decrease in the weight and size of individual pieces. This Act imposed a tax of 9s. 4d. per cwt. on the raw materials used in the manufacture of flint-glass. It may have discouraged waste in the glasshouse, but following as it did closely on the heels of the Perrott furnace and the tunnel leer, it had virtually no effect on prices and none at all on form.

The improved glass made possible by the Perrott furnace was more manipulative than the earlier slow-moving metal, permitting the glassworker to make the more delicate styles long wished for by the trade and public alike. More pieces of glass could now be produced from each pot of metal than formerly. Undecorated flint-glass increased in price per pound only because of the labour involved in producing a greater number of lighter pieces. In 1746 when the Excise Act became operative best undecorated flint-glass was advertised by the glass-sellers at 9*d*. per lb.; by 1752 the price had risen to 10*d*. per lb.

The new metal—new only in manipulative properties—brought a rapid development in ornament, with engraving, enamelling and cutting and stems of filigree spiralwork. Decorated flint-glass was sold by glass-sellers by the dozen, price depending upon the amount of ornament put into each piece.

Contradicting the opinion of many authorities, academic and otherwise, it must be emphasized that more than one quality of metal was produced from a single pot. Metal taken from the top of the molten mass was known as tale and ware made from this was sold at about two-thirds the price of the ordinary quality glass fashioned out of metal taken from the lower part of the pot. Also in the same furnace were piling pots, each capable of holding about 100 lb. of "a finer and more nice metal, fit for the nicest works". Coloured glass, such as Bristol blue, green and red, was also prepared in piling pots.

Under the Glass Excise Act of 1745 cullet, that is, broken flint-glass, was not accounted as a raw material, and so many wasters were produced that the amount of cullet might exceed half the weight of the batch. The figures are: a tax of one penny on raw materials, with certain allowances for waste and half the amount in cullet, would amount to less than a halfpenny on table-glass weighing less than one pound. On a dozen wine-glasses weighing four ounces each, 3 lb. the lot, the tax might be 1½*d*. Surely no reason to bring about drastic changes in form.

A statute of 1777 doubled the glass tax which was now levied upon "materials or metal [cullet] that shall be made

PRICES OF FLINT GLASS,

1829.

	per s.	s.	d.
ANTIGUGLARS, see Funnels			
Apparatus		2	6
BASINS, blue for Sugar, Tale		1	4
Ditto, ditto edged		1	8
Ditto, oval, with flat covers		8	0
Baskets with handles		2	6
Bell Glasses, for Flower, half pint and under		1	9
Ditto, larger		2	6
Bee Hives and covers		1	8
Bird Boxes, uncut		1	4
Bowls on feet			
Bottles, moulded best flint for patent medicine, perfumery, &c. weighing two oz. and under		8	0
Ditto above 2 oz		1	8
Basins, moulded clear blown, weighing 8 oz. and under		2	1
Ditto above 2 oz		1	9
Ditto, ordinary metal moulded for patent Medicine, Perfumery, &c. weighing under half an ounce each		8	8
Ditto 1 oz and under 1 oz		2	2
Ditto, 1 oz and under 3 oz		1	1
Ditto, 2 oz do 4 oz		1	1
Ditto, 4 oz do 8 oz		1	8
Green 1d per lb under			
Breast Pipes		2	6
Butter Boats, with Handles		1	8
Basins, Covers, and Plates			
CADDY Bottles			
Cake Shades or Figure Shades		1	6
Cans, Solid Flint		8	6
Cans, Lemonade, Best		2	0
Ditto, do		0	10
Candlesticks		1	10
Ditto for Shades		1	0
Ditto handled		1	10
Caraffs		1	6
Caraffs as decanters			
Ditto Stopper, ring tops		2	6
Celery Glasses, no feet		1	6
Ditto, ringed do		1	8
Ditto, on feet		1	10
Ditto, do. ringed			
Chimney and Moons all sizes and shapes weighing 2½ oz and under		2	6
Ditto above 2½ oz		2	0
Champagne, as Piano			

	per s.	s.	d.
Fountains		2	0
Funnels, common		1	7
Ditto, Green		2	0
Ditto bent or Antigular		2	0
Ditto, lining		1	11
Funnel perdue			
Ditto, ring tops		1	8
GOBLETS, tale plain Stem, all sizes		1	4
Ditto, button Stem no morsse		1	5
Ditto do mule			
Ditto, best plain stem, weighing 10 oz and under		1	7
Ditto, above 10 oz		1	8
Ditto, and covers			
Ditto, best button Stem weighing 10 oz and under		1	6
Ditto, above 10 oz		2	0
Ditto, thistle and ringbowl		19	0
Godfrey's, green, ——per Gross			
Ditto, white do		20	0
HUNGARYS, green, per lb		1	4
Ditto, white		1	5
Hemispheres for French Lamps		1	10
Ditto do Sincumbras		1	11
Hock Glasses, common shape, 2d per lb more than Wines			
Ditto threaded and pruned, 1s. per lb more than Wines			
JARS, best		1	8
Ditto, common for pickle, or the over Rounds		1	5
Ditto, green		1	4
Jellies, best		1	2
Ditto, button Stem		2	0
Ditto, tale		2	2
Jeweller's Globes and Tops		2	10
Ice cups tale		2	11
Ditto, tale		1	9
Ice plates		1	10
Inkt, best		1	8
Inkt, Wedgewood		2	6
Ink fountains			
Ditto, for every extra nozzle 4d per lb additional			
Inks, tale round or square		1	9
Ditto, green		1	6
Ditto, Eccleman		2	8
Ink Cistern and Sand Cups		2	7

	per s.	s.	d.
RETORTS and Receivers, like weight and upwards		1	6
do muller		1	8
do subulated		2	8
Root Glasses		1	6
Rounds and Stoppers, ½ oz measure and under		2	8
do 1 and 2 oz		2	0
do 3 and 4		2	0
do 5 and 8			
Rounds specie mouths the same as Rounds and Stoppees		1	6
Rounds, preparation, 1d per pound more than do			
do do oval 2d per lb do			
SALVERS		2	0
Salts, blow over oz, moulded, uncut		1	4
do for cutting		1	4
do tops blown off		1	4
Salts, cut, or plain cut		1	1
do, with or without feet		1	10
Salt and Soap Lining		1	0
Salt and Smelling Bottles, common		2	4
Shades for Figures		1	6
do India		1	4
do Ceiling		1	10
do do with Rings		1	10
Shaving Glasses		1	2
Sharp Drams			
do Coburg shape, as Wines			
Show Glasses, on feet and covers			
Smelling Glasses, pinched		1	6
Do do lapidary and for cutting; 1 oz weight and under			
do do under 2 oz weight		2	6
do do above 2 oz		2	0
do do ringed		2	0
Square, best, with Stoppers, and do for Medicine Chests			
Containing ½ oz measure and under, per lb		2	8
——1 oz and 2 oz	ditto	2	4
——3 oz and 4 oz	ditto	2	0
——6 oz and 8 oz	ditto	1	7
——12 oz	ditto	1	8
——16 oz	ditto	1	6
Stochinger's Globes			
Sweetmeats, double, as Salts		1	9
Syllabub, best		1	6
do tale		2	8
Sugar Basins, for cutting, with or without		2	7

COLOURED GLASS 1d der lb extra.—Allowance for Cullet 12s. per cwt.

LEEDS PRINTED AT THE PATRIOT-OFFICE, BY JOHN FOSTER,

List of flint-glass prices issued by the manufacturers, September 1st, 1829, adopted as a net list for the country trade and subject to a discount of ten per cent to the London dealers. In 1833 the price of coloured glass was raised to twopence per pound.

use of in the making of all flint-glass". In spite of this increased duty and because of the new design in leers, flint-glass table-ware began gradually to increase in weight and new forms were evolved. The tax itself had now become a serious matter. By 1820 the excise duty on glass had been raised to 10½d. per lb. The duty was abolished in 1845.

During the second half of the eighteenth century there were progressive improvements in the clarity that could be achieved in flint-glass as chemical processes were applied to remove certain impurities contained in the ingredients. For instance, in 1785 talc earth was mixed with Stourbridge clay to make the melting pots resistant to the effects of the lead oxide. Metal worked from such pots produced distinctly clearer table-ware. Records prove the immediate use of such pots in the Stourbridge, Dudley and Birmingham areas and at Waterford.

The glass furnace so far was heated directly by the fires situated close to the chamber containing the pots. This allowed a light ash to be carried into the chamber which had an adverse effect on the hue of the metal contained in the covered pots. The defect was overcome by the introduction of the Donaldson furnace, patented in 1802 and first installed by Ricketts, Evans & Co. of Bristol. The patent claimed that this furnace used only one-third of the amount of fuel formerly needed, yet provided such intense heat that the materials fused in half the time and, for the first time, a crystal-clear glass could be produced in the piling pots. This invention was not immediately effective throughout the flint-glass trade, but when a furnace needed replacing a Donaldson furnace was usually installed. W. S. Wheeley of Brettell Lane, Stourbridge, further improved the glass furnace in 1824, producing "a glass of purity and crystalline appearance".

In the glass furnaces so far described impurities rose at the sides of the pots and flowed towards the centre, "causing a quantity of scum commonly called stones or cordes on the surface of the metal, rendering it necessary to be skimmed from time to time". This was overcome by the Bacchus patent of 1834.

That flint-glass had not been fully cleared even by the

mid-nineteenth century is shown by the *Reports of the Juries, Exhibition, 1851.* Here it is recorded that "English manufacturers have lately been making important experiments with a view to discovering a method of producing glass free from tint and striae", and that English flint-glass "is charged with the defect of colour, of striae, of globules, and of undulations".

When Albert Hartshorne wrote in *Old English Glasses,* 1897, that "Waterford glass is usually to be distinguished by its pale blue tinge" he started a legend that has persisted for sixty years. Even though Westropp, in *Irish Glass,* 1920, emphatically denied that there was "a distinctive blue tint" associated with Waterford, the canard continued. Mrs. Graydon Stannus, however, in a lecture on *Irish Glass* delivered to a distinguished audience at the Royal Society of Arts in 1925, produced a number of marked Waterford specimens for inspection. Every example displayed this blue tint.

The truth is that this peculiar depth of tone is found in a large percentage of flint-glass—English and Irish alike—made before 1810. Its presence is due to the fact that the lead oxide used in this glass was manufactured from lead mined in Derbyshire. Flint-glass workers in the 1760s had noticed that lead oxide prepared from Derbyshire lead possessed characteristics which greatly improved the quality of their flint-glass. It also contained an impurity, well known to the glass industry of the period, which gave a faintly bluish tint to the glass. This was recognized as a defect which for long chemists had endeavoured to eradicate. In every other respect Derbyshire lead oxide was preferred to that found elsewhere.

This tint, known at the time as Derby blue, was eliminated from red lead processed by the firm of Blair & Stephenson, Tipton, Staffordshire, in 1810. They naturally supplied all the Stourbridge, Dudley, Birmingham and Warrington glasshouses with their improved red lead and even despatched supplies to Waterford. From 1815 every firm of repute was using red lead from Tipton. The manufacture of this processed lead oxide proved a profitable monopoly for rather more than a decade. Then Blair & Stephenson's manager joined the firm of Adkins & Nock, Smethwick. Henry Adkins, a partner in this firm, communicated these facts to the British Association in 1864.

Not every batch of Derbyshire lead contained the impurity responsible for tinging glass with a faint blue, but it was a hazard users were compelled to contend with. There is, therefore, no consistency in the presence of Derby blue in glass during the period concerned and its depth of tone varies. The presence of Derby blue was infrequent between 1810 and 1815, and most examples may be dated earlier. It is now customary to believe that Waterford glass never displayed this tint. But Mrs. Graydon Stannus's display of marked examples tends to discredit this. Efforts to reproduce the genuine Derby-blue tint have been unsuccessful, but a bogus "Waterford blue" was made for many years.

Plate 5
Drinking glasses with solid-based, drawn conical bowls and welted feet. These are in a dark, heavy glass such as was used before the 1730s.

Wine-glasses with welted feet, three of them domed: (*l. to r.*) pointed funnel bowl, with multi-knopped stem; trumpet bowl with single-knopped stem; round funnel bowl on combined baluster and knopped stem; toasting glass with easily snapped stem; ogee bowl with plain stem.

Plate 6

Wine-glasses with air tears, all with welted feet: (*l. to r.*) bell-shaped bowl on light baluster stem knopped at each end; trumpet bowl on light baluster stem; trumpet bowl with drawn stem on ball knop; trumpet bowl with solid base on centrally knopped stem.

Chapter Two

MANY collectors specialize in wine-glasses: it is surely remarkable, then, that so few can display a complete chronological development from the late seventeenth century until the introduction of mechanism in the early nineteenth century. The stems of drinking vessels have been classed into five main groups and twenty-two subsidiary types.[1] These again may be subdivided according to bowl forms and the styles of feet, but it must be recognized, of course, that these were liable to overlap considerably.

ANGLICIZED VENETIAN GLASSES (1676–95). These were adapted from the Venetian importations that preceded flint-glass. Because of the less viscous nature of the early flint-glass when molten, however, the delicacy associated with the Venetian soda-glass was necessarily abandoned in favour of simple sturdy styles.

Hollow and Solid Knop Stems (1676–90). In attempting to copy Venetian styles in flint-glass, the glassmen at first produced stems that were short, hollow-blown in pear- or melon-shaped knops, ribbed or plain, and collared. These, failing to withstand the strains of changing temperatures and the joltings of seventeenth-century transport, were quickly superseded by solid knops similarly shaped, ribbed and collared. By 1690 these had been replaced by squat, bulbous, smooth-surfaced knops without collars.

Quatrefoil Knop Stems (1676–95). A solid button knop might be ornamented by pinching into four lobes, the stem

---

1 *English, Scottish and Irish Table Glass*, by G. Bernard Hughes, 1956.

being known variously to collectors as quatrefoil, lobed or winged. A short, fat, ball knop was pinched with a tool resembling spring sugar tongs into four vertical lobes or projections pressed with strawberry or raspberry prunts. A taller stem was soon demanded to harmonize with the heavier bowl. This was accomplished by mounting the quatrefoil on a knop or thick collar.

Bowls. Bowls at this period were short, wide-mouthed, V-shaped funnels. At first the circumference of the foot was strengthened by folding it over on itself, forming a narrow, hollow rim on the upper surface. This soon developed into a flat welt folded beneath the rim and measuring about one-quarter inch wide.

For *Feet* see page 34.

BALUSTER GLASSES (1690–1800). The quatrefoil stem was outmoded by a short, urn-shaped knop or stem.

Heavy Baluster Stems (1690–1750). By 1690 the urn-shaped knop had extended into a tall, sturdy baluster known at the time as the Portuguese swell. To ensure safety in lifting, an inverted baluster or urn-shape was generally preferred with the bulge of the shoulder towards the bowl, thus preventing the smooth stem from slipping through the fingers, wasting the wine and probably breaking the glass. Flint-glass drinking vessels were expensive at this time. A large wine-glass weighing eight ounces and costing three shillings a pound would be priced at about half-a-crown by the glass-seller, equal to about fifty shillings in today's currency.

In the case of best-quality glasses the simple austerity of the heavy baluster was soon enlivened by incorporating into the stem one or more knops of various forms. During the 1690s a wide, angular knop might be placed between stem and bowl, and by 1700 the cone and drop knops had appeared, followed during the next decade by the acorn, cushion and annulated knops. These have all been noted in the baluster stems of seventeenth-century silver standing cups. The knop was conveniently placed above the baluster, enabling a safer grip to be taken upon the so-called "greasy" metal of the period.

Double balusters were placed head to head between a pair of knops with, sometimes, a matching knop between: in other instances three knops, each of a different shape, were tooled. The mushroom knop was particularly favoured and by 1710 cylinder, egg and dumb-bell knops were added to existing patterns. By about 1715 triple and multiple rings, angular and swelling knops, round and compressed balls, which might be plain or vertically ridged, were also in use. A basal knop might have set upon it a baluster topped by one, two or three knops of differing forms, and some of these might be enriched by the silvery brilliance of air-bubbles or tears placed either centrally or above the baluster motif. In some examples the tears are so large that the bulge of the baluster appears to be hollow.

The formation of a tear was simple. The glassworker dented the surface of the metal and picked up a second gather of metal over this. The heat expanded the entrapped air into a spherical bubble. This was elongated into tear-shape whilst the stem was being drawn. Heavy baluster stems with and without knops continued to be made until the mid-1740s and in tale metal considerably later.

Bowls. Heavy baluster stems, inverted and true, are to be associated with all bowl forms made during the period. At first these bowls were straight-sided, conical or in the grace-fully tapering round funnel design. The former was set directly upon the baluster and might have a thick, solid base, its interior depth usually measuring rather more than half the total height of the glass. The stem might be welded directly to the bowl, or, less frequently, drawn from the bowl and tooled into shape. These thick-bowled, heavy-stemmed drinking-glasses were found better to withstand the stresses and strains caused by atmospheric changes than thin-section glass with its ever-present tendency to fly (see Chapter 1). Others were purled or otherwise strengthened around the lower part of the bowl.

Early Georgians delighted in wine-glasses in which the solid base of such a bowl displayed a group of spherical or comma-shaped air-beads. From about 1715 the brim of the round funnel bowl might be expanded and the sides grace-fully incurved, thus forming the bell-shaped bowl. Because

31

of lack of harmony between bell-shape and stem, however, this bowl is infrequent on heavy balusters.

Feet. The foot might be plain with a well-formed conical instep at the stem joint, and concave beneath, thus lifting the punty scar above the table. This was less transparent than the thinner-sectioned, flatter-welted foot, its edge folded, a feature associated with good-quality glass. Domed, and domed and welted feet were also used.

Light Baluster Stems (1715–80s). Balusters of less cumbrous design and lighter in weight date from the accession of George I. Known to collectors as light balusters, their greatest bulge seldom exceeded the diameter of the largest knop. Knops were well-proportioned in curves harmonizing with those of their associated baluster. Wine-glasses of this type, on the evidence of trade cards, and engraved glasses were made in fine flint-glass until the 1780s. A second-quality metal appears to have been used concurrently with best glass from the 1740s.

Bowls. Bell-shaped bowls were most frequently associated with light .baluster stems, although the conical and round funnel bowls also continued concurrently. The thick base of a bowl might be drawn into a short neck to which the stem was welded. Such drawn-neck balusters have been noted on heavy baluster glasses depicted on paintings of the Queen Anne period. This neck eventually gave way in favour of a collar.

For *Feet* see page 34.

KNOPPED GLASSES (1715–1770s).

Heavy Knopped Stems (1715–30s). Stems composed entirely of knops were also made, at first sturdy and well-modelled. The heavy knopped stem was designed to contain several knops varying in size and form, each shaped by pinching upon the stem. They were made throughout the reign of George I and afterwards, and are to be found in best-quality glass and also in tale metal—often a series of mis-shapen knops hand-tooled at considerable speed.

Plate 7

(*Upper left*) Tall-boy with round funnel bowl, baluster stem with tear, welted foot; height 11 inches; about 1700. (*Upper centre*) Wine-glass with bell bowl, tear in straight stem, welted foot; height 8¾ inches; early Georgian. (*Upper right*) Cordial glass with bell bowl, knopped stem, welted foot; height 4½ inches; early Georgian. (*Lower left*) Wine-glass with funnel bowl engraved with band of fruiting vine, plain stem, domed foot: height 6½ inches; 1750s. (*Lower centre*) Wine-glass with bucket bowl, engraved with band of flowers, plain stem, welted foot; height 6¼ inches; mid-eighteenth century. (*Lower right*) Wine-glass with waisted bell bowl, engraved with portrait of Prince Charles Edward and Jacobite inscription AUDENTIOR IBO; welted foot; height 6⅝ inches; 1750s.

Plate 8

Two of a set of six matching drinking glasses of the mid-eighteenth century. They are in a heavy, dark metal displaying cords and striae, seeds and stones, the results of imperfect fusion. Variations in height, and in formation of bowl, stem and foot are typical features of the period. The diameters of the rims vary and the bowl on the right is appreciably the deeper, The bell-shaped bowls have solid bases and are engraved with flower sprays and insects, finished with clear-cut edges. The three-ply twist consists of a central vertical gauze within a pair of spiral threads, all in opaque-white enamel, enclosed within a pair of red spirals. There is a punty scar beneath each foot. Neither glass is accurately built upon its central axis. Height (*left*) 6¼ inches; (*right*) 6½ inches.

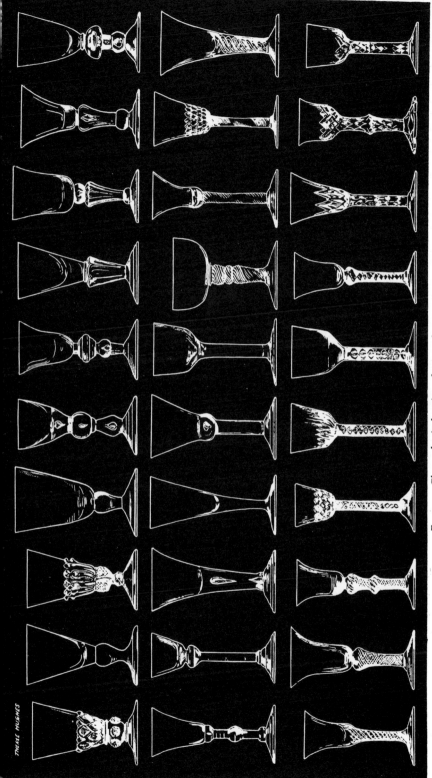

THERLE HUGHES

Fig. 2. Chronological series of wine-glasses, 1680–1780.

Light Knopped Stems (1735–70s). By the mid-1730s knopped stems were more slender and lighter in weight. They continued to be made until the last quarter of the century and very often are composed of three or four bulges in the stem associated with one or more carefully tooled knops.

Feet. These might be plain, welted, domed, or domed and welted, but in every instance the foot diameter exceeded that of the brim. From the days of Elizabeth I it had been customary to raise the wine-glass from the table with the left hand and carry it to the lips by holding the foot between the first finger and thumb of the right hand. This has appeared so surprising that some have queried whether the custom was general, but there is considerable contemporary evidence. Nor is it surprising when viewed in conjunction with other table manners of its time. Various reasons have been propounded, such as the fragility of the early hollow stem in soda-glass, and the necessity to handle the wine with careful attention because even when decanted it contained sediment that would mar the drink if jolted thoughtlessly. These, doubtless, were contributory factors, but it appears more than probable that the main reason was, after all, one of convenience: a glass so held, although requiring a steady hand, was most easily returned to its normal resting place between drinks, not on the table but inverted in monteith or individual wine-glass cooler. From this it would be withdrawn in the same manner, by the projecting foot rather than by the damp stem.

SILESIAN GLASSES.

Flat-faced Silesian Stems (1700–30). These and the reeded silesian stems are also known to collectors as shouldered and pediment stems. They have been termed silesian only by twentieth-century collectors, in the mistaken belief that this form was of West German origin. This shouldered design was adopted by English silversmiths compulsorily working high-standard silver from 1697 to 1720. Candlestick stems with a silhouette resembling that of a four-sided tapering inverted baluster have been noted with hall-marks ranging from 1699 to 1728, and from 1705 might have hexagonal or octagonal shaping. The silesian stem is the glassmen's version of this form and continued in production on drinking and sweetmeat glasses until 1790.

The earliest silesian stem was a high-shouldered four-sided inverted pyramid with plain flat sides and a domed shoulder. By 1710 the plain shoulders were pinched into the form of four arches. Occasionally a long silvery air-tear is found within such a stem. From 1720 a collar or triple merese might be placed above the wide foot, which might be plain or welted. Powell refers to wine-glasses with such stems as "square-stemmed Windsors", a name used for similar-shaped cut stems of the mid-nineteenth century.

The flat surfaces of the stem might be diamond-inscribed with a toast or a political slogan. One series is found with the shoulder faces impressed with "God Save King G R"—a single word to each face. These are thought to be Hanoverian propaganda glasses issued at the time of the Jacobite rising of 1715, but may equally well have been coronation glasses for George II in 1728. Others were issued with the royal crown, crossed sceptres or the cypher GR on the four shoulders.

Reeded Silesian Stems (1720–90). The smooth surfaces of early silesian stems were less successful than balusters and knops in disguising flaws in the metal, such as tiny irregular bubbles and specks. These defects were concealed by pinching the stems with deep vertical flutes or reedings. The six-faced stem had arrived by the mid-1720s. The lower part of the reeded stem was slimmer than formerly, accentuating the shoulders. Stems were usually footed and capped with knops or single, double or triple mereses, and might be given a slightly spiral twist. Clusters of tears are to be found in compressed ball, bullet and bobbin knops, but not in the stem itself. There was a vogue for the inverted silesian stem and the double-silesian in which two short, reeded members were placed head to head with an intervening knop.

The eight-sided silesian stem dates from the 1730s. This is a less attractive style to modern eyes than the six-sided, the pinched moulding lacking the clear definition of the earlier type which still continued to be made. It was appreciably lighter in weight and appears to have been hand-tooled in the chair. In tale glass the silesian stem appeared in a slender twisted form. During the fourth quarter of the eighteenth century some finely-proportioned silesian stems were made, basically pinched but improved by clever manipulation of the cutting wheel.

Bowls and Feet. Silesian stems on wine-glasses are usually associated with round funnel and waisted bowls. Feet may be domed, but are usually welted. The most desirable silesian stems are found on candlesticks and sweetmeat glasses. They were used on early Georgian hemispherical champagne glasses.

DRAWN GLASSES (1690s–1850). Two-piece glasses in which the stem—the straw shank as it was termed by eighteenth-century glassmen—was drawn from a trumpet-shaped bowl, date from the introduction of flint-glass, but few pre-Georgian examples remain. Early examples were in large heavy forms with thick stems and from the 1730s tens of thousands were made every year. They were the standard form for public drinking and ordinary domestic use, ranging from pint-size vessels to tiny drammers in cloudy tale metal. Waisted, thick-based bowls on drawn stems date from the early 1720s, always in fine-quality metal. From the 1750s the straw shank with a trumpet-shaped bowl appears to have been made infrequently, the type continuing with a funnel-shaped bowl.

Drawn Stems with Tears (1700–60). Long, slender tears decorated many straw shanks. At first these were short, but from the 1720s they developed into long slender air-threads running the full length of the stem. In an example with a waisted bowl there might be a group of spherical air-bubbles or comma-shaped tears enclosed within the thick base.

STRAIGHT-STEMMED GLASSES

Plain Straight Stems (1725–60). These are found on three-piece glasses in which a separate stem known as a stuck-shank was welded to the bowl. These were uncommon until the late 1730s. Dated engravings show them to have been in use a few years earlier and a few engraved examples suggest manufacture in the mid-1720s. At first the weld of the stem to the bowl was seldom clean, the joint usually being visible as a distinct flaw. The stem, although thick and heavy, possesses a slight but distinct narrowing in the centre and occasionally contains a tear. A knop was sometimes worked at the top of the stem, giving it a shouldered appearance. After the 1740s straight stems tended to be thinner than formerly. Until about 1760 they were often of best-quality glass: afterwards tale quality was usual.

Hollow Stems (1760–75 and mid-nineteenth century). These appear to have had a brief vogue in mid-Georgian drinking-glasses, the intention being that the sediment from the wine should sink down into the tube of the stem, leaving clear liquor in the bowl. This would then remain undisturbed when the glass was lifted. Hollow-stemmed drinking-glasses were advertised in 1765 and Sir Ambrose Heal possesses a bill from the London glass-seller, Colebron Hancock, dated 1768, in which are included "12 Hollow Shank Wines". Body and stem were drawn in a single piece, the stem and lower part of the bowl being cut with vertical fluting with the intention of obscuring the thick sediment. The plain foot was made with a nipple on the upper surface to fit into the tube to which it was welded. It was difficult to clean such stems, hence the briefness of their vogue.

A second series of hollow stems was made in the mid-nineteenth century. The tazza-shaped bowls of some champagne glasses were set upon hollow stems. In a set of twelve still remaining intact, bowl and stem are undecorated.

Bowls. Almost every shape of bowl is to be found on straight stems. First came the funnel-shaped, waisted and bell-shaped. From the mid-century ogee and bucket bowls were usual, and from 1780 the ovoid bowl was in use.

Feet. Feet for the most part are of plain conical form: welted and domed feet are also found.

TWIST-STEMMED GLASSES

Twisted-Rib Stems (1680–1720). This was a method by which the baluster stem might be made easier to grip securely. The inexpert quality of the tooling produced ribbing in a graceless series of alternating crests and troughs. They were never popular. Some obviously hand-cut examples exist. A method was devised in about 1700 by which the spirals were made uniform. Balusters of this type were made until about 1720, probably much later.

Incised Twist Stems (1740–1800). Straight stems from about 1740 might be incised with spirals, more uniform than the ribbing found on earlier balusters. The incisions were made by tooling the plastic glass with vertical ribs and immediately twisting the stem. These are easily recognized by an almost imperceptible lessening of diameter in the centre of the stem. Occasional examples will be found with a half-knop at the top of the stem.

A technical improvement in about 1760 permitted finer corrugations: these are very closely spaced and stem diameter is uniform.

Bowls and Feet. The incised twist is usually associated with a round funnel bowl, the lower half pinched with "hammering" or shallow flutes. Feet for the most part were plain, but welted and domed feet have been noted. Drawn stems with conical bowls were incised from about 1780 until the end of the century, the spiral being carried out by the method used between 1740 and 1760.

Air-Twist Stems (1735–60). The filigree thread-work which gave graceful elegance to fashionable drinking-glasses from the late 1730s until the 1780s included spirals of air and of white and coloured enamels. Although such ornament appeared to Georgians almost magical, such work was often carried out by children. The finer specimens are notable for uniformity of thread and the precise regularity of the spiralling.

The air twist, a development of the late 1730s, was the first of these filigree traceries to be made commercially. Glassmen of the period referred to glasses enriched with air

spirals as "worm'd glasses", and as such they were advertised until the 1760s. Their cost at the glasshouse was about
twenty-five per cent more than the baluster and knopped
stems which they superseded on the fashionable table. In
1746 John Cookson of South Shields invoiced "6 dozen
Worm'd Brittanick Wine, 32 lb." at 10*d.* per lb. or about
4½*d.* each. Ordinary "plain Britannick wines" invoiced on
the same account were 8*d.* per lb., that is, twenty per cent
less.

The air twist obviously burgeons from the air-tear drawn
into a slender vertical thread of air. The earliest air-twist
stem consisted of a pair of such threads loosely spiralled
about each other. These are not necessarily earlier than the
more carefully spiralled stems : being simple to make they
continued throughout the period and were possibly the type
advertised as wormed. The more elaborate spirals could be
costly in time.

The earliest air-twist stems probably appeared in straw-
shank glasses. A symmetrical cluster of tears, or blows as
they were called by their makers, was introduced into the
thick base of the bowl and drawn out with the shank. These
spiralled down what was usually a plain unknopped stem.
Few two-piece air-twist glasses are found with knopped
stems, and very rarely indeed do such stems display more
than a single series of spirals.

Flaws can usually be found in pre-1750 air twists. Filaments might be weak and thin; spirals not extending the
full length of the stem or too wide apart; and when stems
were knopped the spirals might be broken. Irregular spacing
of the inceptive tears in the bowl base brought about un-
symmetrical coiling of the air filaments and one or two of
the air beads might fail to draw. For some years little
attempt was made to deviate from the simple cross-hatching
effect of multiple spirals, the only variation being in the
spacing and number of the spirals. Corkscrew twists or
spirals in pairs or fours date from the mid-1740s. By then
the air-threads possessed a silvery brilliance and threads
began to be made of uniform thickness, spaced uniformly
and coiled with precision.

The most attractive air twists are found in the stuck

shanks of three-piece glasses: the bowl was blown, a length of air-twist stem stuck to its base, and the foot attached. These stems with fine-drawn air-threads were cut from rods or canes produced by a newly evolved and more reliable process than had been used in connection with the straw-shank. The method of manufacture is fully described in my book *English, Scottish and Irish Table Glass.*

The new method ensured uniformity of diameter throughout the stem. One's finger-tips may detect a slight depression following the line of each spiral when it is near the stem surface. This single-twist multiple spiral was later made more elaborate. For example, it might coil around one or more independent air-threads, forming the compound twist of which more than a dozen variations have been collated, including a pair of air threads spiralling around a gauze column; a vertical column within four spirals; a spiral gauze enclosed by a pair of corkscrews. Early examples of the stuck shank often display constructional faults such as irregularity of threads and coiling. These irregularities were overcome by 1750 in single twists and ten years later in compound twists which are found only in association with unrelieved straight stems.

The air spirals in a knopped air-twist stem were magnified by the knop in a way that proved popular in Georgian days. Shoulder knops and central knops are found singly or, more frequently, in combination, the upper one being the larger. Stems are to be met with having as many as five knops in gradually diminishing sizes and the spiral unbroken. These stems were costly to make owing to the large proportion of wasters. In some uncommon examples the air twist is placed between a pair of knops each enclosing carefully arranged spherical air bubbles. An applied band of clear metal might break the line of a straight air twist without interrupting the continuity of the air spiral. This narrow band might be cable-moulded or shaped as a triple ring. Some of the later close air spirals have collars at the ends, flush against bowl and foot.

When stem motifs have been used to reduce the length of the air twist, the glass is usually considered to be early. Such a composite stem formation may consist of a drawn stem welded above a short inverted baluster; two short air-twist sections joined by a central knop which might contain tears; a section of plain stem either above or below the air twist.

Mercury Twist Stems (1740–60). These air-twist stems with their highly brilliant spirals do not, as is so often asserted, contain mercury. The outstanding refractory effect was achieved by using metal of the finest quality, prepared in piling pots. The threads consist of a pair of thick corkscrew air twists spiralling down the centre of the stem in wide or close coils.

Opaque-White Twist Stems (mid-1740s–80s). These display spirals in white enamel ranging from hair-like filaments to broad tapes. Coming at a time when fine table-glass was demanded in greater quantities than formerly, they immediately became fashionable.

The enamel used for making the opaque-white filaments was specially prepared so that distortion would not occur when molten flint-glass came into contact with it. Enamel-making was a specialist branch of the glassman's craft. The enamel was sold in brick-shaped blocks for conversion into short, slender cylinders known as canes. In 1748 white enamel canes were advertised at 10*d*. per lb. Wine-glasses with stems containing opaque-white spirals cost about seventy-five per cent more than plain-stemmed of similar form.

They were made with stuck shanks owing to the difficulty of shaping the spiral accurately in a drawn shank. The collector will meet with two types: single and compound twists. Treble twists exist but are seldom seen. The single twist consists of one formation of white enamel threads spiralling around a clear glass core, or in the form of a pair of reciprocal spirals. The single twist—at first a spiral of multiple threads—preceded the compound type, but both were in production during the 1780s. A few years of practical experience appear to have been needed before carefully spiralled fine threads were produced. Single twists are generally contained in straight stems; knopped examples are uncommon.

The compound twist, in which two formations of enamel

threads spiral within one another, is more frequent than the single twist and is found only in straight stems. The number of varieties exceeds one hundred. To produce such stems, two, four or eight of the white enamel canes were placed in grooves around the inside of a cylindrical earthenware or gunmetal mould. The mould was filled with clear plastic glass and the resultant solid cylinder of glass was withdrawn with the canes attached. More clear glass was added around this, and the cylindrical shape regained by manipulation. This cylinder was reheated and drawn out by two men walking backwards away from each other, twisting it as they went. The eventual pattern depended on the number, thickness and arrangement of the enamel canes, for the drawing process merely reduced the cylinder to stem thickness, without distortion. Thus the familiar gauze twist was created by placing the canes near the centre of the cylinder, and the lace twist with two parallel lines of canes. The corkscrew twist required a flat ribbon of enamel across the diameter of the mould and this could easily be given coloured edges.

Colour Twist Stems (1760–80). These are but a variety of the opaque-white twist, made by the same process, coloured canes being associated with white, although a single colour might be used, or even two or three colours. Blue, green and ruby were the most frequent, but lavender, yellow, black and a greyish blue are found.

Mixed Twist Stems (late 1740s–75). This is a combination of air twist and opaque-white twist. Usually a single air column spirals down the centre of the stem within a multiple opaque-white twist. Tubes of flint-glass were used to produce the air-threads. In association with colour twists they are rarities indeed: an occasional example is found in which air twist, colour twist and opaque-white twists are associated. Stems are seldom knopped.

FACETED AND CUT GLASSES

Early Faceted Stems (1745–70). These were made concurrently with late air twists and early opaque-white twists, always in a two-piece construction, the shank being drawn from the bowl. The glass produced by the Perrott furnace and passed twice through the tunnel annealing leer was quickly found to form an ideal medium for the cutter's wheel with much less danger of fracture than formerly. The elongated facets were never made small, as this subdued scintillation by candlelight.

The facets were cut across the stem and not down it. At first they were but slightly concave, cut with an almost flat-edged wheel, stems being encircled with staggered rows of simple elongated diamonds, their length two or three times greater than their width, and their angles approximately 120 and 60 degrees. Elongated hexagonal facets soon followed and continued concurrently. Such a stem of this period was straight until about 1760, when it might have a central cusped knop, the facets from above and below meeting at the extreme width of the knop in triangles. Closely spaced scale facets were shallow depressions resembling in shape the fashionable fish-scale motifs enamelled on porcelain of the period and were laboriously cut with a rounded wheel.

Late Faceted Stems (1780–1800). During this period the facets might be emphasized by deeper cutting.

Cut Stems (1780–1850s). The final phase of stem decoration within the collector's period was made possible by the introduction of the improved annealing leer in about 1780. Stems cut with vertical fluting ran concurrently with facet-cutting for about two decades. During this period the stem was centrally knopped, being fluted above and below, and the knop grooved: occasionally the knop was facet-cut. In many instances the crests of the fluting were notched. The flutes above and below the knop might be staggered.

Plain vertical fluting was then fashionable until the mid-nineteenth century. From about 1820 cut knops of all shapes and sizes might be introduced into wine-glass stems, above and below the fluting and centrally.

Bowls. There is little variety among wine-glass bowls on facet-cut stems, the outline suggesting a compromise between the round funnel shape and the ovoid. Cresting or bridge fluting, consisting of six shallow flutes, was well suited to this design. Early cresting was short, merely

43

ornamenting the junction of the stem and bowl: from the late 1750s simple designs might extend over the bowl base. Cresting then began to be elaborated with shallow flutes rising from the vertical columns of stem facets, sometimes reaching almost halfway up the bowl from the late 1770s. A circuit of double or treble sprigs might be added, or two circuits of scale cutting, incised with a sharp mitre-edged cutting wheel. More sprigs might appear on the foot.

Feet. Facet-cut stems seldom appear on glasses with folded feet, although this is frequent in reproductions. Usually the foot is plain and its rim circular. Occasional surface decoration includes sliced cutting, a sprig circuit or fine radial cutting, and the rim may be scalloped or in petal outlines, or, rarely, in the arch-and-point outline. One may sometimes note a solid conical foot, and a thick heavy disc foot is occasionally observed.

PEDESTAL FEET (1676–1810).

The hollow pedestal foot blown in trumpet-shape with its end opened out to form a flat rim, folded for strengthening purposes, was introduced by the Venetians and included among the wine-glass feet made at Verzelini's glasshouse in Crutched Friars. In flint-glass the pedestal foot was used during the first few years, existing examples being mainly associated with salvers and jugs. This foot does not appear to have been again in production until the late 1740s. It is illustrated on several glass-sellers' trade-cards from the early 1750s, where it is shown on wine-glasses, on goblets used for cider, on bowls and jugs. Wine-glasses and goblets show pedestal feet to be tall and narrow; jugs and bowls, short and wide. Caricatures of the 1770s incorporating drinking scenes almost invariably depict glasses with hollow pedestal feet. Sheraton's *Cabinet Maker's Dictionary* published in 1803 illustrates hollow pedestal-footed wine-glasses consistently, thus suggesting that they were in fashionable use at that period. Many hollow feet associated with purled bowls and attributed to the seventeenth century will be found, by careful inspection of the metal and the fold of the foot, to belong to the later period.

44

Chapter Three

FLUTE-GLASSES have been made in England since the days of Charles I, probably much earlier. These were in lightweight soda-glass capable of being drawn into long conical bowls of thin section without much difficulty. The slender, conical-bowled vessel, measuring 10 to 14 inches in height, was attached to a foot by means of a short decorative knop. Until about 1800 it was impossible to make it in flint-glass because the thick section made it too cumbersome for use. From the late 1670s until 1850 short flute-glasses in flint-glass were the preferred form of drinking-glass for cider, champagne and strong ale. All these liquors deposited a sediment which collected in the apex of the flute-glass and was not stirred and mixed into the clear liquor when carefully lifted for drinking.

The earliest reference to the flute-glass so far noted dates to about 1650, when the poet Lovelace wrote that "Elles of beare, flutes of canary, They well do wash down pasties, Mary". The elle or ell-glass was an abnormally long flute containing at least a pint, but no more than a quart.

The outline of a short flute, 6½ inches in height, occurs in Greene's drawings in the British Museum This outline sketch shows a slender V-shaped bowl rising from a short pedestal foot, its diameter measuring nearly one-third greater than the brim, and rimmed with a narrow, hollow fold. A ribbed knop separates bowl from stem. These were in soda-glass and were the flutes made at the Duke of Buckingham's glasshouse. Flutes are not entered in Ravenscroft's price list of 1677, suggesting that they were not among the early productions in flint-glass. There is no doubt that flint-glass flutes were made in the 1680s, however, with solid knops.

When the first Lord Scudamore in the 1640s evolved the art of blending and bottling fine cider he recommended that it should be served in tall, graceful flutes, a fashion that continued into early Victorian days. Bucket, ogee and other bowls on tall stems were fashionable during the third quarter of the eighteenth century when an effort was made to popularize bottle cider.

Draught cider, according to Philips in 1707, was preferred in "bellying goblets", defined by dictionaries of the period as beakers with convex sides. An inn-keeper's window display bill issued in the mid-eighteenth century illustrates draught cider being drawn into carafes and served in flutes with hollow pedestal feet, as shown by Hogarth in 1737 for the service of champagne.

Bottled cider in the 1730s and 1740s might be served in flutes with deep funnel bowls engraved with all-over sprays of apple foliage and fruit. During the 1740s such bowls might be associated with single-knopped and double-knopped air-twist stems. At this time, too, appeared cider flutes in flint-glass of excellent quality. These resembled champagne glasses with air-twist or opaque-white twist stems, but were engraved with motifs associated with cider, such as a fruiting apple spray and a large codlin moth, or a conventionalized apple tree.

By 1760 cider might be served in straight-stemmed glasses, their capacious bucket bowls engraved with such motifs as a fruiting apple tree on one side and a cider barrel on the other, or an espaliered apple tree with a codlin moth on the reverse. A more frequent series was issued in which the rim of the bucket bowl was encircled with a border of scrolling and fruiting apple sprays. The engraved border might be oil gilded and the edge of the bowl above the engraving enriched with a wide band of gilding. In some instances the name CYDER was engraved in an expansive cartouche with an apple spray on the reverse. All such glasses have straight stems and plain conical feet.

Cider became subject to excise duties in 1763. Two years before the event an anti-excise propaganda campaign was begun, financed by the cider-masters. Fine-quality drinking-glasses were engraved with the slogan "No Excise" and a motif such as a fruiting apple tree or a cider barrel with a cock. One example has been noted engraved with an appropriately labelled cider bottle. This propaganda was partially successful, for in 1766 the Marquess of Rockingham modified the tax, which was shown to have discouraged the drinking of cider in favour of Continental wines. The cider tax continued, however, until 1838.

Cider glasses, obviously, were no longer engraved with the "No Excise" slogan after 1766. There was no immediate reversion to the flute: bucket bowls with filigree stems continued and were joined by ogee bowls. In the Elkington collection was a cider glass of early rummer shape with a short, plain stem and domed foot, engraved with a fruiting apple tree and two barrels. Bottle cider was in little demand between the early 1770s and 1790. Reduced imports of Continental wines then brought about a revived interest in English cider. This was served in deep flutes distinguished from wine-glasses by their twisted stems. In 1829 a catalogue issued by the Rotherham Glass Company listed "cyders with twisted stems and welted feet at 1s. 8d. per lb.", and "cyders purled" at 1s. 10d. per lb. The presence of purling indicates that bottle cider had not yet been cleared entirely of sediment.

The celebrated epicure M. St. Evremond, Governor of the Duck Islands, a sinecure worth £300 a year under Charles II, decreed that champagne should be served in flute-glasses at a time when the wine was selling at six shillings a quart bottle.

Champagne was served in flutes until about 1715 when the Prince of Wales (later George II) made champagne the royal drink. He brought with him from Hanover the preference for tazza-shaped glasses for champagne. These had expansive bowls, almost hemispherical in form, usually on moulded silesian stems. The baluster-and-knop stem is also found. Frequently the bowl was thinly blown and smooth of surface, but in some specimens the bowl was thicker of section, the lower part being closely ribbed.

Champagne was a costly wine: from 1703, like all French wines, it laboured under a tax of £55 per tun upon arrival at English ports: wines of Portugal were taxed at only £7 per tun. This champagne, unobtainable outside London, was drunk from the finest flint-glass it was possible to produce. Cider was sold in the taverns under the name of champagne and at several times its real worth, served in glasses of thicker metal in order to obscure its cloudiness. A bill in Sir Ambrose Heal's collection shows that in 1755 the fashionable glass-seller Thomas Betts was selling half-ribbed champagne glasses with air-twist stems at 10½d. each, and half-moulded egg-shaped champagne glasses at a shilling each. When in 1763 the champagne duty was increased by one-third to £73 a tun, oddly enough the consumption of champagne increased whilst other French wines were virtually no longer imported.

It is doubtful if the champagne flute ceased to be used during this period. Maciver Percival illustrates a champagne glass copied from Hogarth's drawing "Tartuffe's Banquet", 1736. This is a trumpet-shaped flute, its drawn stem encircled with a cable coil. The date when the tall flute such as was used for strong ale was introduced to champagne drinkers is uncertain. Edward Gibbon in 1773 paid eight shillings to Colebron Hancock, the Strand glass-seller, for "a dozen champagne flutes", and Zoffany's conversation piece, "William Ferguson celebrating his succession to Raith" painted in the 1760s, depicts a table with several tall champagne flutes and a quart bottle of champagne. Three more flutes and several bottles of champagne are in a brass-bound wooden wine-cistern. The deep, narrow bowl with a rounded base was generally supported by a plain stem: knopped examples are known and an authenticated set of twelve has silesian stems. The foot with welted rim has an exceptionally large diameter and a punty scar beneath: the majority are plain and hollowed. The drawn bowl graduating in curves to a plain or faceted stem is also found, and in the case of faceting this is carried into the base of the bowl above. In later champagne flutes the feet are flatter and of smaller diameter. The air twist is infrequent on genuine champagne flutes; such vessels may have domed and folded

late 9

Upper row) Wine glasses with air-twist stems: (*l. to r.*) waisted bucket bowl, four knops and plain foot, height 5¾ inches; double-ogee bowl, two knops in stem, plain foot, height 5⅞ inches; double-ogee-bowl, mercury-twist, height 6 inches (*Lower row, l. to r.*) Waisted bell bowl, incised twist stem, collared at each end, height 7½ inches; double-ogee bowl, double spiral air-twist, welted foot, height 8 inches; waisted bell bowl, collar on centre of air-twist stem, height 8⅞ inches.

Plate 10

(*Upper row*) Wine-glasses with trumpet bowls and drawn air-twist stems: (*l. to r.*) engraved with ros
and two buds, height 6½ inches; engraved rose, two buds and star, height 6⅝ inches; twist startin
in bowl, welted foot, height 6⅜ inches. (*Lower row, l. to r.*) Drawn flute with stuck air-twist stem
height 8⅜ inches; drawn double-ogee bowl engraved with flowers and grapes, air-twist stem with tw
knops, height 6⅝ inches; ale glass engraved with hops and barley, air-twist stem, height 10 inches

feet. The opaque twist is frequent with a plain hollowed foot. The champagne flute with cut flutes encircling the lower part of the bowl is not uncommon.

Tall champagne flutes held a gill of sparkling liquor, but on formal occasions the glass was only half-filled—another tribute to its high cost. The slight sediment associated with champagne was allowed to sink to the bottom of the glass. This urged glass-sellers to reduce the clarity of the lower part of the bowl with facets or slightly concave flutings. These vessels were listed as "champagnes with cut-bottoms". This increased the apparent brilliance of the champagne. These and other champagne flutes were usually slightly flared until about 1790.

Engraving was a feature of eighteenth-century champagne flutes, the fruiting vine being most frequent. Similar motifs were enamelled in white and colours. Flutes were also used for cider and strong ale and if undecorated there is no differentiation between the types, although ribbed stems distinguish the cider glasses. The flutes made from the more expensive piling-pot metal, however, were undoubtedly intended for costly champagne.

Very little champagne came into England between the early 1790s and about 1817, the old-style flutes continuing in use. With the after-war revival of champagne drinking, ordinary straight-sided flutes were used, the catalogue issued by the flint-glass trade in 1817 listing them "Champagnes, as Flutes". Fifteen types of flutes were made: (1) welted and plain feet (these were with drawn stems), 1s. 8d. per lb.; (2) button-stems, no maree (merese), 1s. 9d. per lb.; (3) button stems, mule, 1s. 10d. per lb.; (4) best plain stem, under 3 oz. weight each, 3s. 2d. per lb.; (5) 3 oz. and under 4 oz., 2s. 3d. per lb.; (6) 4 oz. and under 5 oz., 1s. 10d. per lb.; (7) 5 oz. and under 8 oz., 1s. 9d. per lb.; (8) 8 oz. and upward, 1s. 8d. per lb.; (9) plain stem, goblet feet (square feet), 1s. 9d. per lb.; (10) button stem, under 3 oz., 3s. 6d. per lb.; (11) 3 oz. and under 4 oz., 3s. per lb.; (12) 4 oz. and under 5 oz., 2s. 3d. per lb.; (13) 5 oz. and under 8 oz., 1s. 10d. per lb.; (14) 8 oz. and upward, 1s. 9d. per lb.; (15) thistle and ring bowl, 4d. per lb. extra on above prices.

Champagne was made more limpid and lively by the

4.

removal of sediment by the disgorging process introduced in the late 1820s. Byron in *Don Juan* hailed this as "Champagne with foaming whirls, As white as Cleopatra's melted pearls".

Glass-sellers were urged to design a new glass permitting champagne drinkers to appreciate the wine's sparkling brilliance. This they did by reverting to the early Georgian form, a hemispherical bowl with expansive brim and tall slender stem, issuing it under the name of a coupe. The finest metal available was used but its crystal clearness was obscured by lavish engraving and cutting on stem and bowl. Disraeli recorded his first acquaintance with such a glass in 1832, when he was served with champagne in "a saucer of ground glass mounted upon a pedestal foot". A series of champagne glasses was made at this time with cylindrical hollow stems into which the sediment still associated with champagne was allowed to sink, but they were never greatly used because of the difficulty in cleaning.

The discovery in 1840 of a less hazardous method of fermenting champagne brought about a sensational fall in its price, soon 11*s.* to 22*s.* per dozen quart bottles in London bond. Coupe champagne glasses with bowls all-over engraved in a wide range of patterns were made in large numbers, but from the late 1850s tulip-shaped bowls were preferred.

Toasting flutes were a late Stewart and early Georgian conceit. Their stems were so slender that after toasting a celebrity they could be snapped between finger and thumb and not used for a lesser toast. The custom of naming the reigning beauty as a toast became fashionable in the early 1690s. Although Congreve in 1700 spoke scathingly of "a decayed beauty or a discarded toast", Sir Richard Steele could announce in *The Tatler*, 1709, that "Toast is a new name found by the Wits to make a Lady have the same effect as Burridge [borage, a flower used for flavouring cordial, floating decoratively in the glass] in the Glass when a Man is drinking". It was an affectation to believe that the lady's mere name flavoured a glass of wine like borage. In 1711 Swift wrote that Lord Rochester's daughter was "just growing to be a top toast".

Toasting glasses were made with stems drawn to a diameter no thicker than ⅛ inch, and bowls blown in fine metal of section thick enough to withstand engraving of the toast in delicate script with a diamond ring. No existing example has been noted. The toasting glasses now remaining have more substantial stems, either plain, air-twist or opaque-white twist, and date around the middle of the century.

Ale flutes date from the 1680s and were made in progressively increasing numbers for nearly two centuries. Sir Hugh Platt in 1594 explained that "it is the Hoppe onlie which maketh the essential difference between Beere and Ale", adding that the beer, which contained the hops, was drunk from "streight upright glasses". Sir Robert Mansell in a statement to the House of Lords in 1639 recorded that he was then making "cristale beere-glasses at 9/– and 10/– dozen and 11/– for extraordinary fashions", these prices being about half those charged to the glass-sellers before he acquired the monopoly.

Beer glasses were of tumbler shape such as were illustrated by John Greene, plain, speckled with white enamel, perpendicularly and horizontally ribbed. They were all rounded at the base, with sides very slightly sloping outwards, and with their diameter equal to their height. Nests of six and twelve in graduated sizes were also made. Greene's drawings also illustrated stemmed glasses intended for beer. These were more capacious versions of the funnel-shaped glasses marked "for French wine", and Morelli was instructed that "the lower partt of these beer glasses and the buttons must be of solid mettall and all ye Rest of ye glasse I would have to be blowne thicker than useally especully ye feett must be strong". Ale-glasses are not specified, neither are they listed by Ravenscroft.

Ales during the Stewart period were thick, opaque and strongly alcoholic, served in tiny tumblers known as thimbles. The first flutes for ale appear to have been made in flint-glass with the lower two-thirds or more of the bowls spiralled, the twist obscuring the murky appearance of the ale. These were of small capacity, as evidenced by Fryer in 1698, complaining of this defect in "the Glasses as we drinke Somerset Ale out of". Somerset at that time was celebrated as the source of the most potent of strong ales made in England. Ale flutes at this time cost 8*s*. a dozen and on the same bill wine-glasses were charged for at 5*s*. a dozen. Lady Grisell Baillie in 1715 noted in her domestic accounts that she paid half as much again for ale-glasses as for wine-glasses. The metal of ale-glasses was thicker in section and the spiralling an extra charge. The spiralling in some late seventeenth-century ale-glasses terminated in an irregular flammiform fringe. The hand-tooling of the spiral work ensured that each spiral widened in harmony with the increasing diameter of the flute towards the brim. Stems, often surface-spiralled to match the bowls, might be straight, or in baluster-shape, double-knop or dumb-bell form on feet flat or conical and gilded. Examples of ale-glasses have been noted with the base of the bowl purled.

There seems little evidence that fine strong ale was a fashionable drink until after the imposition of the heavy tax on French wines in 1703. Strong ales then tended to replace wines on the dining table. A method of clarifying strong ale was introduced in the late 1730s and by 1740 the tall ale-glass with a clear blown bowl displayed the rich amber hue of the liquor, which might now cost as much as £10 a gallon. Such a flute, used also for champagne and cider, has a deep, narrow, round-based bowl with slightly everted brim. The tall stem may be plain, silesian, air-twist or opaque twist, or facet-cut, and the bowl may be engraved, enamelled or gilded with hop and barley motifs. This distinguishes it from the champagne glass. Typically, one side of the bowl is engraved with two stalks of barley diagonally crossed and each bearing two or four ears: on the reverse is a single hop blossom between two leaves and some tendrils. Grant Francis lists ten other variants.

Tall ale-glasses were invoiced in July 1746 by Cookson & Company, Newcastle-upon-Tyne: "1½ dozen Worm'd Ale Glasses 10½ lb. at 10*d*. lb., 8*s*. 9*d*.; ½ dozen Plain Ale glasses 3½ lb. at 8*d*. lb., 2*s*. 4*d*." This records that drinking glasses with air-twist stems were about 25 per cent more costly than plain. These were, of course, wholesale prices. In 1749 the Earl of Carlisle paid two shillings each for "12 ale glasses, new fashion", and in 1760 "six long enamelled

(*Left to right*) Champagne flute with waisted bowl, multiple spiral air twist stem, welted foot; bell bowl with solid base, composite stem, plain foot; funnel bowl with facet-cut stem and scalloped foot; decorated ovoid bowl, knopped facet-cut stem and scalloped foot.

Plate 11
Drinking glasses with opaque-white twist stems and plain feet: (*l. to r.*) ogee bowl engraved with fruiting vine; bell-bowl with tears in solid vase; waisted bucket bowl; bell bowl engraved with flower motifs.

Plate 12

(*Upper row*) Jacobite glasses: (*l. to r.*) engraved with portrait of Prince Charles Edward, laurel wreath, rose, thistle and star; engraved with portrait of Old Pretender with inscription, height 8 inches; engraved with the royal crown, cypher J R, and the Jacobite anthem, height 7 inches. (*Lower row, l. to r.*) Jacobite glass with drawn air-twist stem, inscribed "Fiat", password of the Cycle Club; Williamite glass engraved with portraits of William and Mary, height 9⅞ inches; Jacobite glass engraved with rose and two buds.

ale glasses" cost him four shillings each, double the cost of air-twist. Long ale-glasses from the 1770s might have deep, straight-sided conical bowls, vertically fluted from the base. The bowl was either set directly upon a plain foot or separated from it by one or two knops. The Carlisle accounts for 1776 record their cost to have been four shillings each undecorated. From about 1780 they might have thick, square, hollow-based feet.

Dwarf ale-glasses continued concurrently with tall-stemmed flutes. The bowl was no longer obscured by spiralling but was crystal clear in funnel or conical form. The stem consisted merely of a single knop, of which many variations are found: the foot might be plain or welted and an occasional domed foot is to be noted. Hop and barley motifs are to be found engraved on ale-glasses with barrel-shaped or wide bucket-shaped bowls of the 1780s. Their bowl-stem junctions are strengthened, dating them late in the century, and feet plain or welted.

The nineteenth-century glassmen classed ale-glasses under the heading of flutes and these were no different in form from those for champagne. These were made in large numbers in ordinary metal, closely resembling the dwarf ale-glasses of the late eighteenth century, with both folded and plain feet.

Yard-long flutes, from which beer was drunk, were of two types. First came the footed ell-glass (page 45), which was, presumably, originally so named because it was a flute measuring an ell, or 1¼ yards overall. John Evelyn in his *Diary*, February 1685, noted that after the proclamation of James II at Bromley, Kent, the sheriff, commanders, officers and chief gentlemen drank his majesty's health "in a flint glass of a yard long". The yard-of-ale glass made in the eighteenth century has a highly domed and folded foot of about the same diameter as the rim, and a ball knop, sometimes containing air bubbles. In the nineteenth century the flute was joined directly to a flat foot. Hartshorne has recorded that in 1872 many a country inn possessed such flutes measuring exactly a yard in length with engraved lines dividing the bowl into halves and quarters.

The trick yard of ale flute became popular in the second

quarter of the nineteenth century and many coaching inns and clubs hung an example on the wall with coloured ribbon. In these the flute terminated in a hollow ogee bulb about 4 inches long. To empty such a glass at a single draught was considered a test of skill and sobriety on convivial occasions. When the bulb was partially emptied of beer, air-pressure passing down the tube to replace the liquid was strong enough to force out the remaining beer with a sudden rush and drench the head of an unskilled or unprepared victim. In 1843 J. Ward of Stoke-upon-Trent was made a freeman of the borough "for the drinking off a yard-length-glass of ale at a single draught".

Chapter Four

AMONG the many forms of drinking-glasses which
appear to have been created solely for the delight and
bewilderment of collectors, few are more disconcerting
than that sturdy old yeoman the rummer. As if to make
confusion doubly sure, four entirely different glasses—
different in style, in age, in purpose—have come down to us
under this name. These are the English adaptation of the
German *roemer*; the purled drinking rummer; the Georgian
stemmed drinking goblet; and the toddy rummer. All are
worthy of note: the more is the pity that they have been
subjected to muddled classification.

These four types of drinking-glasses were spelled and
pronounced "rummer", a word which probably came to
the court of Charles I with that connoisseur of German
wines Sir Anthony Vandyke. The English version of the
German *roemer*, although seventeenth-century writers
spelled it "rummer", has no association with the spirit
rum: it was intended to contain straw-coloured Rhenish
wine.

John Greene imported *roemers* from Venice in the 1660s,
annotating his drawings "rnish wine-glasses". The majority,
however, were imported from Holland and Germany in
various shades of delicate green soda-glass, described at
the time as sea green, yellow green, apple green and olive
green. The imported *roemer*, according to Hartshorne, was
made in two parts, the bowl and stem blown together, and
the foot. The bowl shape resembled an elongated sphere
with a slice removed from the top, the circle of the brim
being smaller than the greatest swell of the bowl. From this
was drawn a hollow cylindrical stem, studded with small

prunts to prevent slipping from the fingers. This was supported by a hollow pedestal foot. A crimped thread of glass was usually applied where the bowl merged into the stem.

There is yet no evidence to show that *roemers* were made by English glassmen in the pre-flint-glass period. The evident demand is proved by the existence of examples sealed with the raven's head, made by George Ravenscroft from 1677 to 1681. The English version in flint-glass was a close copy of the Venetian type, and lacking all the thread-work found on German varieties. The sealed example in the Victoria and Albert Museum has an almost spherical bowl vertically ribbed, supported by a thick hollow stem applied separately, vertically ribbed and decorated with eight raspberry prunts, and a ribbed pedestal foot with a narrow fold. The bowl-stem junction is encircled with a wavy collar. This measures $6\frac{1}{2}$ inches in height, the bowl about 3 inches deep. Another similar example, sold in 1946 for 620 guineas and now in the Corning Museum of Glass, is "nipt diamond wais". This pattern, under the name of "rummer", was approved by the Glass-Sellers' Company.

Its hollow stem was intended to collect the sediment for which Rhenish wines were then notorious. The vessel charged with wine was allowed to stand for a few minutes before drinking, to ensure the clarity of the liquor in the bowl, and allow the sediment to settle. The flint-glass masters soon designed a rummer with a solid stem, slightly thinner than the hollow type, but still retaining the raspberry prunts, and with a flat folded foot. The deep, incurved bowl was narrow—purled at the base, making the glass at that point just sufficiently opaque to conceal the ugly wine sediment from view. The interior of such a glass could be cleaned efficiently, a difficulty never overcome with the tubular stem of the *roemer* proper.

Purled rummers continued to be made until the 1760s with the usual chronological sequence of stems. Baluster, knopped, silesian, air twist, opaque-white twist are all to be found (Chapter 2), sometimes with sea-green bowls. Such purled glasses might also be used for champagne. The rummer was defined by Bailey in 1730 as "a broad-mouth'd large drinking Vessel of glass: or such a one fill'd up to the Brim".

It is improbable that hollow-stemmed *roemers* were made in flint-glass during the eighteenth century, difficulty being experienced in drawing the hollow stem in a piece with the bowl. Improved furnace conditions in the early nineteenth century enabled this to be overcome. The catalogue of the Edinburgh and Leith Glass Company issued in about 1816 (the paper upon which it is printed bears the watermark for 1811) illustrates *roemers*. One example on a tall pedestal foot is drawn in section to emphasize the wide, hollow stem: another is in dark-green glass with a low conical foot covered with a close spiral of glass thread. The same page illustrates four Georgian rummers with similar convex bowls: one for toddy with an expansive reinforcement disc between bowl and stem; and three drinking rummers with drawn stems and plain, conical feet.

The drinking rummer with its capacious ovoid bowl and short stem was gracing the Georgian scene by the mid-eighteenth century. This was not a new form in England: glasshouse excavations have proved it to have been an Elizabethan type of drinking glass. It was an ideal shape for long drinks such as rum and water. Rum, under its original name of rumbullion, had been a congenial drink in England from the 1640s and rum-punch houses were established in the 1670s. The officers of the Cromwellian army carried rum in their baggage, and from Marlborough's day both navy and army issued rum as a standard ration. In 1740 Admiral Vernon ordered the rum ration to be diluted with six parts of water. Vernon invariably wore a cloak of grogram, hence his nickname "Old Grog". This one-to-six rum thereupon became known to the navy as grog: to civilians, who preferred their rum in the proportion of one-to-two, it was "seven-water grog". Soon, however, flavoured with nutmeg, grog was a popular drink, taken at first from tumblers and then from the short-stemmed goblets known to collectors as rummers.

Georgian engravings support the contention that rummers were quickly taken into use for any long drink. They are illustrated equally in association with comfortable social accessories around the domestic fireside and with rowdy hunting breakfasts. They do not appear to have been included in the lavishly cut 500-piece table services dating between about 1810 and 1830.

Grog obviously needed a capacious glass. At first the vessel followed the earlier rummer shape without purling and came into use on a short straw shank and round foot. The short stem lowered the centre of gravity near to the table, thus permitting the use of a relatively small foot at a time when on wine-glasses the diameters of brim and foot were equal. These two-piece grog-glasses were the first stemmed vessels to be termed goblets by the glassmen, who continued the name throughout the collector's period and beyond. To the public, however, they were known as rummers, the name associating their purpose with the name of their predecessor, the purled rummer.

Rummers with straw shanks and the lower part of their ovoid bowls encircled with twelve hollow flutes form a numerous group among existing specimens. The hand-cut series date from the 1770s; the blown-moulded type in a coarse metal from about 1805; and the blown-moulded specimens with clear-cut edges given by fire-polishing from about 1840. In a nineteenth-century example the blown-moulded fluting might continue into the stem and both might be slightly spiralled: the bowl itself might also be spiralled from the brim, but examples are rare. In the case of hand-cut flutes the upper part of the bowl might be encircled with a band of wheel-engraved ornament, extending from one-quarter to half its depth. Drawn rummers have been noted, very infrequently, in a style with a vestigial stem in the form of a cyst on the surface of the foot.

The drawn stem was tooled at the end to form an expanded, dome-shaped cyst. To this was welded the round foot, its diameter approximately two-thirds that of the bowl. The foot was most usually flat or slightly conical. Beneath a large number of fluted rummers—even of the mid-nineteenth century—are punty scars; the finer examples are, of course, hollowed.

Rummers in which an ovoid bowl and round foot are joined by a short, spool-shaped stem form another numer-

ous group. The stem was collared at the top for attachment
to the bowl and expanded into a spreading dome at the
lower end, where a thick flat-surfaced foot was welded.
From about 1805 its underside might be star-cut, a motif
more frequent after about 1815. Heavy square feet in drinking rummers date from about 1790.

The fashionable drinking rummer from about 1800 had a
bell-shaped bowl cut with wide flutes covering as much as
two-thirds of the area between base and brim. The knopped
stem was cut. In these the depth of bowl was half of the
total height.

The quality of the metal varied. Those in fine metal cost
2s. per lb. at the glasshouse early in the nineteenth century;
1s. 10d. per lb. in tale metal; in coarse glass 1s. 4d. per lb.
Rummers with square feet were made only in fine metal
and cost 2s. 2d. per lb. The price list of the Verreville Glasshouse, Glasgow, dated 1811, and quoted in full by Fleming,
lists goblets in three forms: "rummers with round feet 2s.
per lb.; with square feet 2s. 2d. per lb.; with pulley stem
2s. 6d. per lb."

In England rummers were issued in eight standard forms:
(a) drawn with plain stem, in all sizes, tale glass, 1s. 4d. per
lb.; (b) with button (knopped) stem and no merese, 1s. 4d.
per lb.; (c) button stem mule, 1s. 5d. per lb.; (d) drawn with
plain stem in best glass, 10 oz. and under, 1s. 7d. per lb.;
(e) above 10 oz., 1s. 5d. per lb.; (f) as (e) with covers 1s. 8d.
per lb.; (g) best glass with button stem 1s. 6d. per lb.;
(h) thistle and ring bowl, 2s. per lb. The Excise Commis-
sioners in 1835 reported that the best rummers weighing
7½ lb. per dozen—10 oz. each—were selling at 8s. 6d. a dozen
in comparison with 5s. 5d. ten years earlier.

The toddy rummer, destined to become lavishly ornamented with wheel engraving, appeared in the late 1780s.
This is a purely English form of glass vessel possessing no
counterpart elsewhere. These capacious vessels, too heavy
and unwieldy for comfortable drinking, were the characteristic vessels in which hot toddy was prepared. The whole
design of a flint-glass toddy rummer was planned to ensure
the avoidance of any weak point susceptible to heat: it is
therefore one of the most sturdily built objects made in

flint-glass. *Chambers' Journal* in 1838 referred to the "universal practice of toddy-drinking among the middle classes and county towns".

Toddy was a new drink in the late 1770s, being then defined as "hot grog with the addition of sugar, lemon juice, and grated nutmeg". By about 1810, when toddy had become a favourite drink in social circles, the rum might be replaced by whisky, brandy or gin. Toddy-making was a social accomplishment requiring a small kettle of boiling water, one or two toddy rummers, drinking-glasses, glass or silver toddy-sticks or sugar crushers, and a toddy-lifter. The hot toddy was prepared in a rummer holding a pint and a half or more—or perhaps in a china bowl with a thick, high foot rim—then served into drinking-glasses by means of the toddy-lifter. Sugar was added to the individual glasses, which were two-thirds filled, and stirred with the toddy-sticks. The glasses might be small drinking rummers or tumblers.

The early glass toddy rummer continued the ovoid bowl design which became a field for wheel-engraved ornament, occasionally accompanied by sliced cutting and notching. Stability was given to the bowl by fitting a thick, square foot, either solid or hollow beneath. The stem-bowl junction of such a toddy rummer was encircled by one or more thin collars.

Ovoid bowls began to be displaced from about the turn of the century by flat-based bowls such as the bucket shape which became most popular in best glass and continued throughout the rummer period; the cylindrical or straight-sided bucket; the near hemispherical; the barrel shape and ogee forms. At the same time the square foot tended to be displaced by a round one, usually thick and flat-surfaced with a central dome or cyst at the foot of the stem. These new features all appear on toddy rummers engraved with designs in memory of Lord Nelson and dated either October 21, 1805, or January 6, 1806, the date of his funeral at St. Paul's Cathedral.

The bucket bowl, with sides sloping towards the base, tended to take on a more pronounced shape during the ten-year Regency period, with the lower part encircled with

Drinking glasses with white opaque-twist stems: (*Upper row, l. to r.*) Conical bowl, collar at each end of stem, plain foot, height 7¼ inches; cordial glass with pointed funnel bowl, impressed fluting, domed foot, height 6½ inches; ogee bowl with gilded rim and ornament of fruiting vine, plain foot, height 6 inches. (*Lower row l. to r.*) Ovoid bowl, impressed fluting, knopped stem, plain foot, height inches; lipped bucket bowl, white gauze within air spiral, plain foot, height 6 inches; ogee bowl, ed, white and light green twists, plain foot, height 5¾ inches. All third quarter of the eighteenth century.

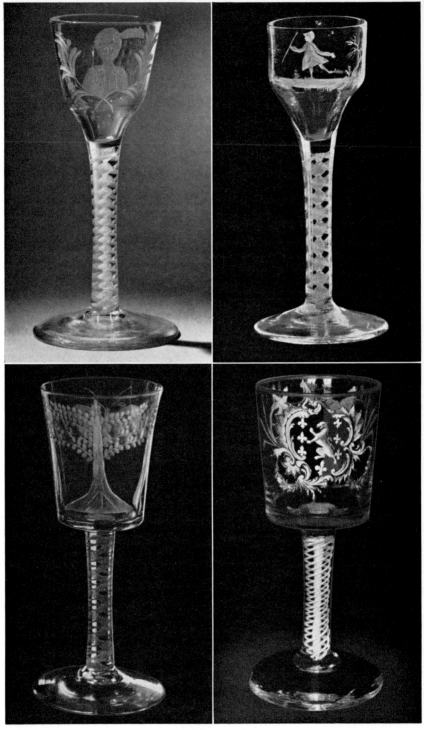

Plate 14

Drinking glasses with opaque-white twist stems: (*Upper left*) Engraved with Turk's head. (*Upper right*) Ogee bowl enamelled with a skater in a winter scene; twisted cable and spiral ribbon in opaque stem; height 5¾ inches; about 1760. (*Lower left*) Cider glass with bucket bowl engraved with espaliered apple tree and codlin moth; height 7 inches; about 1760. (*Lower right*) With bucket bowl decorated in coloured enamel with coat of arms, and with gilded rim; height 7⅛ inches; late eighteenth-century

flat-cut or hollow flutes. From the beginning of the century
the bowl of a flat-based rummer was reinforced beneath
by a disc with rounded or bladed edge extending to more
than half the diameter of the base, and to which the stem
was welded.

The short thick stem, seldom measuring as much as
2 inches in length, and rising from a round foot, allowed
little scope for variation. These round stems may be grouped
into four types: plain cylindrical, knopped, cut and spool-
shaped. In later examples the stem was made with a spreading dome for attachment to the foot, perhaps occupying as
much as two-thirds of its surface.

The earliest knops were in the form of centrally placed
flattened balls, a type which continued throughout the
period of toddy rummers: from about 1805 such knops
might be all-over facet-cut with small diamonds. Early in
the nineteenth century the annular knop appeared, followed
by the bladed knop and still later by the triple knop.

The bowls of toddy rummers provided an excellent field
for the engraver, enabling him to work with artistry and
outstanding technical skill. Much of this work consisted of
stock designs such as the garter star or cartouches enclosing
coats of arms, crests or cyphers. Stock patterns included
portraits of naval and military heroes with scenes depicting
the exploits that had brought them fame. Royal, historical,
political and social events were pictured. Suitably inscribed
and engraved toddy rummers were awarded as souvenirs or
prizes associated with fox-hunting, racing, hare-coursing,
cock-fighting and the like. Coaching scenes encircling the
bowl were popular. Engraving might have a personal
significance such as the tools of leading crafts, arms of
guilds or masonic emblems. Others were described as wedding gifts or christening cups. Toddy rummers engraved
with sheaves of oats were intended for the preparation of
Atholl brose; and the frequent examples displaying hops
and barley were for serving mulled ale.

Toddy rummers enriched with diamond and other cut
motifs in deep relief date from about 1805. These, with
hemispherical or barrel-shaped bowls, are to be found with
square or thick circular feet. The cutting forms most

frequently illustrated in pattern books are an encircling band, and a deep, plain band around the rim. The base of the bowl might be fluted and an oval blank left in the cutting design for the reception of an engraved crest or cypher. A fairly representative collection of drinking and toddy rummers may be assembled at no great cost and include some six dozen variations of form.

The most distinctive feature of the toddy ritual was the glass-lifter, described in Simmond's *Dictionary of Trade*, 1858, as a "small instrument used for conveying whiskey toddy from a rummer or bowl to a wine-glass". The flint-glass toddy-lifter is an instrument of the pipette type having a long slender, tubular neck terminating in a bulbous container with a hole in its flat base.

The dispenser of hot toddy would take the glass lifter by the neck, his first and second fingers supporting the lower neck ring. He then plunged the body of the lifter into the hot toddy which entered through the lower hole. When the vessel had filled, he created a vacuum by placing his thumb over the hole on the top at the mouth of the neck. He could then convey the toddy safely to the glass: when the lifter was above the glass he merely had to move his thumb to release the toddy into it.

A toddy-lifter may measure between about 4 inches and 8 inches in length, 6 inches being the average size. The two forms most frequently found have short bodies resembling either high-shouldered miniature decanters or, more rarely, pear-shaped bulbs. Scottish examples mostly follow the club shape with a less expansive base. The body of a toddy-lifter, capable of containing exactly a wineglassful of liquor, is generally smoothly plain. In some specimens the lower part is encircled with six or eight wide flutes, and shoulder and neck may be fluted also. One series of club-shaped toddy-lifters has been noted cut with narrow flutes extending from the base rim to the under-surface of the thumb-rest. Fine Regency and George IV examples may be elaborately diamond-cut in deep relief or ornamented with wheel-engraving.

In a blown example the punty mark on the base was ground smooth and slightly concave, the hole drilled and slightly bevelled. In the blown-moulded toddy-lifter the hole was pierced in the glass while it was plastic. Drilled holes might measure as little as $\frac{1}{8}$ inch diameter; pierced examples up to $\frac{5}{16}$ inch diameter.

The elongated neck might be drawn in the same way as required for a bottle, wide at the shoulder and tapering towards the thumb-rest: in others it was drawn as a tube with a bore measuring about $\frac{1}{4}$ inch. In flint-glass examples the neck is often enriched with six or eight finely-polished flutes extending from the shoulder to the under-surface of the thumb-rest, but more often broken by the presence of one or two applied neck rings: in some examples the flutes extend only from the shoulder to the under-surface of the lower ring.

The neck is usually encircled with a single wide neck-ring applied between one and two inches below the thumb-rest. Sometimes there is a second matching neck-ring a short distance below: ringless examples are infrequent.

The thumb-rest is applied over the neck opening in the form of a thick circular disc of glass, frequently placed off-centre. Like the base, it might be pierced whilst plastic or else drilled. On the cut-glass toddy-lifter the upper surface of the thumb-rest was ground flat and polished. The thumb-rest usually has a rounded edge, but one may also note the facet-cut ball, the knife-edged outline, and cheese-shaped, flat hexagonal and annulated forms, usually matching their accompanying neck-rings. Occasionally the thumb-rest is expansive and may measure as much as $1\frac{1}{2}$ inches across. A rare type is the heavy mushroom-shaped thumb-rest, deep and expansive, enabling the flat under-surface to rest on the fingers. In one series of lifters the end of the neck is shaped in an upward curve, ground flat on top, without the addition of a thumb-rest.

Neck-rings might be omitted and replaced with one, two or three groups of closely spaced incised rings with knife edges, three rings comprising each group. When three groups are introduced the lower incisions encircle the top of the shoulders.

The earliest toddy-lifter in the Firmin Leek collection of about one hundred examples dates from the late 1790s and measures 8 inches in length with a 5½-inch neck or stem. It is thinly blown from a lightweight metal such as was used for phials and suggests the work of a bottle-maker, to whom the unusually elongated neck appears to have given trouble, for it is distinctly bent. The sides of the body have a slight inward slant from the shoulder to the base which has a rounded lower edge, showing it to be a blown-moulded specimen. There are matching sets of six in the collection and one in blue glass.

Toddy-sticks, described by Judd in 1845 as "glass spatulas for stirring toddy", are now referred to by collectors as sugar crushers. These short glass rods, measuring from 4 to 6 inches in length, have plain, cut or incised stems terminating in hemispherical or flat-surfaced pestle-like knobs. The tops are usually pressed into decorative finials. Those used in taverns were made of the cheapest metal and at the beginning of the nineteenth century cost one shilling and sixpence a gross.

Drinking glasses: (*l. to r.*) ovoid bowl, facet-cut drawn stem; welted foot; ogee bowl encircled with engraved Chinese motifs, facet-cut drawn stem with cusped knop, plain foot; funnel bowl with ball knop above white opaque-twist stem, plain foot; saucer-topped bowl, facet-cut stem, plain foot; ogee bowl engraved with flower, facet-cut stem, welted foot.

Plate 15

Drinking glasses with engraved bowls: (*l to r.*) lipped bowl, white opaque-twist stem, plain foot; pointed funnel bowl, air-twist stem with knops, welted foot; short flute with mercury-twist stem, plain foot; bell bowl, opaque-white twist stem with single air spiral, plain foot; pointed funnel bowl, opaque-twist spiral stem, plain foot.

Plate 16

Trade card engraved by Colebron Hancock, the well-known glass cutter and engraver. This card illustrates the range of fashionable glass illuminaries, including a six-light centre-piece for the table, candelabra,

John Jacob's trade card showing the fashionable demand for lavishly cut glass, including a narrow-shouldered facet-cut decanter, a two-branch mantelshelf chandelier, and samples of dessert glasses with a dry

Chapter Five

CORDIAL, DRAM, FIRING, PUNCH, SHAM-DRAM AND TOAST-MASTER GLASSES

———————

THE majority of stemmed drinking-glasses were brought into duty for the service of red wines and the heavy wines of Portugal and Spain. Flutes for the most part were used for sparkling and other light-coloured wines and cider. There were in addition special-purpose glasses such as those for the service of tea-time cordials, punch glasses, firing glasses, drammers, small-capacity toast-master glasses and sham-drams.

CORDIAL GLASSES. The mahogany tea-table of the Georgian drawing-room might be a gorgeous spectacle of silver, porcelain and flint-glass. The fashionable, formal dinner began at four o'clock and after the dessert the ladies left the gentlemen to their wine and withdrew to the drawing-room, sweet with the delicate fragrance of English beeswax tapers. Here, at seven o'clock, they were served with tea, bread-and-butter and cordials. When evening visitors were expected coffee would be served at six o'clock, tea at eight, and the last guest would have departed by eleven.

The English custom of combining tea with cordials was discussed in the *Female Spectator*, 1744: "Tea, whether of the Green or Bohea kind, when taken in excess occasions dejection of spirits and flatulency, which lays the drinker of it under a kind of necessity of having recourse to more animating liquors. The most temperate and sober of the sex find themselves obliged to drink wine pretty freely after it. None of them nowadays pretend to entertain with the one without the other, and the bottle and the cordial-glass are as sure an appendix to the tea-table as the slop-basin. Brandy, rum and cordials are become the usual accompaniment to tea."

When Sophie von la Roche visited England in 1786 she recorded in her *Diary* that cordials were served in small decanters matching those of the wine decanters used by the men. She had already been thrilled by the display of cordials in the spirit booths: "Here crystal flasks of every shape and form are exhibited. Each one has a light behind it which makes all the different coloured liquors sparkle."

Joseph Farrington in his *Diary* for September 1801 noted the Scottish version of this custom: "Our party went to dinner at 4 o'clock to Mr. Bell's at Leith. After the dinner was removed, before the fruit was put on, a case of cordials was placed before Mrs. Bell who helped her guests to small glasses of Cherry Brandy, Lemon Brandy, &c., &c. This is the Scottish way and the Ladies partake of it."

Aromatic cordials containing 50 per cent of alcohol and 25 per cent of sugar, flavoured with fruit juices or herb essences, were the English-made equivalent of French liqueurs throughout the eighteenth century. Direct descendants of Chaucer's "grate delycious wynes aromatiques", they were known also as compounds. Their cost, early in Queen Anne's reign, was about two shillings a pint when spirits of wine was sold retail at four shillings a gallon. So potent were cordials that no more than a sip could be taken at a time, thus bringing into use the dainty pint-size decanters and small-bowled cordial glasses that delight present-day collectors.

The existence of silver cordial pots bearing hall-marks of the 1690s suggests that already cordials had found a place on the fashionable tea-table, but no further evidence is available. The silver cordial pot was a small version of a teapot, without a strainer to the spout entrance, and measuring about 4½ inches in height. Cordial decanters are discussed in Chapter 8. Cased squares were used for carrying cordials in the coach and elsewhere. When in May 1776 the Duchess of Kingston stood her trial in the House of Lords for bigamy, she was plied with cordials from a case of squares in the charge of one of her three maids of honour.

The earliest reference noted by the *Oxford English Dictionary* to a drinking-glass intended specially for cordials dates to 1663, when Cowley wrote: "Fetch me the cordial-glass in the Cabinet-Window." Because of the potency of these liquors cordial glasses were made with small bowls and filled no more than two-thirds. No example made before the introduction of flint-glass in the 1670s appears to have survived. Until the 1740s they followed modish designs in wine-glasses with small funnel- or bell-shaped bowls rendered even less capacious by thick walls and thick bases. The stem with its heavy baluster, drop knop or, from the 1690s, acorn knop, might display a brilliant, elongated air-bubble, matching a fellow caught in the heavy base of the bowl. The foot might be domed and folded. From the first years of the eighteenth century the vessel might have a straight stem drawn from a trumpet bowl and tooled at each end to form a knop. Then came a straight stem in a three-piece glass. This might be plain or with a central swelling, ball or angular knop, or with a merese or button knop immediately beneath the bowl and a baluster rising directly from the foot.

Cordial glasses to accompany tea-table silver and porcelain from the mid-eighteenth century were as gracefully designed and ornamental as possible. Air twist and opaque twist and facet-cut stems were usual, with bowls either plain, crested, all-over engraved, flowered or sometimes shallow-cut. Bucket, bell, ogee and trumpet bowls were numerous. Occasionally the base of the bowl was encircled with shallow, moulded fluting or dimpling.

Some tea-drinkers delighted in the fruit cordials known as ratafia, a brandy infusion of fruits. Most of the soft fruits were used for these brandy infusions, black cherries, strawberries, raspberries, currants and mulberries picked at their prime. Ratafia was sold by the bottle in three qualities, fine, dry and common. Collectors consider that these were served in long, deep, extremely narrow tapering flutes, often with drawn stems of equal length. The foot was always plain, its diameter more than half as much again as that of the bowl rim. No evidence seems available to prove that such flutes were used for ratafia to the exclusion of other cordials. But the majority were engraved with all-over flower sprays, making them harmonize most charmingly with the flower-decked porcelains more usually associated with the richly furnished tea-table. The cordial itself might be bespangled with gold leaf.

SURFEIT WATER GLASSES. Glittering with tiny fragments of gold leaf, or flushed with oil of poppy or gillyflower, surfeit water took its place among the fashionable cordials that concluded the mid-Georgian evening orgy of eating and drinking. Despite its uncompromising name it was in fact an extremely potent brandy distillation, finding a place among more ornamental delicacies in recipes for the dessert table and requiring its own style of slender and often particularly ornamental glass.

Drinking-glasses intended for this purpose were so designed that they would be distinguished immediately from other cordial glasses which had bucket, ogee and bell-shaped bowls. Surfeit-water glasses were flutes, with narrow, tapering drawn bowls very slightly convex but never curved at the rim, and with straw or straight stuck stems of about the same length. Collectors have tended to give these the more picturesque but inaccurate name of ratafia glasses implying that they were intended exclusively for ratafia, a Georgian brandy infusion that possessed only about half the alcohol content of surfeit-water, and consequently had less need of the peculiar narrow rimmed design.

The bowl of a surfeit-water flute might be encircled with faintly moulded or writhen flutings extending about two-thirds of the distance between stem junction and rim. This obscured the cloudiness of the white, undecorated surfeit-water most frequently used. The upper portion of the bowl might be left plain or be engraved with a flowered border. Other bowls, of clear glass throughout, were engraved with flower sprays. The stems might be plain, or in one of the immensely decorative air-twist or opaque-white twist styles. The foot in every example noted has been plain, and to ensure stability its diameter has been about twice that of the rim which has usually measured as little as three-quarters of an inch, rarely as much as one inch.

The bowls of surfeit-water glasses are too small for wine or champagne. The narrow bowl exposed but little of the surfeit-water to the air, thus minimising evaporation of its 80 per cent alcohol content. The recommended quantity to be taken was two spoonfuls and of necessity it could be no more than slowly sipped from such a glass. The ordinary silver spoon of the period, twice filled, held the amount of cordial necessary to fill the glass two-thirds full, at a period when this was the fashionable proportion to fill all flutes, whether wine, champagne or ale. Surfeit water was served directly from one-pint black bottles.

DRAM-GLASSES and the style of drinking known as dramming were associated with "distilled Spirituous liquors or Strong Waters"—as spirits such as brandy, whisky, rum and gin were defined by Act of Parliament in 1763. The distillation of spirits had been a profitable occupation for more than two centuries and the premises at which they were sold known as strong-water houses. These liquors were served in small vessels known under various names. Goldsmith remarked of a friend early in 1662 that "by flourishing a dice-box in one hand, she generally comes to brandish a dram-cup in the other". The *London Gazette* of the same year referred to dram-cups; ten years later the term dram-glass was in use and continued until the 1860s, although dram-pot and dram-dish were early Georgian alternatives.

Dramming was the name applied to the quick gulping-at-a-breath of strong waters from miniature beakers, the earliest being thimble-shaped, measuring no more than $1\frac{1}{4}$ inches in depth and raised on four tiny feet. They might be undecorated, but were usually made safer for fumbling fingers by encircling with raised icicles in the Venetian style, or small rough-surfaced seals. These were in soda-glass, but finer-quality footless dram-glasses were imported from Venice.

In flint-glass the tiny vessel was raised upon a short, heavy stem tooled to a baluster or knop shape and rising from a heavy foot. By the end of the seventeenth century a good-quality dram-glass resembled a short drinking-glass of fashionable form with a straight-sided, thick-based bowl, the lower half solid, containing no more than the former miniature beaker. Until 1713 the distillation and sale of spirits had been severely restricted. The removal of restrictions in that year started a craze for spirit-drinking, particularly gin, causing intense havoc among the poor until 1736 when its sale was again restricted.

By 1715 had appeared a series of short, trumpet-shaped dram-glasses. At first the design had a plain disc foot, quickly followed by a foot pinched with radial flutes, or with a substantial dome to which a drawn or blown bowl was welded. Terraced feet, both pinched and tooled, have been recorded, and later each terrace was rounded instead of square, and the rim welted. Although the bowl shows variations in shape, and the stem may be thick or slender, and contain a tear, the diameter of the foot always exceeds that of the brim. Until the 1740s the cost of such dram-glasses at the glasshouse was 1s. 6d. for a dozen of fourteen.

Finer-quality dram-glasses were also made, the metal of the bowl considerably thinner in section. Short air spirals have been noted, but rarely, and the opaque-white stem was also used. Those who could afford it had their dramming-glasses engraved with crest, cypher or other ornament and, during the third quarter of the century, the rim might be gilded. The majority were drawn with thick bowls, and rough punty marks were usual until Victorian times.

In the nineteenth century dram-glasses sold by the pound might have ovoid or hemispherical bowls and longer stems than formerly. The 1811 price list of the Verreville Glasshouse, Glasgow, quoted by Arnold Fleming, prices "drams, ribbed, sham or thick", at 2s. per lb. The thistle-bowled dram-glass was of nineteenth-century origin, catalogued by the Edinburgh and Leith Glass Company in about 1810.

There was an immense demand for dramming-glasses from 1827 when the duty was again removed from gin. According to Thomas Creevey, writing in 1828, gin "is now so cheap that a whole family may and do get drunk with it for a shilling".

Dram-glasses of tumbler form were made with thick ribbed bases and everted rims; they were 2 to 3 inches high and were filled two-thirds. Large numbers crudely made in poor-quality metal were produced between 1750 and the 1840s.

FIRING GLASSES are an amiable byeway of glass-collecting. These short, stumpy drinking-glasses with thick, heavy feet and bowls of small capacity were a type of dram-ming-glass, although not necessarily used for spirits. They were the successors of the bumper or thumping glass noted by D'Urfey in 1676 when he wrote that "full bumpers crown our Blisses", and again in 1719 when he referred to them as thumping glasses. The *Oxford English Dictionary* defines the bumper as "a large thumping glass".

These thumpers were cylindrical vessels of the tumbler type and had thick solid bases with which drinkers expressed their appreciation of a toast or sentiment by hammering them vigorously upon the table. Bumpers of this form were made throughout the eighteenth century, and from the 1770s might be waisted.

It appears highly improbable that straw-shanked dram-ming-glasses of flint-glass with thickened feet were ever used as bumpers until after the introduction of the annealing tunnel (see Chapter 1). Oven-annealed flint-glass stems could not possibly have withstood bumping.

Bumpers or thumping glasses were used for the most part on public occasions, such as political committees, guild dinners and meetings between groups of friends. When drinkers hammered their glasses upon the table in honour of a speaker or a toast they produced a sound resembling a ragged volley of musketry fire—hence the term firing glass. This style of applause is reminiscent of the old "Kentish fire", after which it was probably named. Political dinners such as those associated with the Williamite clubs of the late eighteenth century and the Pitt clubs dating from about 1810 might be followed by as many as seventy or eighty toasts, each of which was applauded by firing.

The majority of firing glasses belong to the late Georgian period from 1760, but sets are known engraved with dates of the 1850s. The shapes of bowls followed those of dram-ming-glasses and were of small capacity, convenient for repeated filling and emptying. The Elkington collection contained fourteen examples, height ranging from 3 to 5½ inches. The larger specimens, however, invariably of excellent metal, were drinking-glasses intended for wine or punch in the unstable surroundings of ships' cabins where their low centre of gravity and thick, flat spreading foot held them firmly to the table top. An excellent example of such a glass with a plain drawn bowl and stem is illustrated on Hogarth's conversation piece showing George Graham, son of the 1st Duke of Montrose, in the cabin of his ship. Its very thick disc foot measures more than half as wide again as the brim. Towards the end of the eighteenth century ships' glasses might have ovoid bowls with ½-inch drawn stems and massive disc feet, vertically rimmed. A set of three, measuring 4½ inches in height, has been noted engraved "Lord Howe", but these were probably souvenirs sold in the shops following his successful naval victory over the French in 1794.

Masonic firing glasses were made in sets and engraved with the emblems of the craft. A matching set of six from the Elkington collection are engraved with the fruiting vine on one side and, on the obverse, two with the Prime Master's jewel, two with P.R., one with S reversed, one engraved with the treasurer's jewel. These measure 3 inches in height. In addition there was usually a tall "constable" or master glass of a capacity six times greater than each of the smaller ones. The constable stood unused upon the table except on ceremonial occasions. A Masonic firing glass in the Victoria and Albert Museum was among those included in the service of glass presented to the Duke of Sussex when he was elected Grand Master of the Freemasons of England and Wales in 1810. This has a straight-sided, wide-mouthed drawn bowl engraved with masonic emblems and the Garter ribbon enclosing the letter S cut against a matted ground. The diameter of the thick foot is no more than twenty per cent greater than that of the brim.

The firing glasses provided by keepers of taverns and other places of public resort were usually of tale glass, often with almost hemispherical bowls of thick section and stuck stems, but more usually of flute or trumpet-shape. They were known as hammering glasses in taverns.

Many existing ships' glasses and firing glasses proper are of excellent metal and may have gilded rims. The trumpet-shape was the most frequent bowl form until the 1790s, when for the most part they were straight-sided. Bell-shape, ovoid and ogee bowls have also been noted, the latter some-times with dimpling encircling the base.

The stems of these glasses are always thick and short, measuring between ½ inch and 1 inch, seldom more, to minimize the risk of fracture with continual concussion. For the most part the stem is drawn from the bowl and stuck to a disc foot. Rare examples are found with air twists, the corkscrew being most frequent: a section of such twist was usually welded between bowl and foot, making a three-piece glass. Others have opaque stems and here ogee bowls might be used. Some ships' glasses have facet-cut stems. In late examples the foot was pinched with a slight dome greater in diameter than the stem, making the junction boldly convex.

The feet are heavy discs of glass measuring between ¼ and ½ inch thick and appreciably larger than bowl rims: on ships' glasses they are sometimes more than fifty per cent greater. They are almost always plain, but late firing glasses may have radially moulded feet, or corrugated with con-centric circles, and there is a type which is deeply recessed beneath by encircling the rim of the under-surface with a flange. Terraced and square feet have been noted, but neither proved successful on firing glasses. A firing glass foot was often pinched with a rounded rim and traces of the fin mark encircling the edge are visible. Punty scars were ground from ships' glasses, but are frequently present on eighteenth-century firing glasses. One may sometimes note marks indicating vigorous use.

PUNCH GLASSES do not appear to have been of any specified form. It was essential, however, that the bowl should be clear, neither purled nor with its transparency obscured by ribbing or cutting. The cloudless liquor had to be displayed in its full brilliancy. Although punch as a seafarer's drink reached London in the 1620s, and was well known by 1675, it did not become fashionable until favoured by William III in the last decade of the century.

Punch clubs were then established in London, and by early Georgian days the drink had so captured the imagination and the palate that rich folk equipped their homes with puncheries. Here were displayed punch bowls, punch glasses, sugar bowls, spice dredgers and nutmeg graters, long-handled punch ladles and bottles with parchment labels naming the liquors from which the modish punches were made. Punch-making in the eighteenth century was a distinguished social accomplishment, enthusiasts vying with each other as successful punchifiers.

Conversation pieces and portraits suggest that punch was usually served in glasses with straight-sided bowls that would be about two-thirds filled by a ladle of punch. The use of the drawn glass is confirmed by Hartshorne, who records a number of punch bowls accompanied by plain drawn drinking-glasses, all known to have been used at the "Congresses" held at Houghton by Sir Robert Walpole during his ministry, 1721–42. George Knapton's portrait of Sir Bouchier Wray, c. 1750, presents the sitter in a ship's cabin dispensing punch with a silver ladle from a giant punch bowl into a glass with a plain trumpet bowl, drawn stem and plain foot. Many another painting and engraving illustrates the drawn drinking-glass used in association with the punch bowl.

Hogarth in several paintings of low life shows an entirely different type of glass in use by punch drinkers. This has a bell-shaped bowl, a short, knopped stem and a highly domed foot. Joseph Highmore preferred his punch drinkers to use glasses with conical or trumpet bowls and light baluster stems. Queen Mary possessed such a light baluster glass with a cover, the rims of bowl and cover being gilded; this bore an inscription connecting its use with punch.

The fashion for hot punch, popularized by George III during the early 1760s, brought with it the handled punch glass—a glass mug known then and later as a can and used also for lemonade, then always prepared hot. "Punch glasses with Handles" were advertised in the *General*

Advertiser, 1766, among other plain glass-ware. Handled punch glasses were announced elsewhere as being "double annealed" to withstand the effect of hot punch. Until the improved annealing tunnel was introduced in about 1780 glasses for hot punch required to be warmed before the liquor was ladled into them or poured from a punch-pot, as annealing was far from satisfactory, a point discussed in various government reports on the glass industry of the late eighteenth century.

Handled punch glasses resembled thick-based tumblers, at first with vertical sides, later widening from the base. A set made for Queen Charlotte in the early 1780s, now in the collection of H.M. the Queen, are encircled with shallow-cut flutes and the brims enriched with deep borders of gilding, the bodies engraved with the crowned cypher C.R.

Punch glasses were differentiated from wine-glasses in the 1780s, as is shown, for instance, in a *Newcastle Journal* advertisement of 1781 and the sale catalogue of the Holly Hall Glasshouse, Dudley, in 1784, where punch glasses and tumblers were differentiated from other drinking-glasses, including rummers. At a later period, however, the drinking rummer was used for punch (see Chapter 4).

SHAM-DRAMS are deceptive glasses of the toast-master type, but instead of displaying the latter's elegance they were cheap, substantial glasses commonly used by tavern-keepers and others when invited to drink with customers. They were often in tale quality metal, priced on the 1817 list at 1s. 6d. per lb. at the glasshouse. Listed also in 1829 were Coburg sham-drams at prices ranging from 1s. 9d. per lb. to 3s. 9d. per lb.

Sham-drams are to be found with drawn flute bowls, bucket bowls on stuck stems, plain fluted on knopped stems. Many have folded feet although of nineteenth-century origin. Earlier examples were solid-bowled editions of contemporaneous dramming-glasses.

TOAST-MASTER GLASSES outwardly resembled ordinary drinking-glasses. They were deceptive, however, for the bowl was solid save for a narrow V-shaped depression at the top capable of holding a bare half-ounce of liquor. The Georgian toast-master held an important position in company conviviality, where the drinking of toasts might start after mid-afternoon dinner and continue uninterruptedly until the early hours of the morning. It is uncertain when the office of toaster was introduced to public entertaining, but City Company records until the 1660s indicate that the toaster's functions had been carried out by the butler. A Toasters' Club was prospering in 1690 at the Globe Tavern in Fleet Street, suggesting that the occupation was then widespread. Brown's *Humorist*, 1704, refers to "the chief Toaster at a Drinking-Match" as though customarily an assistant was required to carry through a strenuous evening of toasting. It was essential that a toaster should officiate soberly however long and arduous his task, for it was the custom for him to announce and drink to every toast.

The toaster was first styled a toast-master in the late 1740s and a special form of glass designed for his use. This outwardly resembled a tall-stemmed cordial glass with a straight-sided, but deceptive, bowl and a solid conical foot. On special occasions, such as at the country-wide dinners commemorating the centenary of the "Glorious Revolution" of 1688, he would be presented with a suitably inscribed toast-master's glass. Toast-master glasses will be found with air and opaque twist stems with appropriate bowls and feet. They were always well-made and of fine quality.

Chapter Six

A SOCIAL occasion in Stewart and Georgian days was graced by the service of a banquet—not the many-course meal usually associated with the word, but a collation of fruits, sweetmeats and wines displayed ostentatiously in the drawing-room. Guests were not seated but stood or strolled about the room in the manner of modern cocktail parties. The *London Gazette*, 1703, in reporting a ball, noted that it "ended in a very handsome Banquet of Sweetmeats". This repast, which might be either a separate meal or a continuation of dinner, became known after the accession of George I by the less cumbrous name of dessert, defined by Bailey's dictionary, 1730, as "a service of fruits and sweetmeats".

Instructions for the preparation of a dessert or banquet of sweetmeats are available from such authorities as Giles Rose, master cook to Charles II, Queen Anne's cooks who issued the *Royal Cookery Book* in 1710, and the celebrated mid-eighteenth-century Mrs. Hannah Glasse. In *The Complete Confectioner*, 1762, Mrs. Glasse described the "dressing out of a dessert" in several arrangements with imposing centre-pieces such as "a high pyramid of one salver above another, the bottom one large, the next smaller, the top one less; these salvers are to be filled with all kinds of wet and dry sweetmeats in glass baskets or little plates, colour'd jellies, creams, &c., biscuits, crisped almonds and little knicknacks, and bottles of flowers prettily intermix'd, the little top salver must have a large preserv'd Fruit in it". At each end of the table were arranged "whip'd syllabub and Ice cream, different colours", and along the sides "lemon creams, clear jellies in glasses, bloomage stuck with almonds, and fruits".

These sweetmeats were displayed in glasses specially designed for dressing out a dessert. For example, Thomas Mayo, mayor of Cork, bought from Nat Berry of Bristol: "2 dozen glass saucers for holding sweetmeats at 4s. 4d. dozen; 4 dozen glass fruit baskets at 6s. 6d. dozen; 6 dozen jelly glasses at 1s. 9d. dozen; 2 dozen Whip Sillibub glasses."

The commercial confectioners, who were also glass-sellers, offered a wide range of sweetmeats. Typical were those announced on the trade card of D. Negri, "Confectioner at the Pine Apple in Berkeley Square, Makes and sells all sorts of English, French and Italian wet and dry'd Sweet Meats. Cedrati and Bergamot Chips, Naples Diavolini, Common Sugar Plums, Syrups, Capilaire, Orgeate, Marsh Mallow, Apricocks, Jordon Almonds, Raysons, Drogea, Comfits and Flower Candy, Harts Horn Jellies and Blomanges. Sherberts, Rout Cakes, Ice Cream Whips, and Blanshmange. Glassware also sold." The pineapple was the emblem generally adopted by confectioners of the eighteenth century.

Sophie in London, 1786, described the interior of such an establishment: "It is surrounded, like a large spacious room, by glass cases in which all kinds of preserved fruits and jellies are exhibited in handsome glasses. In the middle of the shop there stood a big table with a white cover containing pyramids of small pastries and tartlets and some larger pastries, and sweetmeats; wine-glasses of all sizes with lids to them, and full of cordials of every conceivable type, colour and taste, were attractively set out in between at a large and very elegant table. What we women liked best of all, though, was a large but delightful covering made of gauze which hid nothing from view and at the same time kept the flies off."

The collector of dessert glasses distinguishes between those used for wet sweetmeats and those for dry—between the custards, ice-creams, jellies and syllabubs, which all required fairly deep, capacious glasses, and the dry suckets or candied fruits, dried orange chips and the like, lifted with the fingers from open, tall-stemmed bowls, baskets or

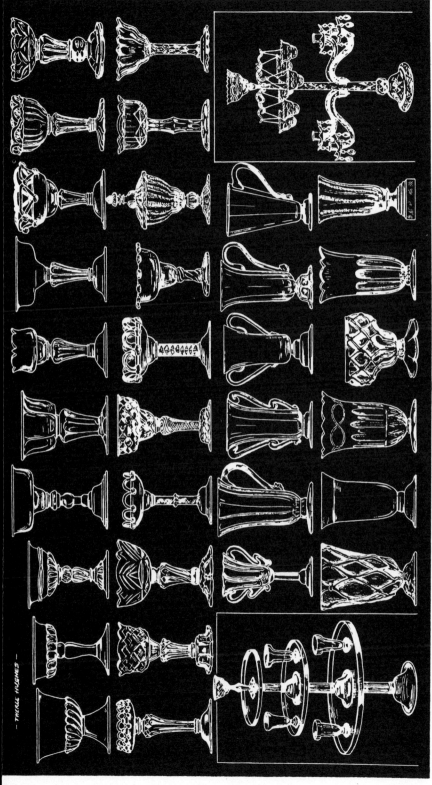

FIG. 3. Chronological series of sweetmeat glasses and a pyramid and an epergne, 1680–1800.

— THERLE HUGHES —

saucers. The typical dry sweetmeat or sucket glass of the early eighteenth century had a capacious bowl, hemispherical or in a waisted double-ogee outline. This was mounted on a highly domed foot somewhat smaller than the bowl in diameter, to allow of close-setting on the salver. From about 1720 the bowl-rim might be scalloped, and by about 1725 the familiar arch-and-point outline had been developed (see Chapter 12). Such ornamentation continued for half a century, but by 1730 the glassmaker was delighting in more elaborate escapes from the conventional style of rim required for drinking-glasses and was introducing open-work loops of trailed glass in three or even four tiers above the rim. Even in the conventionally smooth-rimmed sucket glass, however, its purpose was never forgotten. Whereas for drinking a thin rim was required, in the sucket glass this could be strengthened and made more convenient by folding over the brim to thicken it and provide an everted edge. These features and the small foot at once distinguish the sweetmeat glass from the thin-rimmed, wide-footed champagne glass of the period.

In many sucket glasses the bowls themselves are decoratively shaped. Radial rib moulding, for instance, was popular for half a century. Such bowls are often on silesian stems with their flutes cut after moulding. At first a bladed knop or a more or less spherical swelling linked bowl and stem. Then came the use of triple rings above and below the stem; then, from about 1750, a return to a knop, large and round. There were other shapes of stem at this period, too, but these are rarer. Variously swelling knopped and baluster stems are sometimes noted, also spiral and facet-cut. The typical small, high-domed foot to the eighteenth-century sweetmeat is appropriately decorated with radial ridging, moulded bosses, panels of slicing and the like.

Sucket glasses with tazza-shaped bowls on short stems rising from squat, spreading domed feet were fashionable until the 1760s, and continued to be made until the end of the century. These were advertised as sweetmeat stands and their bowls might be plain-surfaced, moulded or purled. Many, from the mid-century, have tooth-lipped rims, the teeth irregularly spaced, their ends alternately rounded and

Plate 17

these cost the author one shilling each. (*Upper left*) A pair of water-glasses engraved with oak and acorn sprays. (*Upper right*) Jacobite glass with plain stem, ogee bowl engraved with formalized rose, buds and a jay. (*Below*) Tall stems, small bowls, welted feet. (*Below right*) Flute with long conical bowl on bifurcated and twisted stem, engraved with sprays of roses, thistles and shamrocks in vertical panels commemorating the union of Britain with Ireland in 1801; height 14½ inches.

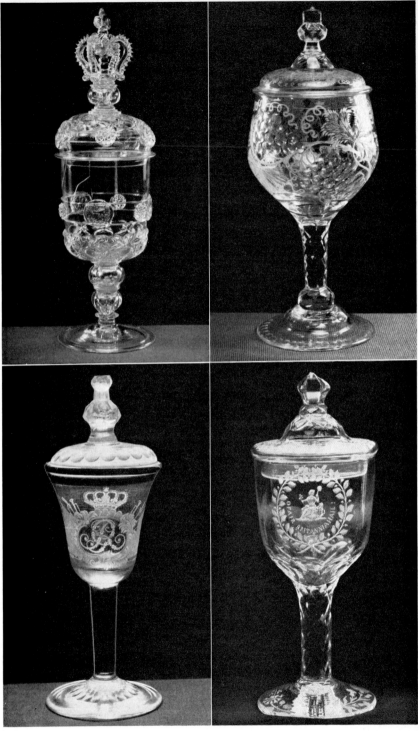

Plate 18

Covered goblets: (*Upper left*) With base of bowl pinched with trellis decoration in relief and encircl above with trailed decoration and strawberry prunts, large and small alternately; the lid has crown finial on a cushion knop; late seventeenth century. (*Upper right*) With facet-cut stem and dom mid-eighteenth century. (*Lower left*) With slightly everted funnel bowl and smooth stem cut hexago ally; rims of bowl and cover heavily gilded; engraved with cypher of George III; early 176 (*Lower right*) Britannia glass on diamond-faceted stem; 1760s.

sheared off more or less squarely. These are often in good-quality metal but of poor craftsmanship.

Dessert glasses, tall and short, containing candied fruits, took their place with others specifically designed for wet sweetmeats—jellies and ices, syllabubs and custards. Jelly glasses date from the early years of flint-glass making. The earliest reference so far noted is in Robert May's *The Accomplisht Cook*, 1678. Fashionable cooks are here directed to "serve jelly run into little round glasses four or five in a dish". These were footless, basin-shaped bowls with folded lips and base kicks. They were sold by the set of eight for general household use at a price of one shilling in 1698. After about 1700 a rim foot might be added.

A cookery book published in 1714 recommends that jelly be "poured into narrow-bottomed Drinking Glasses" as more capacious alternatives to the little bowls. A year or so later "new-fashioned jelly glasses" were on the market. This design is a gracefully-waisted, trumpet-shaped bowl on a straight stem rising from a plain folded foot and with a pair of double-looped handles. By 1720 such a bowl, without handles, was welded directly to a high-domed foot with a high instep and radial ribs. Like the sweetmeat glasses the vessel has a foot diameter considerably smaller than that of the brim. When dining with Lord Carlisle in 1722 Lady Grisell Baillie was vastly entertained by the table centrepiece, "a salver with 6 jelly glasses, with 3 of biskets hip'd as high betwixt each 2 glasses and a high scalloped glass in the middle containing orang chips".

Jelly glasses, according to Francis Buckley's index, were most frequently advertised of all table glasses between 1725, when they cost 1s. 9d. a dozen, and 1771. Such glasses, until the 1740s, were usually twist ribbed, vertically ribbed or pinched with diamond or hexagonal diaper work as some protection against cracking when the warm liquid jelly was poured in: hot jelly most certainly would have cracked them. A thick, flattened knop with moulded edge was introduced between the bowl and foot from the mid-1720s. When these knops were plain they usually enclosed clusters of air beads. The knop eventually decreased in size and importance and after the mid-century might be abandoned,

6   81

the bowl once again being attached directly to a foot, now plain. The deep, bell-shaped bowl from about 1740 was plain, the expansive brim enabling the cook to top the jelly with clotted cream. The foot might be low-domed, but more usually was conical or plain and thick.

In the 1750s fashionable jelly glasses began to be decorated with engraving or shallow cutting, brim and foot rim sometimes being scalloped. After about 1790 deep relief cutting was applied for at least half a century, the bowls being thick in section to accommodate the elaborate ornament which usually included a wide band of diamonds below the brim. Square feet with high, solid domes were used, and from about 1820 round feet radially pinched. Cut flutes were also popular and the vertical crests of these might be notched. Jelly glasses of the late Georgian period are nowhere recorded with handles. The 1829 price list names three types of undecorated jelly glasses then in production: in best flint-glass 1s. 9d. per lb.; in second quality 1s. 8d. per lb.; and best glass with button stem 2s. per lb.

Syllabub was a favourite English drink throughout the Tudor, Stewart and Georgian periods. Bailey's dictionary, 1721, says the term is a contraction of swilling bubbles and defines it as "a potable Liquer made by mixing [whisking] the Milk of a Cow with Cyder, Sugar, Spice, &c.". More recently the word has been said to come from *selig*, meaning silly or merry, and *buc*, belly. In Derbyshire the drink was known as "merribouk".

The earliest reference to syllabub glasses so far noted appears in the Duke of Bedford's accounts of June 1676, when "ribb'd flintt sulibub glasses, marked", were bought at 1s. 6d. each, the marking being that of the raven's head (see Chapter 1). In June 1682 the duke bought "4 fflint sulubub glasses 4s. 8d." and "one large sulubub glass 3s. 0d." The latter was probably a spout pot (see page 88) in which the syllabub was prepared for serving into drinking-glasses. It is evident, however, that a glass of special design was used. That syllabub continued a fashionable drink is shown by a letter written in 1698 by Sir J. Verney: "I send down tomorrow in the Linnen Box a large Paper Box, you must take it out very gingerly because it is filled with Sullybub Glasses."

The whipped syllabub sweetmeat was a Hanoverian innovation and recipes are found in early Georgian cookery books. A recipe from *The Compleat Housewife*, 1732, reads: "Take a quart of cream, not too thick, and a pint of sack, and the juice of two lemons: sweeten. Put into a broad earthen pan and with a whisk whip it, and as the froth rises take it off with a spoon and lay it in your syllabub glasses: but first you must sweeten some claret or sack, or white wine, and strain it, and put it into eight glasses, and then gently lay on your froth. Set 'em by: do not make 'em long before you use 'em."

That syllabub glasses were double the size of jelly glasses is confirmed by several accounts. Both the Oxford University and the Cutlers' Company account books for 1733 record the payment of two shillings for six syllabub glasses, and six shillings for three dozen jelly glasses. Flint-glass at that time was retailed at eightpence a pound. Syllabub glasses, then, weighed eight ounces—twice the weight of the jelly glasses. Glass-sellers' trade cards from the 1750s illustrate salvers bearing syllabub glasses of about double the capacity of accompanying jelly glasses.

"Whip sullibub" and "jelly glasses" were frequently consecutive items in glass-sellers' accounts and advertisements from as early as 1725. The "whip syllabub" continued in table-glass advertisements until the 1750s, when "whip" was dropped, suggesting that the syllabub drink was not a fashionable dessert. That whip syllabubs continued fashionable is proved by Mrs. Delany's comment in 1758 that "Mr. Brownlow gave us two whip syllabub lessons, perfectly neat".

The collector, then, will no longer consider the whip syllabub glass and the jelly glass as one and the same thing. Their forms differ: the syllabub glass has a deep, exceptionally wide mouth to a double ogee bowl with almost horizontal shoulders forming a saucer opening into the deep, narrow lower portion which contained the sweetened liquor, the shoulder giving support to the airy froth. Early whip syllabub glasses were plainly blown and undecorated.

Advertisements from the late 1760s announce two qualities: common ribbed and best diamond-cut. Trade cards show these with short knopped stems on scalloped feet cut to match the expansive brims above. Handled syllabub glasses were also made.

The demand for syllabub glasses continued until Victorian days. The 1811 list of the Verreville Glasshouse, Glasgow, prices them at 2s. 6d. per lb., and in the 1829 trade list they are priced "best 1s. 9d. per lb." and "tale 1s. 8d. per lb." with no description.

Custards from special recipes and distinguished from baked custards were a favourite Georgian dessert. Baked custards were customarily served to morning visitors. Mrs. Nicholas writing to Sir John Verney in 1697 invited him "to mett my daughter at long spoon and custard between twelf and one of the clock". In Queen Anne's day baked custards were poured into individual cups "and put them soon after in a stew-pan, containing as much water as will rise half way up the cups. Set the stew-pan over a charcoal fire and let it simmer so as to have them of a proper thickness." The assumption is that such cups were made from thick bottle-glass to withstand the heat.

The Georgian dessert was more flavoursome. Mrs. Hannah Glasse bade her readers to pour orange and almond custard, the latter perfumed with ambergris, into individual glass cups. These resemble a small tea-cup, about 1½ inches in height and 2½ inches in diameter at the brim, with a kick in the base lifting the punty scar. The handle, drawn cylindrically, extends slightly above the brim and down to the base, terminating in a curly tail.

Custard cups with handles continued throughout the eighteenth century, plain, shallow-cut and, by about 1805, cut in deep relief. Capacity, however, became rather greater. Illustrations in the Waterford pattern books show custard cups with convex and straight sides, with and without handles. One pattern is shown with a foot and a cover. All are decorated with encircling bands of diamond-cutting. Another design has a tulip-shaped bowl. The list issued by the Verreville Glasshouse in 1811 enters "custards with handles" at seven shillings a dozen. The Flint-Glass

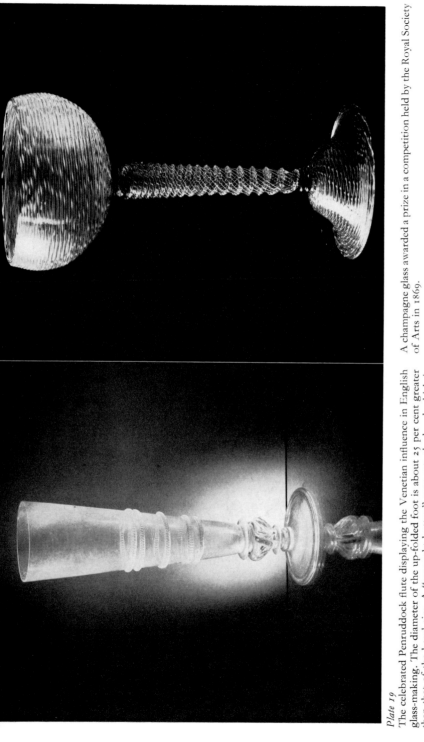

Plate 19

The celebrated Penruddock flute displaying the Venetian influence in English glass-making. The diameter of the up-folded foot is about 25 per cent greater than that of the bowl rim. A "wrought button" supports the bowl which is encircled with applied trails of rigaree ornament Height 10¾ inches.

A champagne glass awarded a prize in a competition held by the Royal Society of Arts in 1869.

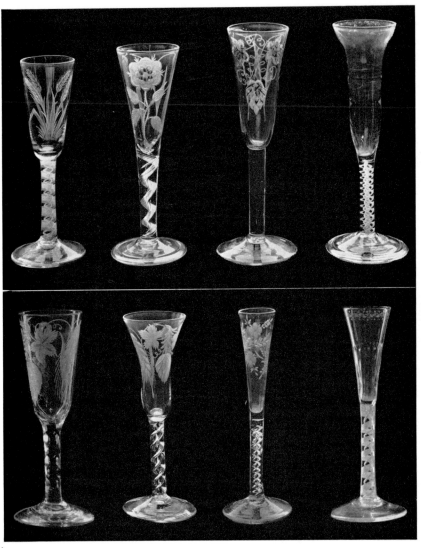

Plate 20

(*Upper row*) Three tall ale flutes engraved with hop and barley motifs and a champagne flute with saucer-topped bowl: (*l. to r.*) with compound-twist stem, 1765; drawn stem with air spiral on welted foot, engraved on front with Jacobite rose and bud, 1750s; with plain stem, 1740s; with gauze and corkscrew opaque-white stem and welted foot, 1760s. (*Lower row*) Two tall ale flutes and two surfeit water flutes: (*l to r.*) with facet-cut stem, 1770s; with mercury twist and waisted bowl; engraved with flowers and foliage with air-twist stem; moulded flutings around lower part of bowl, with flowered border, white opaque-twist stem.

Manufacturers' Association listed four types in 1829: "(*a*) custard cups, best, 1*s*. 10*d*. per lb.; (*b*) with handles 2*s*. per lb.; (*c*) custard cups, tale, 1*s*. 9*d*. per lb.; (*d*) with handles 1*s*. 10*d*. per lb."

Ice-cream glasses date from the 1680s when fruit-flavoured iced creams were a fashionable sweetmeat. Then, and ever since, they have been served in a straight-sided conical glass, wider at the brim than wine-glasses and of thick section to withstand the cold. These hybrid bowls stand direct upon crudely shaped disc feet or short knopped stems rising from conical feet. Many were used by confectioners and these were in poor-quality tale metal. Engravings illustrate such glasses until early Victorian times with little variation of form, although some early examples are shown with short pedestal stems.

Glass salvers in the form of flat circular plates supported by hollow pedestal or stemmed feet were made throughout the flint-glass period. Stemmed salvers, loaded with wine-glasses, were carried by liveried servants at formal functions. The servant held the salver in his left hand and a wine bottle in the right. Stems are usually of the silesian type which offer a firm grip to the fingers. These were known as waiters. Salvers with wide-rimmed hollow pedestal feet were used upon the table, at first "to set Glasses of Wine, Cups of Liquer upon, to save a Table-Cloth", and later as platforms for desserts.

Salvers are recorded in the early seventeenth century: there is an excavated example from Charles I's reign in the London Museum. This has the under-surface of the plate impressed with a design composed of circles. Salvers were among the early consignments of glass acquired by the Duke of Bedford. In 1682 he paid £1 6*s*. 0*d*. for a salver, this price suggesting its weight to be 6½ lb. An existing example of this period, its plate 13¼ inches in diameter, has its rim tooled with a shallow, turn-over edge to the upper surface. This stands upon a hollow, bell-shaped pedestal, its expansive rim strengthened by welting. Such hollow pedestals continued to be fitted to salvers until the 1690s.

Salvers dating from the 1690s may have sturdy solid stems in various baluster forms rising from high, spreading domed feet, their rims strengthened with thick, wide welts. The majority of existing examples have silesian stems, a pattern that continued uninterruptedly until the mid-nineteenth century. Air twist and opaque twist stems are rarely found. Cut salvers were advertised consistently from 1740, Jerom Johnson using the term "middle-stands". Cut, flowered and plain salvers are noted in 1772 and in the same year H. & D. Ayckbown advertised "new fashioned salvers and pyramids". Salvers illustrated on glass-sellers' trade cards at this time show the hollow pedestal stem to have returned, and this may have been the "new fashion", although the term might probably refer to the heavy salver with its plate revolving on a gilded brass pivot fixed in a massive, bell-shaped pedestal.

Fashionable salvers were cut during the second half of the eighteenth century. The under-surface of the circular plate might be cut with flat stars or other simple geometric patterns and from about 1770 the highly up-turned rim might be scalloped, or tooled in some resemblance to the pie-crust rims of silver waiters. This was supported on a substantial pedestal foot with the spreading foot-rim either welted or cut and scalloped to match the plate rim. The plain salver, and these were in the majority, was rimmed by a low gallery projecting above the edge: during the second quarter of the century the gallery might project downward too.

In the early nineteenth century the pedestal salver acquired its place on the tea-table to display a cake. This was known as a tea salver and the price, plain, was fifty per cent greater than that of an ordinary salver with a silesian stem which might now be cut in flutes and rise from a square foot.

Pyramids for displaying a dessert in all its abundance and colour were fashionable from the days of Charles II until early in the nineteenth century. The *London Gazette*, 1681, reports an occasion at which there were "Four Tables, covered with high Piramids of all sorts of Banquet". Lady Grisell Baillie records in her household diary of 1719 that she attended a London dinner party where "in the middle of the table a Pirimide, sillibubs and orang cream in the lower part, above it sweetmeats wet and dry". Orange cream was a jelly.

The account books of the glassmakers Cookson, Jeffreys & Dixon, Newcastle-upon-Tyne, under the date September 2, 1746, contain the earliest reference so far discovered to the parts composing a single pyramid. The total cost was 42s. 4d. for four salvers, one top glass, five top sweetmeats, thirty-two jellies and custards. Each pyramid was formed by placing several salvers one above the other in progressively diminishing sizes, the topmost being centred by a master glass containing preserved orange chips costing tenpence a pound in 1745: such glasses were advertised in 1772 as "orange or top glasses". This was an ordinary tall-stemmed sweetmeat glass and might be plain or cut.

Dessert as a dining-table accompaniment was fashionably displayed from the early 1740s on a facet-cut centre-piece which by the mid-1760s had evolved into a scintillating epergne. The centre-pieces were giant, tall-stemmed glasses with plain, double-ogee, scalloped-rimmed bowls and expansive domed feet. Upon a large knop below the bowl were welded six or more upward and downward curving branches, hooked at the end for suspending hemispherical glass baskets. In another design a central column, terminating in a bowl, rises from the centre of a heavy pedestal-stemmed salver.

Epergnes are elaborations of these, with curved branches, facet-cut or notched, extending from several silver or gilded brass fittings set in a tapering facet-cut stem. This rises from a spreading domed foot and terminates in a fixed bowl at the top. These branches were cut to match and fitted with loose hanging baskets. Such an epergne might be further enriched with pendant lustres.

In a specimen made towards the end of the century the lower portion of the stem is shaped as an urn, pineapple or other moulded form rising from a scalloped, moulded, domed foot or a large, thick, square foot. To the top of the urn is fixed a metal attachment supporting the central sweetmeat bowl and several notched branches terminating in smaller matching bowls. Suspended from each branch is a pendant lustre, and these are linked with smaller lustres.

Plates and saucers of glass for the service of sweetmeats were included in the table appointments of Henry VIII. An inventory of his household possessions taken in 1542 shows that he then possessed nine spice plates—spice being the Tudor name for sweetmeats—of green and blue glass, three of them partly gilt; seven in jasper colour; sixty trenchers and sixty-six platters, dishes and saucers of glass. These were all of Venetian manufacture.

Glass plates for the service of fruit and sweetmeats continued in use during the Elizabethan period, many of them "graven about the brims", others gilded, sometimes over "sinque foil on the brims". The Duke of Rutland's MSS. record that in 1598 glass plates were hired for fruit banquets. In 1602 the duke bought three dozen with engraved rims at a cost of 6s. 2d. a dozen. Similar entries were frequent until 1615, including one in the Howard Household Book, 1612, for "6 Glasse Plates xij^d", but these were not engraved.

Plates for serving the ice that accompanied pungent sauces from the seventeenth to the early nineteenth centuries are usually ornamented with engraving or impressed design. Early in the nineteenth century they were made by the blow-over method and elaborately cut. Apsley Pellatt issued a long series of these with cut rims, the centres set with sulphides (see Chapter 18).

Plates of flint-glass follow the shapes of those made by contemporaneous silversmiths, chiefly in the depth of bouge and width of rim. Only by examination of the metal, however, may an accurate attribution of date be given. The majority, of course, are plain, but by the 1730s diamond-cut and scalloped plates were advertised as well as engraved. Plates for desserts were sometimes advertised as sweetmeat saucers. Glass plates made before the introduction of the blow-over process in about 1800 are rare. Pressed plates (Chapter 14) are comparatively common in many designs.

Spout pots, although not associated with the formal dessert table, are to be found in glass, their use being for the drinking of possets. Early spout pots in silver were used for the service of wine and were known as skinkers, a term used until the mid-seventeenth century. The 1614 inventory of

William Middleton, Stokeld, Yorkshire, described such a vessel as "j skinker or a spout pot of pewter". Spout pots in metal for the service of wine were outmoded in the early seventeenth century by the introduction of such ware in tin-glazed earthenware.

Spout pots of small capacity were made for the individual service of posset and caudle: this design is lidded, has a loop handle on each side, and stands upon a trencher. They were made in silver, pewter and earthenware.

Spout pots in flint-glass date from the late seventeenth century. Their clarity enabled the user to see that the spout was clean. The early form has a cylindrical body with a thick, heavy gadrooned base, purled to give stability, and a pair of short loop handles placed low. The tubular spout, of unvarying diameter, emerges immediately above the gadrooning and travels upward flush against the vertical side of the bowl, projecting outward at rim height.

Glassmen by the 1690s were copying the curved delftware form, a low, heavy foot ring protecting the table from the punty scar. The spout was given a more graceful curve than formerly, wide at the bowl junction, tapering towards the end. Handles extended the full length of the body. These, with domed covers, continued to be made throughout the eighteenth century, when they were outmoded by the now rare spout pots in glass resembling diminutive teapots, but with handle and spout at right angles. These were feeding cups for invalids.

Chapter Seven

MANY a glass collector starts with a gradual accumulation of old wine bottles. But it would be interesting to find how many wanded bottles have lost their true identity along with their osier coverings, and how many beginner-collectors, or how few, realize the significance of the "kick" in the base of the typical wine bottle that was so essential to the early bottle-maker with limited means of annealing or toughening his vessels.

Fruit with wine was a between-meal repast favoured by Tudors and Stewarts alike. Guests were regaled with claret imported by the tun by the vintners. These merchants sold wine by the barrel to tavern-keepers and others who bottled and sealed the wine for sale. These retailers were notorious for diluting the wine with water, thus bringing into operation a statute of 1636 prohibiting the sale of wine by the bottle, to the great advantage of the Vintners' Company who thus held a monopoly.

The rich now bought their wines by the barrel, providing the vintner with quart-size wine bottles marked with a glass seal impressed with the owner's crest or cypher. Into these the wine was bottled, corked, and sealed by the vintner, wine connoisseurs making it a duty to be present at the filling, thus preventing unauthorized dilution. Samuel Pepys's *Diary* for 1663 records his visit to "Mr. Rawlinson's where I saw my new bottles, made with my crest upon them, filled with wine, about five or six dozen of them".

The filled bottle was stoppered with a cork tied down with thread anchored beneath a string-ring encircling the neck a short distance below the mouth. At first, to prevent access of air or leakage of wine, the bottle was dipped into a mixture of warm resin and pitch. The Georgians preferred to seal their wine with red Spanish wax made from a mixture of heated shellac, resin and vermilion. Each bottle was then labelled with a hand-written ticket of parchment, a custom continued until the nineteenth century.

The sealed bottles were then binned or placed slopewise on the sand or sawdust that covered the floor of a cold cellar to a depth of at least three inches. Contrary to the general belief that binning dates no earlier than the 1730s, a number of seventeenth-century references to binning are available. The inventory of Sir William Ingilby, Yorkshire, taken in 1617, records "a square binge [bin], a glasse case, seaven glasses, another binge and 7 bottles, and a table basket". The inventory of the contents of Beauchief Hall, Derbyshire, in 1691, records that in the pantry were "Thirteen dozen of glass bottles, one pound six shillings; a frame for bottles, six shillings and eightpence; one old bottle frame five shillings".

Until early in the seventeenth century the wine might be filled into stoneware bottles. This was unsatisfactory for the liquor tended to seep through the bottles and to become tainted by the corks. Also, as the bottle-mouth interior was rough, uncorking was difficult. Tin-glazed earthenware wine bottles were also used. Glass bottles were imported for wine bottling, but unless covered with wicker could not be relied upon to resist the rigours of long journeys in the carrier's cart over unmade roads.

Pre-Stewart wine bottles in England were blown with smooth hemispherical bases, and because of their comparative fragility were protected by covers of osier work. They continued in production until the mid-eighteenth century under the name of "wanded bottles" and "flasks". Bailey's dictionary, 1730, defines a flask as "a sort of bottle wrought over with wicker twigs". Obviously these bottles would not stand upright and were tabled in wicker baskets such as were recorded in the Ingilby inventory. Several early eighteenth-century conversation pieces illustrate wanded bottles in use, such as Sir Godfrey Kneller's Kit-Cat portrait of the Duke of Newcastle and the Earl of Lincoln, in the National Gallery. Such a bottle at that time might have its wine decanted, but more usually it stood upright in an ornamental container made for the purpose in silver, pewter, copper, brass, turned wood or basket work. The holder, when of metal, might serve the additional purpose of wine cooler, as demonstrated in the painting "Members of the Hell Fire Club", in the National Gallery of Ireland. This shows a wanded bottle in a silver stand made for Lord Santry in 1700 by the London silversmith Anthony Nelme.

Wanded bottles of one quart capacity cost tenpence each in 1631 and ten years later were listed in the *Book of Rates* at 13s. 4d. per dozen, very costly in present-day values. In *Fogg's Weekly Journal*, 1731, such bottles were advertised at 42s. a gross, and common black bottles 20s. a gross. These bottles were of thinly-blown medium green glass, plentifully displaying the streaks known as cords when on the surface and as striae when within the metal itself. Both cords and striae are visible as swirls caused by the glassblower rotating insufficiently molten metal on his blowpipe. Not until the mid-eighteenth century could glassbottle furnaces raise heat sufficiently to overcome this defect. This type of bottle was blown from the neck as was usual, but possesses no punty mark such as appears in the kick of an ordinary black bottle of the period. The mouth was encircled with an applied string-ring, vertically ridged.

It was customary for bottle houses to employ basket workers to weave and fit the osier covering over the bottles, for which there was a great demand, particularly for bottling champagne. In 1748 Letitia Pilkington in her *Memoirs* noted that champagne was sold by the flask, wine by the bottle. These lightweight bottles were convenient for transporting by wagon or pack-horse or by sea. The osier covering lessened the risk of breaking whilst travelling over rough roads. Inexperienced collectors finding such bottles without their osier covering usually classify them as spa water bottles.

Wine bottles for the most part, however, were uncovered and would stand upright on their own base. These were of two types: (*a*) those advertised as "long-necked French quart wine bottles", known to collectors as shaft-and-globe bottles; (*b*) those with a cylindrical body and short neck.

ate 21

(pper row) Wine-glasses: (*l. to r.*) drawn trumpet bowl with tear in stem, engraved with equestrian ortrait of William III, domed welted foot, height 7 inches; bell bowl, square shouldered stem with ar, plain foot, height 6½ inches; drawn trumpet bowl engraved with Chinese scene, height 6⅞ inches ower row, *l. to r.*): Champagne flute with white opaque-twist stem, height 6¼ inches; champagne te with bell bowl diamond-point engraved "Heck Stanford 1754", on air-twist stem, height inches; ale glass with hop and barley motif, collar at top of stem, welted foot, 7⅝ inches.

Plate 22

Drinking rummers of the early nineteenth century: (*Upper left*) With ovoid bowl engraved with inscription commemorating the launching of H.M.S. *Nelson* in 1814; height 6 inches. (*Upper right*) With bucket bowl, cut flat flutes at its base and engraved with a figure of Britannia holding a sprig olive, indicating freedom of the seas; knop contains a silver coin dated 1815; height 6½ inches. (*Lower left*) With bucket bowl engraved with coach and four and on reverse a castle with the Union Jack flying; height 6 inches. (*Lower right*) With bucket bowl on short stem with annulated knop engraved with a landscape and below a band composed of rose, thistle and shamrock.

These were made from a tougher, darker glass of thicker section than the blown flasks, the metal being prepared from sand, lime, potash, sometimes clay, and when available soapers' ashes. Such bottles are known to collectors as black bottles, but in reality are in various tones of dark green, dark olive green and olive amber. In reflected light they will display a lustrous greenish surface texture, probably due to oxidization. The Excise list of 1695 in levying a tax of one penny each on quart bottles, English wine measure, and a halfpenny on pint bottles, described them as "green glasse and flask glasse, whether the same be plaine or marked or called rounds or squares". In the same year Houghton scheduled thirty-eight bottle houses out of a total of ninety glasshouses then operating in England with an annual production of nearly three million bottles.

Bottle-making was a highly specialized branch of the glass-blower's craft, considerable skill being required in ensuring that the various parts of the structure were of correct thickness. Shaft-and-globe wine bottles with their full-curved shoulders were made by blowing and tooling. Earthenware moulds strengthened by iron ring-bands were used for shaping cylindrical wine bottles from the late 1730s and by 1750 one-piece gunmetal moulds (Chapter 14) were introduced.

The mould mark, visible when a metal mould has been used, is clearly discernible encircling the top line of the body where the curve of the shoulder begins. Where the heavy bottle-glass came into contact with the cooler metal of the heated mould a noticeably pebbled surface was produced. A little-known feature of cylindrical bottles blown in this way is the distinct bulge which encircled the base of the body. It was caused by withdrawing the bottle from the metal mould before the glass had sufficiently cooled to bear its own weight, so that it collapsed slightly. The cure for this was a glass that would stiffen rapidly in the mould, and bottle-glass meeting this requirement was evolved in the 1790s. This bottle-glass could be blown to a thinner section in the mould without loss of strength, and here again the gunmetal caused a slight dappling where it came into contact with the glass. The kick in the base of the bottle

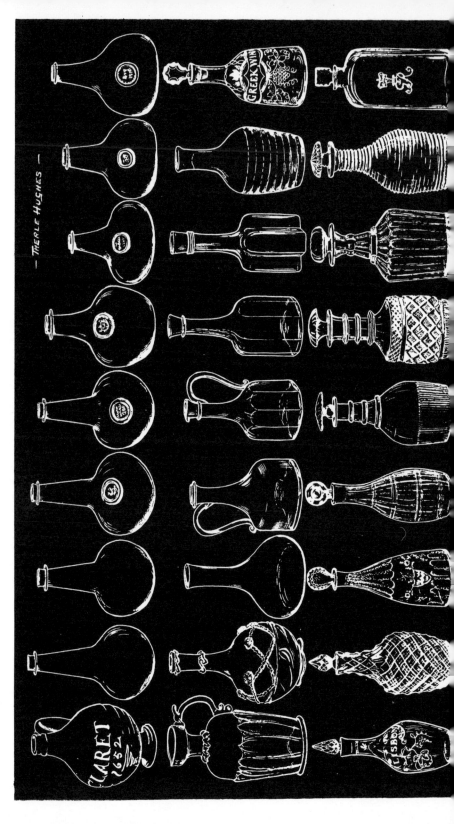

THERLE HUGHES

CLARET 1652

was important until the development of the tunnel leer. So effectively did it assist the annealing process that the bottle might safely be left to cool in the open air.

Dated seals and changes in manufacturing processes enable collectors to class wine bottles into six main periods, although the chronological developments from the shaft-and-globe to the cylindrical form were gradual: 1620–60; 1650–85; 1680–1715; 1710–40; 1735–1800; 1795–1840. Bottles earlier than the mid-eighteenth century will be difficult to acquire and no two will be exactly alike. The earliest dated wine bottle to be noted is sealed with the coat of arms of Raleigh Gilbert and the date 1620. As the importation of wine bottles was prohibited from 1615 until 1805 this may be assumed to be of English manufacture produced under the *aegis* of Sir Robert Mansell (Chapter 1). This well-designed bottle is of the shaft-and-globe design, with a bulbous body, a low kick and a long neck encircled about half an inch below the smooth, flat-surfaced lip with a thin, sharp-edged string-ring. Quart bottles at this period cost six shillings a dozen at the bottle-house.

Bottle outline between 1650 and 1685 tended to have a more pronounced shoulder angle, the sides of the body sloping more steeply inward toward the base, making the kick narrower. The knife edge was retained on the string-ring, which was applied in the same way as on later flint-glass decanters (see Chapter 8). The late Stewart wine bottle, 1680–1715, progressively widened and became more squat, with a high kick in the base. The neck, shorter and tapering, joined the body in a smooth curve which harmonized with the more rounded shaping of the body itself. By the end of the period, however, the sides of the body became perpendicular, some had a slight outward slant, curving into the neck with a shoulder more square and pronounced than formerly. The neck was wide at the shoulder junction and the string-ring raised to a position immediately beneath the mouth.

Wine bottles with cylindrical sides were more convenient for binning than those with boldly curving sides, and with the introduction of the blown-moulded body in about 1740 the earlier form was abandoned. During the 1760s the wine bottle became taller with a slightly tapering neck and a cylindrical body about five inches in diameter. This was reduced during the 1770s and 1780s, the body being taller than formerly, with a tapering cylindrical neck and a rounded string-ring immediately below the lip. The kick was deep. Blown-moulded wine bottles in black glass were of thinner section than those free-blown and tooled to shape, with consequent easing in transport.

The diameter of the cylindrical wine bottle was reduced to three inches from the early 1790s, with the shoulder higher and less pronounced. The finish was smoother owing to the introduction of quick-setting bottle-glass, and the colour considerably lighter than before. The lip rim was deeply collared, with a slightly curved outline, the string-ring, projecting less than before, being immediately below. The shoulders from about 1820 were still further accentuated. A broad sloping lip shaped by a special tool obviated the necessity for an applied string-ring. This feature with variations continued until the 1840s when wine bottles began to be moulded mechanically. Following the introduction of the snap case there was no punty scar beneath.

The embossed seal, bearing the owner's crest, cypher or name, and in some instances the date too, was very frequent until the 1830s. Vintners' bottles were sealed with badge, tavern sign, initials, or other distinguishing mark. Bottle-houses attached and stamped the seals for 4s. 4d. a gross, the customer paying for cutting the brass die. Seals were produced by dropping upon the plastic bottle enough molten glass to form a flat disc 1½ inches in diameter. The die was impressed upon this hot glass, distortion of the bottle being prevented by supporting the interior with a tool. Intersurface bubbles will be noted beneath the seal.

(Left) Rummer for serving mulled ale, engraved with hop and barley motif; fluted base to bowl and bool stem; height 8 inches. (Right) Serving rummer with incurved bowl on plain stem; engraved with hunting scene *The Kill*.

ate 23

rving rummers: (Left) Engraved with the *Victory* and on reverse a wreath and the inscription Lord Nelson, Oct^r, 21, 1805"; height $7\frac{7}{8}$ inches. (Right) Engraved with Masonic motifs: round topped stem, convex disc beneath bowl; capacity 2 quarts; height 10 inches.

Plate 24

(*Top row, l. to r.*) Wine-glass with ogee bowl, plain stem, highly domed and welted foot; cordial glass with ovoid bowl, rim encircled with engraved stars, facet cut stem, plain foot; toastmaster glass with deceptive bowl, opaque-white-twist stem, domed and welted foot. (*Centre row, l. to r.*) Cordial glass with opaque-twist stem, plain foot; two toastmaster glasses with opaque-twist stems, (*Bottom row, l. to r.*) Surfeit water flute with writhen fluted bowl engraved with flowers, height 6 inches; two wine-glasses with air-twist stems.

Chapter Eight

DECANTERS

DECANTING has always been an essential preliminary to the tabling of many wines, consisting of gently pouring the wine from the bottle in which it has been stored in the cellar, so that the sediment is not disturbed. The clarets of France have always been liable to cast a sediment and port wine to throw a crust. The quality and cheapness of these wines during the eighteenth century brought into being a series of magnificent flint-glass decanters through which the appearance of the wines could be appreciated.

Careful decanting became an important social ritual carried out by the host in the presence of his guests. Dean Swift, a typical early Georgian wine-drinker, recorded in 1730 that he pulled from his pocket a little gold runlet, containing a bottle screw, and "opening a bottle of wine, I decanted it off, the last glass being muddy". Every home of importance gloried in its set of flint-glass decanters, yet few existing examples can with accuracy be attributed to earlier than the 1750s.

The name decanter has not been noted in connection with this vessel until the 1690s, although the term decant was used by Wotton in 1633 regarding the service of fruit juice. The name appears to have been unknown to glass-sellers until the 1690s, but is included in the list of tariffs levied on English glass exported to France in 1701, suggesting that it was then in use. The Oxford University accounts early in Queen Anne's reign record frequent payments for "pairs of decanters". An advertisement published in *The Tatler*, August 9, 1710, announced that "At the Flint Glass-House in White Fryars are made and sold all sorts of decanthers of the best Flint". Kersey's *Dictionary*, 1715, defines decanter as "a Bottle made of Clear Flint-Glass, for the holding of Wine, etc., to be pour'd off into a Drinking-Glass".

Engravings of the 1660s make it clear that wide-mouthed bottles blown from soda-glass were in use for decanting. The frontispiece of the *Compleat Gamester*, 1674, illustrates a crystal shaft-and-globe decanter and a baluster-stemmed drinking-glass. Similar bottles of quart capacity were among the first vessels to be made in flint-glass. George Ravenscroft's price list, issued to the glass-sellers in 1677, records that ribbed bottles weighing sixteen ounces were sold at three shillings each and others, "all over nipt diamond wais", of the same weight were four shillings each. The list also stated that these bottles "have stoppers fitted to them and given in at the rates aforesaid and also handled if required".

Existing specimens show that to facilitate transferring the wine from the bottle to such a decanter, the mouth was expanded into an almost hemispherical funnel with a beak spout. Some of those vessels were lavishly ornamented with applied decoration in the Venetian fashion and listed as "extraordinary work at 5/- per pound". Thick trailed threads enriched the body and elaborate frills encircled the lower neck, with the addition of such motifs as pinched wings, strawberry prunts, chainwork and strapwork. The base stood upon a foot-rim, plain or gadrooned, extending half an inch or more from the body. The loop handle was usually plain with a curled tail and often a thumb-rest on the upper curve. The stopper was blown hollow, highly domed with a solid knop finial. Encircling the widest diameter of the stopper was a projecting rib preventing it from becoming jammed in the decanter mouth. The stopper-finial junction was encircled with frilled ornament. Ravenscroft also supplied purled decanters at the same rates as the diamond. Similar decanters were made by his successors, production continuing into early Georgian days.

The majority of seventeenth-century flint-glass decanters followed the shape of the shaft-and-globe wine bottle (Chapter 7) with a spherical body, a full curved shoulder, an intruding base, a neck-ring and a plain mouth fitted with a stopper. It measured 7 to 9 inches in height and was filled through a flint-glass funnel. This funnel was shaped in a curve at the end so that the lower opening was horizontal, causing the wine to cascade down the side of the flint-glass: this revealed its quality and also prevented aeration of the falling wine. Later the wine funnel might be of silver.

A shaft-and-globe wine bottle bearing a dated seal of 1657 is in the Northampton Museum. A decanter of this shape in flint-glass and bearing a Ravenscroft seal (see Chapter 1), thus dating it between 1677 and 1681, is in the British Museum. This is mounted on a gadrooned foot ring and the surface covered with a trellis pattern in relief, but the majority, of course, were plain surfaced. Such globular-bodied decanters continued to be made until the end of the Stewart period, decorated with trailed flutes and ribbons, frills, strawberry bosses and sometimes their owners' seals.

The ring base had been abandoned by the opening of the eighteenth century, the globular body standing flat upon the table as a wine bottle. The high kick in pre-1740 de-canters is almost opaque because it still proved impossible to fuse the lead oxide efficiently with the other materials in the melting pot. As explained elsewhere, the high kick in hollow-ware of this period, and also the pedestal foot, had a functional purpose, facilitating annealing until the develop-ment of the tunnel annealing leer. Shaft-and-globe decanters continued to be widely used until late in the reign of George II in quart and pint capacities. Variations of form are found, but no chronological significance has been attributed to these, except for a late dating to a low kick and a lack of neck. Seldom are such decanters found with ornament, although some late examples were engraved. Georgian shaft-and-globe decanters are heavy and in no way resemble Victorian decanters of similar form, light in weight and of whiter metal of thin section, and frequently with the spherical body compressed.

It is doubtful if any shaft-and-globe decanter of the seventeenth century has survived complete with its glass stopper which would then have been hollow-blown. Stoppers complete with finials from the late 1690s were shaped in the solid by pinching. Ball finials were the rule and from about

1710 these might be embellished with single air-bubbles or groups of several small ones. Comma-shaped tears in this connection date from the mid-1720s. The flat ends of stoppers pre-dating the mid-eighteenth century display tool marks : later the ends were ground flat.

The shaft-and-globe decanter continued fashionable into the period of shouldered decanters. This is confirmed by its presence on the table, with wine bottles and drinking-glasses, in Gawen Hamilton's painting of "The Brothers Clarke of Swakeleys", *c.* 1750. Examples will be found fitted with cut spire-finialled stoppers such as the celebrated Chastleton set made for Henry Jones who died in 1761. Shaft-and-globe decanters of this period might be encircled with Norwich rings.

Mallet-shaped Decanters with hexagonal or octagonal bodies were used during the first three decades of the eighteenth century. The sides of the body were usually vertical but might have a slight outward slope from the base. Body and neck were of equal length or the neck might be the longer. The mouth was slightly expanded to take the ball-finialled stopper, neither being ground. The neck was encircled by an applied ring positioned an inch or more below the mouth. These closely resembled neck-rings of the late eighteenth century and might be rounded, knife-edged, single, double or treble. Shoulders were near-horizontal. An occasional example will be found with a loop handle, the mouth immediately opposite being extended into a beak spout. The kick in early mallet-shaped decanters rose into a high cone : by the 1730s it was no more than a slight uplift raising the punty scar above table level.

Quatrefoil or *Cruciform Decanters* were an early Georgian design in flint-glass dating from the mid-1720s to the 1760s. The body was tooled vertically so that on plan it appeared as a four-sided cross with lobes extending equidistantly. Other features closely followed the mallet shape, including a capacity of one quart. In the British Museum is a trade card dated 1748 illustrating an excellent example in use for the service of cider. The mouth is never lipped and only occasionally found ground for a stopper. The quatrefoil body in the wine cistern offered a greater area to the iced water and was intended to cool the wine more speedily than was possible with a globular body. Associated forms were the decanters with cylindrical bodies tooled into deep vertical grooves, and square bodies with deeply recessed corners.

Shouldered Decanters were advertised between 1740 and the 1760s, but remained on glass-sellers' lists until early in the nineteenth century. Many were outstanding examples of the glass-maker's art: others were of tale glass such as were advertised in the *Dublin Journal,* 1750: "taverns and public houses supplied with quart, pint, and half-pint decanters for wine, cider or ale". They were made in two types: broad-shouldered narrowing inward towards the base; and narrow-shouldered with sides sloping outward to the base. These shapes are found in wine bottles of blue and white hard porcelain imported from China earlier in the century. The early shouldered decanters were slender-bodied and retained the kick of early bottle forms, together with a rough punty scar.

The slender neck was tall and the ground-in ball-finished stopper recessed in the plain-brimmed mouth. This was succeeded by a series of vertical, flat-sided stopper finials, usually hexagonal, rarely octagonal, with each edge slightly scalloped, the flat sides polished. A print published in 1747 by Carrington Bowles, St. Paul's Churchyard, illustrates a pair of narrow-shouldered decanters fitted with stoppers having plainly cylindrical flat-topped finials. Stoppers of this pattern are recorded in prints from time to time during the next half-century, but curiously enough very few such stoppers appear to remain.

Existing decanters demonstrate that in flint-glass they were not ground to receive stoppers until the mid-eighteenth century, the smooth-surfaced stopper fitting closely into the neck, but with little pretence at keeping the contents air-tight. It has been stated by several authorities that stopper grinding was unknown until the early Georgian period: the process was, however, fully described by John Worlidge in 1675 when corks were found unsafe for sealing fine wines. "With a Turn lathe made for that purpose you may grind glass-stopples to each Bottle, that no liquor or spirit shall penetrate its closures: always observing to keep each Stopple to its bottle which is easily done by securing it with a piece of pack-thread, each Stopple having a button on top of it for that end and a glass ring round the bottle neck. These Stopples are ground with the powder of the stone smyris, sold in the shops by the vulgar name of Emery, which with oil will exquisitely work the glass to your pleasure. First grind them rough with coarse emery, then make them smoother with fine. The mouths of your bottles are similarly ground in the Turn." This establishes the original intention of neck-rings on decanters and finials on stoppers.

Decanter mouths and their stoppers were not ground as a matter of routine until the 1740s, their use having been discouraged by the frequency with which the finials broke off, leaving the stopper immovable within the decanter.

Spire-finials to stoppers were introduced by Thomas Betts, the King's Arms Glass Shop, under the name of "Betts' Gothic" during the mid-eighteenth century vogue for Gothic ornament in homes of the gentry. They were smoothly plain cones at first and accompanied undecorated decanters; naturally with faceted decanters the spires were faceted; with engraved ornament the spires were cut into pyramid form. Examples have been noted with a ball-knop containing a cluster of air-beads separating the finial from the stopper end which is sunk a considerable depth into the mouth. At about the same time the stopper, formerly purely cylindrical, was made tapering and the decanter mouth tapered to match. By now the kick in the base was no more than a slight upward bulge and the punty scar ground smooth.

Spire finials began to be outmoded in the early 1760s by the vertical disc finial, a development of the hexagonal type. These at first were flat, vertical discs with plain surfaces, their edges encircled with diamond-cutting. This was followed by scalloping, usually six to each face with a knife edge and the flat surfaces rendered concave. This was followed by the pear-shaped stopper finial with scalloped edges. Contemporary engravings show that flat heart-shaped and clover-leaf finials belong to this period.

Shouldered decanters soon became a field for ornament

with cutting, engraving, gilding and enamelling, carrying decanters for the first time into the luxury class of table-ware. The well-annealed flint-glass was strong enough to accept all-over facet-cutting. At first the facets were no more than flat touches of the wheel, then distinctly hollowed. The body facets were wider than long and arranged in spirals: the shoulders were encircled with wide flutes and the necks with long narrow diamonds. Trade cards issued by Thomas Betts, Jerom Johnson, John Akerman and William Parker all illustrate such decanters. These continued to be made after 1780 in a metal of thicker section with facets more concave. The effect of a field of scintillating facets viewed through facets with intense ruby or other coloured liquor between produced a superbly radiant effect never achieved by the later diamonds cut in deep relief. The original stoppers were spire-finialled cut with small diamond facets.

A small number of shouldered decanters were Norwich cut, their bodies cut horizontally with seven or nine shallow concave corrugations, the sharp crests between each pair being impeccable circles. Shouldered decanters from the mid-1760s might be encircled with shallow-cut designs. A favourite pattern was to cut the body with six vertical classical pillars joined at the top by sprays of curved mitre-cutting. In others the base might be cut with a double row of facets, a circuit of short flutes, a plain zig-zag, or the tulip pattern, the shoulder and neck being enriched with scale or polygonal facets or small detached printies. The body space between these ornaments might remain plain but was customarily engraved with flowers and foliage, fruiting vine, star festoons, and occasionally an all-over pictorial design with an inscription, such as those engraved in 1788 on the occasion of the centenary of the "Glorious Revolution".

Wheel-engraving was used extensively to add interest to shouldered decanters from about 1750. Naturalistic motifs were preferred such as floral sprays, birds, insects, and fruiting vine. By the 1760s formal ornament included the trellis, husk and sprig motifs, swags, festooning ropework, usually polished and in reality light cutting rather than engraving.

The *Norwich Weekly Mercury* in December **1771** contained an advertisement by James and Arthur Jarvis offering "Cut, plain, sprig'd and engraved quart decanters and a few plain half gallon decanters: quart, pint and half pint carrosts".

Shouldered decanters were the first to bear labels specifying their contents, the name of the wine with no other ornament being engraved on one side in large capitals, the reverse being covered with an expansive design of fruiting vine or, less frequently, hop and barley. The earliest reference to labelled decanters discovered by Francis Buckley was in the *Norwich Weekly Mercury* dated December 26, 1755, where Jonas Phillips announced "new-fashioned Decanters with inscriptions engraven on them, Port, Claret, Mountain, etc., etc., decorated with Vine leaves, Grapes, etc.". Advertisements during the next few years described them as "flower'd and lettered decanters". From the early 1760s they were known to glass-sellers as "label decanters" and were so advertised in *Aris's Birmingham Gazette*, January 23, 1764. These decanters were stocked by glass-sellers engraved with the names ale, beer, burgundy, cider, Greek wine, hock, Lisbon, port, punch, rum and white wine. Other wines were engraved to commission, the cost being one shilling.

Although considerable numbers were made and engraved, comparatively few are yet in the cabinets of collectors and these almost invariably have the name engraved in large capitals framed in a simple border in the shape of current bottle tickets in silver. This was further enriched by an ornamental cartouche with mantlings of foliage above and fruiting vine below, except in the case of ale and beer when hops and hop leaves were engraved, and cider when apples and foliage were displayed. Chain-work, extending from the top of the label frame around the neck completed the illusion of an elaborate bottle ticket. In some instances the inscription was gilded. The reverse of the decanter was usually plain so that the label should not be obscured by the presence of irrelevant ornament.

Decanters labelled in coloured or white enamel were the work of independent enamellers of London, Bristol, Birmingham and Newcastle-upon-Tyne, working mainly for the china sellers. The Beilbys of Newcastle-upon-Tyne decorated decanters with skilful ingenuity in colour and in white. Various enamellers advertised for work in enamelling flint-glass-ware. Modern enamelling is sometimes applied to antique shouldered decanters.

A second series of labelled decanters issued during the Regency are of Prussian shape with three rings encircling the neck and with pear-shaped or target stoppers.

Champagne Decanters are a form of narrow-shouldered decanter evolved in the 1750s, with a cylindrical pocket of flint-glass to contain ice, extending from high on the shoulder downward into the body and provided with a metal cover. In an invoice by Thomas Betts, and now in the collection of Sir Ambrose Heal, "one pair of Neat Ice Champagne Quart Decanters" are priced at twelve shillings.

Taper Decanters were evolved from the narrow shoulder decanter in the early 1760s by slimming the body and making the shoulder less accentuated. "New-fashioned decanters" were advertised in London, Bristol and Stourbridge in 1765, no doubt in reference to the introduction of the tapered form. The taper decanter was cut around the base with a circuit of short, narrow, closely-spaced vertical flutings. The neck from shoulder to mouth was faceted with scale pattern or diamonds, or fluted, and from 1780 these might be notched, the base flutes being notched to match. The body was often lightly cut with bands of short, narrow, hollowed concavities. In other instances the space between the base fluting and shoulder fluting was left clear or engraved with an all-over design or coat of arms, and occasionally a label. Cut decanters of taper form were now advertised.

The mouth of the early taper decanter was lipless, but from about 1770 it might be widely flared. A single neck-ring appeared at about the same time and these vessels are uncommon. Scalloped disc finials to stoppers were usual at first, but as the taper became slimmer the finial followed suit and became a flat, vertical lozenge or pear-shape such as was also associated with late shouldered decanters. The edges were often plainly bevelled but more usually scalloped. Taper decanters continued to be made in the early nineteenth century with wide lip rims.

Barrel-shaped Decanters, known also as oviform and Indian club shape, displayed a form borrowed by the glass-sellers from the silversmiths who were using it extensively in hollow-ware. "Curious barrel-shaped decanters cut on an entirely new pattern" were advertised by Christopher Haedy in the *Bath Chronicle*, December 21, 1775. A few months earlier Philip Elliott had advertised in the *Bristol Gazette* "decanters of a new and elegant pattern".

The barrel-shaped decanter was evolved by incurving the body towards the base and accentuating the bulge, thus giving the decanter body a form resembling that of a wine barrel. The body was cut with vertical flutes to resemble staves, widening and then narrowing up the neck to the mouth in a similar way. Incised rings encircling the body suggested hoops. Early barrel decanters were lipless: then came the flaring lip which soon became wider and for the first time on decanters was made with a flat surface and a vertical edge. These decanters are now difficult to find.

Prussian Decanters have been misleadingly called barrel decanters because their silhouette does in fact suggest a squat cask such as was used for the packing of dry goods. John Keeling of Dudley, a specialist maker of Prussian decanters, illustrated an example under the name of Prussian decanter on his trade card of 1784: one of these cards is in the British Museum collection. In the same year the Holly Hall Glasshouse, Stourbridge, advertised "Barrel and Prussian-shaped decanters cut and plain".

Unlike the slender symmetrical barrel decanter with its neatly cut staves, the Prussian decanter was broad-shouldered and an obvious development of the earlier broad-shouldered decanter. The body sides were given a greater inward slope than formerly, the neck was shortened and thickened, and ornamented with two or three widely spaced rings and the mouth expanded into a broad flat lip having an inward slope and a rounder edge. This design emphasized horizontal lines, and although in no way comparable with the delicate grace of earlier decanters this form continued predominant until the 1830s.

FIG. 5. Pinched decanter-stopper designs, 1805–1835.

The Prussian decanter was designed to withstand the stresses and strains which occurred during its passage through Ensall's improved annealing tunnel. There was little breakage either in cooling or using. In annealing shouldered decanters there was a loss of at least one-third in passing through the leer and in cooling. This shape could also be inexpensively blown-moulded (see Chapter 13) with a circuit of comb-fluting around the base.

The finest, however, were free-blown from metal taken from the middle of the pot. A gathering of molten glass was picked up on a blow-pipe and expanded into a hollow sphere. This was elongated to the required shape by swinging from side to side, finally flattening the end and drawing out the neck. The servitor then attached a punty iron against the centre of the flattened part and the blow-pipe was broken away. The decanter was reheated at the glory hole and then tooled to its final shape on the chair.

Rings were applied to the neck by rotating the red-hot decanter on the chair and dropping a thread of molten glass which became welded by contact. The neck and rings were then reheated at the glory hole and a tool resembling a pair of spring sugar tongs with a pair of dies at the ends of the arms was pressed over the hot rings, one by one, impressing them to the required shape and width. The decanter required re-heating for the addition of each subsequent ring. While shaping the mouth lip the rings were well heated to ensure that they would not crack during annealing. The joints are always faintly visible as hair cracks, having the appearance of flaws.

Vast numbers of blow-moulded comb-fluted Prussian decanters were made in England, Scotland and Ireland, but the free-blown examples were of thicker section, the comb-fluting hand-cut, the shoulders cut with wide flutes, with sometimes touches of cutting between the rings. The body might be engraved: in the 1790s there was a vogue for engraving a monogram or crest on one side, a picture of personal interest on the opposite face. More frequently, however, the decanter was engraved with an encircling repeating motif. From about 1805 Prussian decanters were cut in deep relief, diamonds predominating. These patterns are far too numerous to classify here.

A new shape in stopper finials accompanied the Prussian decanter. This was the horizontal or mushroom shape, separated from the stopper end and lifted high above the lip by a polished ball knop on a short stem. The mushroom top was curved into arc outline and pinched with gadrooned or radial grooves, entirely unassociated with the style of body ornament. The finial was flat beneath and had a spread about equal to that of the widely everted lip, which in its turn was of greater diameter than the lowest and largest of the three neck-rings. By the nineteenth century had appeared the target or bull's-eye stopper finial, also shaped by pinching. This might have a central boss with radial ridges on each face and a serrated edge which might be cut. Others were facet-cut on each face. A third type was lightly impressed with trellis or other simple line patterns.

Cylindrical Decanters with perpendicular sides were made in the 1790s. This design is cut with inch-wide vertical flutes which continue, gradually narrowing, over the shoulder to the lowest neck-ring. Such decanters continued in production until the early 1830s, their shoulders accentuated to an angle of about forty-five degrees. From about 1805 the shoulders might be cut in deep relief and from 1820 horizontal prismatic cutting might encircle the shoulders. By the mid-1820s a series of cylindrical decanters was in production with horizontal shoulders.

FIG. 6.   Pincers for pressing glass stoppers

Cylindrical decanters from the early Regency years were elaborately cut. It was fashionable for the body to be encircled with two or three bands of cutting separated from each other by flat polished rings. Typical were a lower band of vertical flutes with a field of small relief diamonds above, and, later, bands of horizontal prism-cutting, strawberry diamonds, and vertical prisms or thin flutes, wide flutes, relief diamonds. The combinations are endless. Some of the most complex and elaborately worked diamond-cutting is found on cylindrical decanters from about 1820 to the mid-1830s.

Cylindrical decanters were fitted with mushroom stoppers until about 1820 when there was a vogue for heavy pinnacle stopper finials. At the same time appeared large globe and hemispherical finials, often hollow but usually solid. All of these were also fitted into Prussian-shaped decanters.

There was a vogue from about 1810 to the early 1820s for the rim of the decanter mouth to be cut with a design matching the cut neck-rings below. The mouth of a fashionable decanter of the Regency and George IV periods flared widely and gracefully outward from the neck, the flare beginning immediately above the neck-ring.

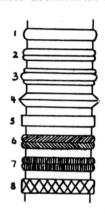

Seven types of neck-rings are found on cylindrical and Prussian decanters: plain single, double and treble round, square, knife-edged, feathered and facet-cut. The feathered ring is a double-ring impressed with shallow lines placed at an angle. Applied neck-rings were omitted from many of the expensive decanters after about 1815, the entire neck being encircled with prismatic cutting or with rings tooled in the solid and cut. Decanters in which the neck rings do not match are uncommon.

FIG. 7. Varieties of decanter ring.

1. Single round. 2. Double round. 3. Triple round. 4. Triangular. 5. Square. 6. Feathered. 7. Double rigaree. 8. Cut.

Cylindrical decanters with sides slanting outward from base to shoulder date from the late 1820s. This was known as the royal shape and was introduced by Apsley Pellatt at the coronation of William IV in 1828. Twelve or fourteen plain bold vertical convex flutes were cut from base to lower neck, and three diamond-cut neck rings with matching bands of cutting encircled the neck between each and the flaring mouth. Stopper finials were of the turned-out fluted type, the low-domed upper surface being cut to match. These were advertised at ten shillings each. In another version the two upper neck rings were omitted and the neck fluted to the rim. Perpendicular sides continued and with wide convex flutes were fashionable until the late 1840s but continued in production until the 1860s.

Fancy decanters was the name given by glass-sellers to the wide range of cut decanters with spire stoppers made from about 1830. In many of these the neck, with a thick expansive brim with a vertical edge, was incurved to the centre, a single ring encircling the top of the shoulder. The body might be globular, barrel-shaped, Prussian shape, or cylindrical with the entire surface cut. Decanters of this period are also to be found with foot-rings, a feature more frequent from 1840. The Prussian shape may have a boldly swirled body, three neck-rings and a large spherical stopper finial also swirled. A long-necked bludgeon-shaped decanter with a balloon-shaped stopper finial was also popular.

Many of these factory decanters were cut on a machine invented in 1833 by John Gold of Birmingham. This would cut, grind, smooth and polish flint-glass decanters. Plain surfaces, grooves, elevated surfaces, and ornamental cutting were efficiently produced by the machine which cut several decanters at a time with all the appearance of hand-cutting.

Cordial Decanters in flint-glass were advertised in 1744, plain, with stoppers, pint-size, at sevenpence a pound. These complied with wine decanter forms, but by 1765 the fashionable tea-table cordial decanter was broad-shouldered and ornamented with all-over facet-cutting. These have been noted in double pairs of quart and pint size intended for wines and cordials.

Towards 1780 a special decanter was designed for the service of cordials. This had a slender, barrel-shaped outline and stood upon a square pedestal foot. Early examples were exquisitely shallow-cut. They continued in production until early Victorian days. A flint-glass price list of 1829 lists undecorated pint-size cordial decanters with square pedestal feet, or ring feet, at 1*s*. 7*d*. per pound.

A now uncommon type of cordial decanter that found a place on tea-tables from the 1790s has a bulbous or globular body divided into four sections by means of interior walls placed at right angles to each other and extending from base to neck-rim. Each of the four openings in the stout neck possesses a stopper. A pair of such decanters would contain eight different cordials, about half a pint of each.

Ships' or Rodney Decanters were fashionable in a day when

ships' cabins for officers and passengers were panelled in fine woods and furnished with specially designed furniture, usually having three or four purposes. Wine decanters of quart capacity were made in heavy metal of thick section in a design suggesting a triangle when viewed from the side. The base was expansive, the sides straight, rising direct from the base to the neck, without an intervening shoulder. Their weight and expansive base gave stability.

These vessels became known as Rodney decanters after the battle of St. Vincent in 1780. "Ten neat Rodney quart decanters with cut rings" were ordered from John Dixon, a glass manufacturer of Whittington in Yorkshire during 1791.[1] In 1799 such decanters are noted in the Waterford records as "Rodneys". Their triangular bodies are for the most part undecorated save for wide fluting, and the three or four neck-rings in graduated diameters are also brilliantly cut. They have been noted cut with Norwich rings. In some instances the base measures 10 to 12 inches in diameter and is radially cut with mitred incisions from centre to circumference, thus giving a firmer grip on a baize cloth. A mallet-shaped series was also made, the body comb-fluted or plain with fluted shoulders. Examples are sometimes noted engraved with a seaman's head.

Square Decanters and *Bottles* were made unceasingly throughout the Georgian period. The earliest were made on the lines of the mallet-shaped decanters, but with square bodies, body and neck being of about equal length. Such decanters are rare, being originally intended for the rough-and-tumble of public service. John Buxton, 93 Watling Street, advertised in the *London Evening Post* during 1769 that he had for disposal "a quantity of square decanters for public houses to be sold cheap".

The majority of squares, however, have high shoulders and very short necks for convenience when packing for transport. From about 1745 blown-moulded squares, slightly tapering from shoulder to base, were made in large quantities. These square bottles were a specialized branch of the trade, and quart sizes of the eighteenth century

---

[1] *Glass-Making in England*, by H. J. Powell, 1923.

Plate 25

(*Upper row, l. to r.*) Tumbler engraved with three-masted man-of-war and inscribed "Prince George Admiral". H.M.S. *Prince George* was launched in 1772. Height 8 inches. Tumbler inscribed "The Glorious 11th Octr 1797" commemorating the Battle of Camperdown. Firing glass with heavy disc foot. Drawn glass inscribed "SUCCESS TO WIL & MARY", height 4 inches; one of a set of six firing glasses engraved with Masonic emblems and fruiting vine, height 3 inches.
(*Lower row, l. to r.*) Firing glass with ogee bowl engraved with crowned thistle, opaque-white-twist stem, height 3¼ inches; firing glass with drawn trumpet bowl engraved with Masonic emblem, height 3⅝ inches; firing glass with conical bowl, height 4⅝ inches; ship's glass with ovoid bowl and expansive thick foot, height 4⅝ inches; ship's glass with heavy foot, trumpet bowl with air-twist stem, height 5⅝ inches.

Plate 26
(*Upper row*) Sweetmeat glasses: (*Left*) Lipped ogee bowl moulded with flutes, collared silesian ste
on domed moulded foot; height 3 inches. (*Right*) Cut and scalloped bowl, silesian stem with tw
knops containing tears, domed foot; height 6½ inches (*Lower row, left*) Money box with handl
trailed decoration; height 6½ inches; early nineteenth century. (*Right*) Covered sweetmeat bow
engraved, with knopped air-twist stem.

usually have faint vertical scratches in the four faces, made whilst drawing the semi-cool square from its mould. The base has neither kick nor punty mark, but is so shaped that there is no danger of creating a vacuum when the vessel stands on the table. Only the tips of the corners are in contact with it. The shoulders are rounded.

Squares were also free-blown in a finer flint-glass, and the faces might be shallow-cut: in some instances the four corners were canted and cut with horizontal mitre incisions, a band of diamonds encircling the body a little above the base. Sometimes one face might bear the owner's cypher engraved or gilded. Many squares were intended for spirits and were enclosed in velvet-lined mahogany, satinwood or sharkskin cases designed to carry two, four, six, eight or a dozen squares which could be locked against the acquisitive.

Smaller squares of pint and half-pint sizes, at first in heavily leaded glass with solid glass ball-finialed stoppers were intended for cordials, medicines, or toilet waters: these were also protected in plain chests. Squares designed for use on the toilet table were enriched with gilded ornament and lips, illuminating the bottles when viewed from above in their cases. Later they were cut on shoulders and lip. Very often this gilding has so worn that only slight traces remain. So similar are plain-faced squares in appearance that it is only possible to date them by the quality of the metal, skill in manufacture, type of stopper—although this may well be a replacement—and the presence of any applied motif, engraved, cut, gilded or enamelled. Sets of three or four squares heavily encrusted with relief diamonds and with faceted ball-knop finials were made from early in the nineteenth century.

Carafes were stopperless bottles of decanter form for holding water on the dining-table, one carafe and a pair of goblets being set before each two guests. A goblet was defined in Bailey's dictionary, 1730, as "a large drinking vessel commonly of round form without either foot or handle". Carafes might also contain wine, but until about 1770 they were invariably advertised as "water crafts". Later they were advertised variously as carraffs and carrosts, in quart, pint and half-pint sizes. In flint-glass they followed the forms of contemporary decanters with curved-over, out-spreading mouths. They were entered in glassmakers' lists of the 1830s as "carafes, see decanters", but by the 1860s the vessel had become standardized with a spherical body and had become part of the normal bedroom equipment with an accompanying tumbler which was inverted over the carafe mouth.

A carafe with the body divided horizontally below the shoulders into two sections, the edges fitted with metal threads for screwing it together, was made during the late eighteenth and early nineteenth centuries. At this time the drinking of medicinal wines immediately upon awakening in the morning was favoured. One of the most common of these, known as the bark, was made from cinchona, the bark of an evergreen Peruvian tree named after the Countess of Chinchon who introduced the drug to Europe in 1638. This medicine, after standing in a carafe for a few hours, deposited a thin coating difficult to remove and leaving a permanent stain and odour. To facilitate cleansing the divisible carafe was devised. Those noted have had cylindrical bodies cut with flat flutes, and the metal threads have been in silver bearing hall-marks of the 1790s. A matching tumbler accompanied the carafe.

Wasp or Fly Catchers bear a passing resemblance to wide-based decanters. This is usually a plain-shouldered or Prussian-shaped vessel standing on three shell or ball feet, but the base, instead of being closed, is open, with the lower rim curled upward and inward to form an encircling gutter about two inches deep. The gutter was charged with sweetened strong ale as an insect bait. The insects soon found their way into the vessel where the fumes made them drowsy so that, casting discretion to the wind, they alighted upon the sweet liquor and were drowned. Those noted have been undecorated apart from neck-rings on early examples. They were made from the late eighteenth century to the 1860s.

Chapter Nine

CANDELABRA AND LUSTRES

THE lustre and refractive power of flint-glass made it an ideal material for candelabra and chandeliers. Hung with scintillating pendants, their rainbow colours flashing and interplaying, they fascinated their Georgian owners. The name candelabrum was first applied to English work by Matthew Boulton of Birmingham, who, in addition to numerous designs in silver and Sheffield plate, made handsome examples combining ormolu with cut-glass, a fashion which continued uninterruptedly for half a century.

Glass candelabra are not known to have been made in flint-glass earlier than George I's reign, when they were called branches or candlestands. The basic design was a candlestick with a deep socket designed to receive a glass peg from which curved several branches. The earliest example so far noted in flint-glass is in the Victoria and Albert Museum. The supporting stem consists of a terraced drop-knop rising from a domed and terraced foot, and has a deep cylindrical socket strengthened with a deeply-rolled rim. Into this fits a cylindrical peg continuing upward with air-bead knops and a terraced finial. From between the beaded knops spring four branches curving downward and upward, terminating in plain grease pans with cylindrical sockets. W. B. Honey dates this 1725-30, and W. A. Thorpe records the metal to be highly leaded. Glass candelabra with loose branches are rare.

Trade cards show branched candelabra to have continued throughout the eighteenth century. Colebron Hancock, near Upper Mews Gate, Charing Cross, illustrates an example with a facet-cut cusped stem supporting an expansive hemispherical facet-cut boss; from this curve four branches terminating in sockets with loose nozzles, and from between them rises a tall urn-shaped finial. A two-branch candelabrum is shown with a central spire finial. William Parker illustrates a six-branch candelabrum, facet-cut all over. The domed foot supports a tall circular tapering standard, so designed that three flat silver rings fit equidistantly spaced. From each extends a pair of curved branches of diminishing spread, with a finialled canopy at the top. Other cards illustrate similar branched candlesticks, some of them hung with lustres.

When clearer, more brilliant glass became available from the piling pots within the furnace (see Chapter 1) by the late 1730s, flint-glass with greater dispersal power than formerly became in great demand for glass lustres or icicles as they were sometimes called. Formerly rock crystal had been preferred as it would withstand grinding at the wheel without fracture. The dispersive power of rock crystal is 14, modern flint-glass 36, and the diamond 44.

Thomas Betts in his trade card of the 1740s announced that lustres could be produced "cheaper and better than hitherto has been done". The preparation of each lustre was costly, few cutters being experienced in this branch of grinding, scalloping and faceting. Mantelshelf chandeliers, redesigned and hung with icicles, were advertised as glass lustres and for more than twenty years the demand was so great, production so small, that they could be obtained only by ordering months in advance. Glass-sellers undertook to clean glass lustres when soiled, as careless servants tended to break them. In 1753 Thomas Betts charged five shillings for this service.

Not until the 1760s were glass-sellers able to meet the demand. Pairs of mantelshelf chandeliers were now designed. A heavy domed foot and a thick cusped stem supported a solid cup-shaped boss containing cylindrical sockets, the centre continuing as a tall vertical spire-shaped shaft, topped by a scalloped canopy hung with pendant lustres. A rayed star or crescent illuminary rose above the apex of the canopy. Into the sockets in the cup-shaped boss were fitted four branches which might be lavishly cut: two at the front, curving upward and downward and ending in

veetmeat glasses in heavy metal of the faintly yellow tint associated with Cork: (*l. and r.*) a pair with rned-over rims and highly domed covers with spire finials, height 14 inches; (*centre*) fluted bowl ith scalloped rim, height 16 inches.

ate 27

vo deep-bowled goblets wheel-engraved with all-over designs composed of vine leaves and grapes reathed around bacchantes in the form of satyrs, and a panther. This engraving is probably the work J. H. B. Millar, a glass-engraver of Leith who specialized in classical scenes. Height 8 inches. 1850s.

Sealed and dated wine bottles showing the progressive change of form during the early Georgia period: (*l. to r.*) 1713, 1722, 1738, 1745.

Plate 28
Sealed wine bottles with names and dates: (*l. to r.*) 1755, 1763, 1776, 1786. These quart-size bottl show a pebbled surface indicating that they were blown in metal moulds. The 1776 example illustrat the narrowing of the body to 4 inches in diameter.

candle-sockets with loose nozzles; two other branches behind, curved sideways and upward to terminate in lustred canopies encircled with pendant lustres and topped by a pair of illuminaries or spires. Ince and Mayhew in 1763 described "illuminaries or disc reflectors" as being cut so that "their several rays will reflect the candles in so many different colours as to render it very beautiful". At this time illuminaries were in diamond shapes or in fluted radial bevels. Eight-rayed star finials with diamond-cut ball centres belong to mantel chandeliers of the 1770s: they were often accompanied by pendant rosettes on the branches. Glass-cutters developed every possible means at their disposal to produce effects that would reveal and exhibit dazzling and prismatic play of colour to the best advantage. Their mantel chandeliers were the delight of rich Georgians sitting around their dark-weather firesides.

Mantel chandeliers of the 1770s stand upon heavy square feet, their flat surfaces highly polished. A pyramidal dome supports a vase-shaped, or, less frequently, a baluster stem from which rises a tall, slender spire, now notched to provide more points for flashing scintillation. As before, this might support a domed and lustred canopy with an expansive illuminary above, but more frequently the curved branches were cut to resemble writhing snakes, with snake's head finials open jawed to hold strings of three or four lustre drops.

The foot from the early 1780s might be highly domed and enriched with shallow diamond-cutting, the surfaces of the three canopies cut to match. The canopies were made with deeper, square domes, and scalloping was emphasized with deeper curves. This was followed by the inverted saucer foot, either banded or completely covered with diamonds in relief in any of the contemporary styles. Domed canopies were displaced by smaller shallow saucers of similar outline to the foot, and from their rims hung strings of short lustre drops, each with a long terminal lustre. Intricate designs skilfully cut on flawless glass produced gorgeously brilliant effects made all the more wonderful to Georgians when an occasional draught produced a melodious tinkle.

Curved branches might now be plain with their upper

surfaces notched, and the top finial might be in the form of a pineapple or a large covered urn enriched with relief cutting. The stem of the chandelier was in matching pattern.

Occasionally four-branched chandeliers intended for the dining-table are discovered, measuring about three feet in height, and originally in pairs. In these the solid glass boss at the head of the standard is more expansive and sunk with eight vertical sockets, from four of which curve branches extending at an angle of forty-five degrees, each terminating in a candle-socket. Between these rise four upward-curving branches with snake head finials suspending chains of lustre drops. From the centre rises a tall spire with a canopy suspending six long chains of lustres, and with a large illuminary finial.

A seldom recognized four- or six-branched table chandelier was patented in 1784 by John Barrett at a cost of about £300. In this design a deep, hemispherical bowl, with a widely expanded lip, stands upon a high bell-shaped or pedestal foot through which runs a central pillar. The pillar supports a boss sunk with deep sockets for the reception of branches, and continues above, being topped by an expansive all-over cut reflecting ball with its canopy and illuminary (see Plate 16). The bowl was filled with water, its surface scintillating in the candlelight at the merest movement of people sitting at table.

Wall-lights in flint-glass date from the first decade of the eighteenth century, probably earlier. Catherine Verney in a letter dated 1710 wrote to her husband, "I would also bye a pare of glass sconces for the side of a chimney", and ten years later Lady Mary Wortley Montagu commented on her wall lustre of rock crystal. These were mirror plates with one or two out-curving branches hanging in a socket. Wall-lights in the style of lustred candelabra are illustrated on trade cards from 1760 to the end of the Georgian period. The early types usually have two branches, a pair of snakes, and a spire with canopy and illuminary. Very few of these are to be found complete with the original brass back-plates which fitted in the wall to hold the glass lights. The reason for this, discovered by Mrs. Graydon Stannus, is because they were left *in situ* on the walls when candles were replaced by gas illumination, the pipes being carried through them.

Early in the nineteenth century the snake branches of mantelshelf candelabra were abandoned, the two remaining lights placed in a line as in silver. Their attractive illuminaries, too, were lost. Every part of the glass surface was now diamond-cut in deep relief. By about 1820 step-cutting was considered the height of fashion on candelabra. Foot, pillar, canopy and the upper surface of the branches might be step-cut, the prisms arranged at angles best suited for catching and reflecting light. At this time the foot might be flat and the canopy a matching disc of cut-glass.

Lustre drops in the nineteenth century became more numerous and were elongated into a drooping slenderness. These were succeeded by long, flat-surfaced hanging prisms found more suitable for reflecting the greater illumination provided. These were pinched in flint-glass to the shape and size required and sold by glasshouses to specialist lustre-makers. The rough lustres were heated at a furnace until plastic: they were then removed by means of tongs designed for the purpose. All flaws such as specks, seeds and microscopic air bubbles were removed by a special hand-tool. It may be mentioned in passing that basic flint-glass, tint-free and flawless, was unknown until the mid-1850s. The Society of Arts in 1834 offered a prize for a process by which flint-glass could be produced without flaws: the prize was unclaimed. The Jury of the Great Exhibition, 1851, also noted these defects in flint-glass. Not until gas furnaces were introduced in the mid-1850s was it possible to obtain the high temperature required to produce flawless flint-glass direct from the pot.

When the lustre had been cleared of flaws the mass was again pinched, thus securing uniformity of shape which might have become distorted whilst plastic. These lustres or prisms were matt-surfaced and exhibited no indication of their potential brilliance. Fins were then filed away, and every facet ground, brightened and polished on the flats of a series of grinding wheels in cast iron, gritstone and hard metal.

Neither lustres nor prisms of fine quality appear to have

been made in Ireland. This suggests that Irish metal was not of the high quality essential for such work. Waterford, for instance, bought lustres from Birmingham, thus discounting the theory that Waterford flint-glass was the most perfect of its period. English lustre drops swell to points on one side or both, and are more richly faceted than the Irish which are typically round or almond-shaped and flatter when viewed sideways, and also deeper-tinted. Prisms with sharp angular corners giving greater reflecting brilliance were the invention of John Gold in 1840.

The illuminaries—stars, crescents, diamonds and so on, measuring 5 to 9 inches in height—used on mantelshelf and side-table candelabra were cast in handled moulds, giving relief shape to one surface, the back remaining flat. After annealing they were faceted.

Chapter Ten

CANDLESTICKS AND TAPERSTICKS

CANDLES in England light a thousand pictures in the mind. They reflect the gay days of Beau Nash: fiddles, hautboys, flashing swords—all the phantoms, laughing or sad, of that wonderful Georgian world. Glass candlesticks in England have had a long history. The inventory of Henry VIII's belongings in 1542 includes eleven glass candlesticks bought from Venice: "oone lowe Candlesticke of glasse, Jasper colour; thr great bell Candlesticks of glass partely gilt; four less bell Candlesticks of glasse partly gilt; thre Aulter Candlesticks of Glass". These, of course, were provided with wide deep sockets and burned fine wax candles of scented English beeswax. Candles which illuminated the personal rooms of nobles were for the most part of imported wax; the gentry burned candles of Russian tallow, less hard and with a tendency to flicker, crackle and gutter.

Silver domestic candlesticks attributed to this period were in a style with a bell foot under an expansive drip-pan supporting a cylindrical stem, turned into baluster and knop-forms and terminating in a socket. These continued fashionable until Elizabethan days, together with pricket candlesticks. It may be assumed that glass candlesticks followed the silversmith's socketed forms in later periods.

Candlesticks of English-made glass are not known to have been used earlier than the end of the seventeenth century owing to the fragility of the metal, but there seems no reason why they should not have been made inexpensively in bottle-glass. They appeared in flint-glass from the early 1680s and at first were blown hollow, from the high foot, in bell or pedestal shape and with a wide-spreading rim, through a knopped stem, to a deep socket. The socket had a thick, rolled, strengthening lip, fitted with a loose saucer-shaped nozzle. At the cost of three shillings a pound, a pair of such candlesticks might cost fifty shillings, with replacement nozzles at about a shilling each.

As the cost of flint-glass tumbled towards the end of the century, chiefly owing to the nation-wide establishment of competitive glasshouses, glassmen found it more profitable to work with solid metal. Candlesticks from the early 1690s were short-stemmed, usually in baluster and knop forms copied from the silversmiths. The dominant central motifs were inverted balusters and acorn shapes, their widest diameter exceeding the rolled rim of a socket, that might have its base purled or pinched into gadrooning. The surface of the pedestal or domed foot might be pressed by hand tools into vertical ridges or diamond patterns.

A candlestick of the early eighteenth century usually contained a slender-waisted inverted baluster with a series of knops above and below, making the stem somewhat taller than formerly, in compliance with the changing fashion in silver. Collared knops date from this period, and others were enriched with silvery air beads, usually contained in a smooth ball, often flattened. The entire range of knop forms was used chronologically as they came into fashion. The foot might be domed with a welted rim, or shaped like an inverted saucer, and in both forms the surface might be either moulded or else a smooth surface ornamented with incised concentric circles.

A candlestick formerly in the Elkington collection, measuring 16 inches in height, is typical of this period. This has a double baluster stem, a true baluster above an inverted baluster and separated by a flattened knop, with a similar knop between stem and socket, and is supported by a high, conical foot (Plate 32).

In the 1730s there was a short vogue for a glass candlestick with a stem containing as its main feature a solid moulded ball, set between heavily ringed collars or knops. This stem was succeeded by one with a large blown ribbed or trellis moulded sphere set between a series of knops and collars, rising from an expansive foot, domed and ringed, or diamond-moulded.

So far as candlestick feet are concerned, the hollow-blown bell-shape with a welted rim was succeeded by the domed foot, free-blown and shaped by hand tools, and with a punty scar beneath. The blown dome may have a round, smooth surface approaching a hemisphere in shape. Others have a squarish outline with a spreading rim strengthened by a half-inch welt, thus protecting the part most vulnerable to accidental chipping. The flat surface of the spread is usually plain, but might be ornamented with concentric rings, sometimes continued also around the dome. A third type has a sloping outline and may be terraced. Seldom are these hand-tooled feet entirely symmetrical.

Sockets were cylindrical and often strengthened by rolling their edges outward into substantial rims, for it was here that damage occurred when unattended candles burned low. It was therefore customary for candlestick sockets to have loose nozzles with saucer rims and tubular sockets closely fitting those of the candlestick sockets. These served a double purpose: they collected melted wax and they would crack before the heat of a low-burning candle penetrated to the socket proper and damaged the candlestick beyond repair. Spares in standard sizes were stocked by the glass-sellers to replace such breakages, and in the early eighteenth century were sold at eightpence a pound: if scalloped the cost was appropriately increased.

Sockets were for the most part plain surfaced, but others might be tooled with vertical ridges, possibly from late in the Queen Anne period. By the late 1720s the socket might be slightly waisted on the outer surface below the lip to which increased thickness was given by rolling the rim, the interior of course remaining cylindrical. From late in the 1730s the lip itself might be slightly expanded into a narrow saucer-shape: this feature was later enlarged into a full-sized grease pan of a diameter exceeding that of the widest motif on the stem.

Wax candles of improved burning quality, emitting greater illumination, came into use during the early 1740s, and these might sometimes be scented, thus to some extent acting the part of the essential pastille burner or perfume pan. Such candles were of rather less diameter than formerly, and instances have been noted where loose nozzles fitting into wide sockets have been designed to contain these brighter illuminants.

A type of candlestick made at this time and continued in production until the end of the century was intended for use in wall lanterns which during the hours of darkness, often throughout the night, illuminated passages and stairways in large homes. This was stemless, consisting merely of a domed foot with an expansive flange and welted rim supporting a plain cylindrical candlesocket. Late in the century the rim might be scalloped.

A long and varied series of candlesticks dating from about 1710 and in continuous production throughout the Georgian period had the style of stem now known to collectors as shouldered or silesian. These were introduced as the glassmen's version of the square or octagonal section baluster stem fashionable in silver until the late 1720s but made until the 1770s. The silesian stem, designed in several varieties with four or five shoulders, occasionally more, is fully described in Chapter 2. The main feature of early Georgian examples was complicated by the introduction of knops above and below, in a range including plain and air-beaded balls, collars and multiple rings. Sometimes the moulded ridges are pressed vertically, at other times curved gracefully, and occasionally moulded bosses ornament the shoulders. The shouldered stem was sometimes reversed and these are noted with a range of foot designs, such as the highly-domed blown foot with and without a welt; the foot with a low dome and an expansive flange ringed on the underside, known at the time as the spreading dome; and the vertically ridged dome foot. The stem proper rises from a clear button or a short spool-shaped member welded to the centre of the base. Inspection of many early examples shows slight flaws in the welds joining the several units, absent in later examples.

An interesting series are those with short shouldered units placed head to head, usually with a flattened knop between. Another type has three short inverted shoulder motifs

Plate 29
(Upper row and lower right) Mallet-shaped long-necked decanters, three with bladed neck rings: 1730s.
(Lower left) Decanter in crizzled flint-glass; body decorated with thick trailed threads tooled into a
trellis pattern and with seven vertical trails pinched horizontally and vertically. About 1675.

Plate 30

A collection of heavy flint-glass decanters machine-cut in deep relief, 1805–1830s: (*Upper left and right*) Pillar-cut bodies and prismatic-cut necks. (*Upper centre*) Neck and base prismatic-cut, shoulder fluted, body encircled with strawberry diamonds; heavy cut stopper. (*Lower left*) Body with horizontal and placed one above the other. Some of the earlier and finer silesian candlestick stems are enriched with flat vertical fluting: later shallow diamond facets are to be noted. The majority, however, were shaped by pinching and finished with hand-tools, the flutes sometimes being twisted.

The rib-twisted baluster is basically a version of the silesian motif: the stem below the shoulder is twisted into a close spiral. Air-beaded knops might be placed above and below, and a plainly blown domed foot with a ringed flange was preferred. The base of the socket might be purled and its rim expanded into a grease-pan about one-third greater in diameter than the shoulder diameter. These appear to have been made from the early 1730s to about 1750, but a pair has been noted of undoubted late eighteenth-century origin.

Sockets and nozzles on silesian stemmed candlesticks follow the chronological forms usual on other glass candlesticks, but pre-1730 sockets might be vertically ribbed. Shallow-cut sockets date from about 1740, but examples made before 1750 are rare. A socket dating to the second period of cut glass might be encircled by long hexagonal diamond facets, and the surface of the foot sliced. Loose sconces and feet might have matching scalloped rims.

The domes of the feet on silesian stemmed candlesticks are usually moulded with radial or vertical ridges. The pinched silesian stem in its inexpensive form continued as a less costly variant of the glass candlesticks made in finer metal during the second half of the eighteenth century. Only by examination of the metal itself is it possible, usually, to distinguish late silesian stems from earlier productions, although for the most part they are less carefully finished.

Candlesticks were less expensive after the introduction of the Perrott furnace (see Chapter 1). In September 1738 the firm of Cookson & Company, Newcastle-upon-Tyne, established in that year with a Perrott furnace in operation, invoiced "6 Candlesticks, best, at 3/- each". These were, of course, plain flint-glass, undecorated, and the prevailing price of fourpence a pound shows them to have weighed nine pounds each. Later in the same year the Cookson firm invoiced "a pair of Wormed Candlesticks at tenpence a pound", and "a four-branch sconce at £1.11.6.".

Glass candlesticks from about 1740 became progressively more beautiful in form and decoration, until eventually, following improved annealing techniques from 1780, the candlelight scintillated in rainbow effects.

First came the wormed or air-twist candlesticks from the late 1730s and these had a quarter-century vogue. The various types of air twists are discussed in Chapter 2. The earliest of these in candlesticks were developed from neatly arranged clusters of small tears inserted in the thick, heavy base of the socket and offer evidence of the craftsman learning a new technique and drawing rather crude air spirals. The majority of air-spiral units are displayed between knops containing a dozen or more air beads, with multiple rings at either end. Such an air-twist stem was inevitably straight. Thin, tight air spirals were possible by 1750 in a single knopped stem, the knop being placed immediately below the socket: others are knopped at both ends, and in some the knop is immediately above the foot.

Opaque-white enamel spirals in candlesticks date between about 1750 and the 1780s. These spirals are tabulated in Chapter 2. Feet and sockets with sconces of both types follow the earlier styles.

Candlesticks of enamel glass were made at Bristol and elsewhere from the early 1760s (see Chapter 15). This style has a baluster stem tapering towards the socket, ring-knopped at each end, and either smoothly plain or enriched with finely incised twist ornament. The flange of the spreading dome foot and the lipped socket are usually hand-painted with floral sprays in full colour, in the style of South Staffordshire enamels. The loose nozzle is usually of painted enamel with a gilded copper rim.

The silversmiths, with their candlesticks encircled by counter-arranged triangular facets around foot, stem and socket, encouraged glass-sellers to facet-cut their glass candlesticks early in the reign of George I. Every possible use was made of flat or slightly concave surfaces to reflect candlelight. The earliest advertisement of these luxury pieces to be discovered by Francis Buckley was published in the *Daily Advertiser*, December 1742, by Jerom Johnson, a celebrated glass-seller "at the corner of St. Martin's Lane",

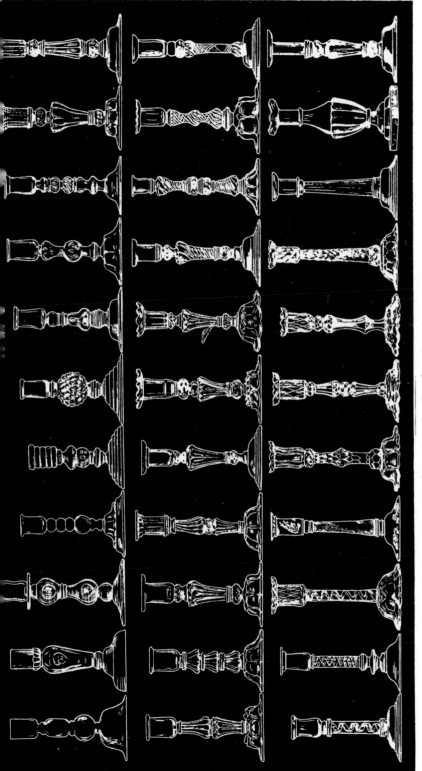

Fig. 8. Chronological series of candlesticks, 1680–1820.

who announced "Diamond-cut and scalloped Candlesticks". A few years earlier he had advertised "Scalloped Dessert Glasses and Lustres done to the utmost perfection". The various types of diamond-cutting are described in Chapter 12.

The introduction at this period of the annealing tunnel and double-annealed flint-glass made possible the more economical production of facet-cutting by further toughening the glass before it was held against the cutting wheel with its ever-present danger of fracture. Enrichment with diamond facets carried cut-glass candlesticks into the homes of the gentry.

The earliest of these diamond-faceted candlesticks are straight-stemmed, knopped at each end, sometimes with ball knops displaying clusters of silvery air-beads. By 1750 knops were larger and facet-cut to harmonize with the stem. At about this time appeared the central knop or cusp. Numerous other knop arrangements followed, including, from the late 1760s, a wide, thin, knife-edged top knop beneath the socket. At about the same time came the vogue for tall, knopless pillar stems reflecting the new classicism. Late examples have been noted with flat-topped relief diamonds made with mitred incisions.

The candlestick stem with faceted double-balusters placed head to head has a ball-knop between each and this, like the shoulders and the upper and lower knops, is cut with facets. The stem proper is encircled with plain vertical fluting. There was at the same time a series in which a faceted cusp and end-knops were joined by flutes.

The foot most frequent on early facet-cut candlesticks is the square dome, with an expansive flange, scalloped rim, the rise and shoulders moulded with vertical ribs or radial ridges, often in high relief, and heavy in comparison with the stem and socket, thus giving greater stability. Less numerous are highly domed blown-moulded feet with welted rims. By the late 1750s the instep of a moulded foot might be cut with large diamonds, flat geometric cutting, plain diamonds or any of the increasing variety of curvilinear motifs. The sliced edges of the scalloped foot match those of the loose nozzle above, which by 1770 might have a diameter approximating half that of the foot. At this time

Decanters showing (*l. to r.*) three, three, two and four neck rings; four rows of prismatic cutting circling the neck; neck cut to simulate neck rings.

Decanters showing (*l. to r.*) target finial to ground stopper; disc finial notched with lunar cutting; bevel-edged pear-shaped finial; mushroom finial with moulded top; two examples of a mushroom finial separated from the ground stopper by a polished ball knop.

Plate 31

Decanters with blown-moulded bodies finished on the cutting wheel; early nineteenth century.

Plate 32
Candlesticks of the eighteenth century. (*Top l. to r.*) Facet-cut; silesian knopped; acorn; silesian and air-twist stems. (*Centre, left*) Knopped stems and domed feet. (*Centre right*) Air-twist stem. (*Bottom, l. r.*) Facet-cut stem; taperstick with silesian stem; double baluster stem, height 16 inches; silesian stem

the domed foot might be blown and shaped by hand-tools, its surface enriched with three bands of cut ornament encircling the flange, the rise, and the shoulder.

The socket is usually plainly cylindrical without a rolled rim and welded direct to the stem without an intervening knop: this suggests the use of loose nozzles throughout the period. A few candlesticks are to be found with their sockets spirally fluted. By 1750 scale pattern, shallow-diamond facets, or full length diamonds placed counterwise ornamented the fashionable candlestick socket which was purely cylindrical, or occasionally waisted.

Tall faceted stems, tapering gracefully from foot to socket, were superseded by stems cut as slender classical columns, with long vertical surfaces highly polished. These stems merge into sockets at first expanded into scalloped wax saucers and later into attractive facet-cut vase shapes fitted with loose nozzles. Some of these stems are hexagonal in section, flat flutes extending from foot to socket base: others are ringed at both ends. Classical stems at first rose from domed and cut feet, sometimes with terraced or stepped rims, then catalogued as "Norwegian feet". Soon the two- or three-stepped square foot was adapted from the Georgian silversmiths, who first used it in the 1760s, every flat surface being carefully squared and brilliantly polished. The vertical corners on the stems of late classical candlesticks might be notched. In some of the finer examples square-rimmed loose nozzles were fitted to match.

In the 1780s the oil-burning argand lamp, with its greater illumination and freedom from snuffing, came into use. This invention gradually outmoded candlesticks in the homes of the gentry. The glass-sellers, facing the loss of a profitable luxury line, introduced less expensive moulded candlesticks for a public that could not afford lamps but was enamoured with the new styles of brass candlesticks in a hue closely resembling gold. The moulded candlesticks were for the most part built from units made by the specialist glass-men known as pinchers (see Chapter 13). With their hand-operated pinching tools they shaped candlestick feet, bodies and cylindrical sockets in separate solid units. Whilst red-hot these were welded into single entities, producing candlesticks measuring from 6 to 12 inches in height at considerably less cost than those worked entirely by hand-tools. The majority of these have "turned" stems with hexagonal sockets; others are hexagonal throughout with free-blown sockets and fixed grease-pans. The petal socket appeared in the early 1820s. There was a vogue for these in colour at twopence a pound extra.

The fashionable barrel shape, a form again derived from the silversmiths, was utilized as the stem in early examples, vertical ribs resembling staves, shallow encircling incisions representing hoops. By the late 1780s the ribs were accentuated into relief, extending from foot to socket, and might be notched. Feet were square and in the various types associated with rummers (see Chapter 4). The loose nozzles were also pinched with expansive saucer rims, the edges often notched. Urn-shaped bodies in candlesticks date from about 1780, the lower part purled, flutes broad. The upper part was enriched with wheel-cutting. Later examples were cut with diamonds in low relief.

This series of candlesticks continued until the end of the Georgian period, being advertised as vase-candlesticks (see Chapter 11). In 1811 they were sold undecorated at the glasshouse at 1s. 10d. per lb. The solid urns provided needed stability. Candlesticks in a brilliant metal with inverted saucer bases and urn stems, the whole prismatic-cut with fine precision, date from about 1820. These may have flat hexagonal feet with honeycomb moulded beneath. Round pressed feet on candlesticks date from this period.

Miniature glass candlesticks, known to collectors as tapersticks, were used to provide small flames in rooms where there was no continuous source of fire, particularly during the summer months. For more than a century until the 1750s they were known as tobacco candlesticks, being used by smokers for lighting their pipes. Specially refined wax candles, non-odorous and costing half a crown each in the 1690s, were sold for this purpose and obviously used only on formal occasions.

Tapersticks, measuring 4 to 6 inches in height, with deep, narrow sockets, often without rolled lips, followed all the characteristics of the candlestick proper, but were never fitted with loose nozzles and never burdened with extraneous ornament. Patterns kept closely to those of candlesticks and were often made *en suite*. The taper-end was wrapped in paper to facilitate removal of the stub end from the deep socket, usually occupying about one-third of the entire taperstick. Complete with lighted taper it was lifted to the smoker's pipe, hence the necessity for a deep socket. By 1700 such articles might be termed tapersticks, and less than half a century later the term tea-candlestick is to be noted. Tapersticks continued to be made until the introduction of friction matches.

Chamber candlesticks in flint-glass are rare indeed and some have been noted as fakes. In 1811 they were listed as "dished candlesticks", and in 1829 as "handled candlesticks". A circular vertical-sided dish with a rolled rim and measuring about 6 inches in diameter carries a short plain socket in the centre. A semicircular handle extends from the side of the socket to the outer rim of the dish.

Chapter Eleven

VASE-CANDLESTICKS AND GIRANDOLES

GIRANDOLE, melodious term for a revolving ornamental fountain, was appropriated by the mid-
Georgians for their most scintillating, lustre-sparkling
piece of glass-ware. This girandole was an elaborate fountain in glass, supporting a pair of candles. But often it is
over-elaborate, and the sense of a rainbow-hued cascade,
its limpid flow held for ever spellbound, is most perfectly
achieved with the simpler lustre-hung candlestick. This is
the girandole-candlestick, encircled with lustre drops and
slender icicles that dance and twinkle and glisten around a
body bright with diamond-cutting.

The collector can trace the exact development of the
girandole-candlestick, and can still find the specimens to
illustrate this byway for the lover of antique glass. Strangely
enough, the more ambitious girandoles considerably preceded the simpler little cascades. Girandoles were being
advertised in the 1770s, but at that time the advertisers were
still coupling them, not with girandole-candlesticks, but
with vase-candlesticks. An instance appears in the *Bath
Chronicle* for December 18, 1777, when the celebrated glass-
seller Christopher Haedy offered "square feet girandoles
and vase-candlesticks".

Vase-candlesticks constitute a distinct group in late
Georgian illuminative glass. They were introduced in the
early 1770s with heavy square feet to give stability, solid
vase-shaped bodies, and cylindrical sockets. These solid
candlesticks, adequately annealed, were found to be an ideal
basis for all-over cutting in deep relief without danger of
fracture. The candlestick units were made by the group of

glass-men known as pinchers, operating chiefly in the Birmingham area.

The stem of an early vase-candlestick is barrel-shaped, and incised with lines suggesting staves and hoops. This pattern was advertised by Christopher Haedy in the early 1770s as "new fashioned". The barrel was succeeded by the pineapple body, and finally by the vase shapes. Trade cards of the 1780s illustrate the three types of stem which were made concurrently throughout the late Georgian period, the vase-shape being by far the most frequent. The incurved neck terminates in a circular flange of slightly larger diameter from which rises a cylindrical socket. Its rim was at first sheared straight: later it was expanded into a saucer-shaped grease pan. In some instances a vase-candlestick of the 1790s or later has a socket rising directly from the neck of the vase without the intermediate flange. These candlesticks display chronologically every fashionable cutting motif of the period.

From the vase-candlestick was evolved the more spectacular girandole-candlestick, merely by expanding the flange and encircling it with scintillating drop lustres. In this way the candlestick made a more fitting accompaniment to the majestic girandole, the name girandole-candlestick distinguishing it from its less glittering predecessor. It measured from 9 to 12 inches in height. Matching pairs were usual, sometimes with a matching table chandelier.

The square foot was completely solid at first; then a hollow dome was pressed on the underside and gadrooned to enrich its refractive properties. Pinched feet and other units were trimmed on the grinding wheel to remove the thin web of molten glass that forced its way between the two halves of the pincher tools. The short pedestal connecting the foot and body was made in a piece with the foot. This might be a spreading spool-shaped unit, or a four- or six-sided pyramid, or a moulded dome rising in steps from the square plinth. The underside might be ornamented with a six-pointed cut star, a feature more frequent after 1820. The sixteen-pointed brunswick star is occasionally seen.

As with vase-candlesticks, the earliest girandole-candlestick, had barrel-shaped bodies; from the mid-1780s the incised lines were omitted from this shape, which was then cut with vertical flutes, slightly concave, the crests cut with intermittent notches. The vase-shaped body, however, predominated, and at this period the lower half might be moulded with gadrooning.

The flange separating body and socket was expanded, being made larger than the foot and slightly dished. The rim was cut with six bold scallops, each bearing pendant lustres—two drops threaded on double-gilded wire, the upper one measuring about one-third the length of the lower. The flange was strengthened beneath by expanding the top of the vase to cover about half of its base. Within the flange was a cylindrical candle-socket, its rim plainly sheared, its base encircled with a thick strengthening ring. The cylindrical socket was quickly outmoded by the tall, urn-shaped pattern, its rim turned over to the horizontal, the edge scalloped, and the upper surface diamond-cut.

From the 1790s the flange bearing the pendant lustres might fit loosely upon the neck of the vase with a brass fitment which enabled it to be revolved, independent of the vase and socket. Such a flange was saucer-shaped, at first shallow, then boldly domed in an upward or downward curve. The lustre drops were succeeded by long slender lustres known as icicle drops, with points often reaching almost to the candlestick foot and tinkling pleasantly against each other in the slightest draught.

The vast majority of lustres were made in England, in swelling shapes characterized by a sharp ridge down the centre of the front, and sometimes also down the back. They were more carefully faceted and smoother than the Irish. The lustres with sharp angular bends for greater brilliancy found on some late girandole-candlesticks may be noted as replacements on much earlier pieces.

Masses of diamonds cut in deep relief ornamented girandole-candlesticks from the early 1800s. A new pattern was designed with a shallow inverted saucer foot, of the same diameter as the flange. Both were cut with matching bands of relief diamonds, their edges either plain or encircled with short, narrow flutes. By 1810 the foot had become more of a dome with deeper, sharper diamond-cutting. Then the umbrella flange was invented and from a heavy facet-cut knop in the centre rose an expansive saucer-shaped sconce or an urn-shaped socket with a spreading horizontal rim. Every available space on body, foot, flange and sconce was lavishly cut. The Regency glassmen produced the double-cascade girandole-candlestick in which the wide rim of the socket was further extended and encircled with lustres reaching almost to the revolving flange below, which still retained its own set of longer, matching lustres.

Girandole-candlesticks with square feet were no longer in fashionable favour by the early 1820s. The foot now took the form of a flat disc, its upper surface radially cut and its edge serrated. In some examples the foot was cut with a sunburst beneath, the points extending to the foot rim. Some round feet were plain with highly-polished single and double step-cutting. The foot and stem were connected by a spool-shaped unit. The vase-shaped stem continued with a large knop above: later there were two knops, the lower being the greater in diameter.

The revolving flange continued, at least as large in diameter as the foot, its up-turned rim cut with a fan, shell or other ornamental border. The socket might be extended into a flat, wide sconce more expansive than the foot, its surface cut radially to match. Foot, stem, flange and socket might be encircled with horizontal prism-cutting. The lustres were long, thin pear-shaped icicles extending almost the length of the body and each topped by one or two jewel-faceted drops.

During the 1820s the vase-shaped body gradually became more slender, reduced, perhaps, to a cylindrical stem, prism-cut and with horizontal grooves, and knopped above and below. By 1830 the stem might include one or two units in burnished silver-gilt or double-gilded brass, placed immediately below the flange and between the flange and the socket. Their high brilliance was found to give the pendant lustres a hint of sunshine colour. The whole flint-glass girandole-candlestick was radiant with a sunshine glow during the 1840s and later when it was placed inside a glass dish lined with a gilded and burnished metal reflector. The Victorian girandole-candlestick with a metal reflecting stand was catalogued as a mantelpiece girandole, whether supporting one light or two.

The final phase of the girandole-candlestick was expressed in coloured glass, but the basic purpose as a candle-holder was lost. Such pieces, made by Davis, Greathead & Green of Stourbridge in the late 1840s, were catalogued as chimneypiece lustres, such as a pattern "in ruby and chrysoprase, with flint drops, cut, enamelled and frosted", colourful, melodious, but solely ornamental.

Chapter Twelve

CUT-GLASS

———

CUT-GLASS, sparkling and lustrous beneath flickering candlelight, is far more than a collector's enthusiasm. On the table or in an illuminated cabinet it scintillates with all the colours of the rainbow as light plays upon facets or flashes from raised diamond points.

The *History of Worcestershire* by T. R. Nash, 1782, states that "Crystal Glass has long been made here [Stourbridge]; but the art of cutting and engraving has not long since been brought from Germany to London, and from London hither". It has been proved conclusively, however, that glass cutters were operating in London during the reign of Queen Anne, and in 1725 more than thirty cutters were named individually as members of the Society for the Art of Glass Grinding.

Glass-cutting on flint-glass developed gradually through distinct phases during the eighteenth century into a highly specialized craft. Glass-sellers employed cutters to decorate flint-glass blanks bought from the glasshouses. These men might work in the glass-sellers' workshops, but were usually garret-masters working in their own homes. Some glass-houses in the 1770s established glass-cutting workshops on their own premises, such as the Holly Hall Glasshouse, Dudley, and Michael Glazebrook, Kingswinford, both of whom were advertising cut and plain flint-glass in the 1780s.

Specialist glass-cutting firms, known as glass-cutting manufacturers and employing as many as fifty workers, began to establish themselves from about 1800, buying blanks from the glasshouses, decorating them to order or to stock patterns which for the most part reflected fashionable

Parisian styles. These were sold to glass-sellers and to export merchants.

The London Post Office Directory, 1811, records forty-five glass-cutting manufacturers, some of whom were also glass-sellers, such as Pellatt & Green, 16, St. Paul's Church-yard, Cut Glass Manufacturers to the King; Boucher & Guy, 271, Strand, Cut Glass Manufacturers to the Prince of Wales; William Collins, Cut Glass Manufacturer to Her Majesty and the Royal Family; Haedy & Lafont, 287, Strand; W. Wilson, Steam Mills to Cut Glass, 40, Black-friars Road. A copy of Wilson's trade card, preserved in the British Museum, illustrates nine examples of flint-glass cut in deep relief, including an all-over diamond-cut decanter with disc stopper and three neck rings, and an ale glass with a cut bowl and single-knopped stem.

At this time Birmingham possessed about twenty-five glass-cutting firms, including the Patent Cut and Flint Glass Company, Charlotte Street, and Thomas Docker & Son. Bristol, Newcastle, Liverpool, Warrington, Glasgow and Edinburgh supported considerably more than fifty glass-cutting establishments. The amount of cut-glass produced by these firms must have been tremendous. The blown shapes, heavy and long annealed and known as blanks, were the raw material upon which the glass-cutter displayed his art and skill. Blanks were bought by the pound, and in best annealed metal could be more costly than finished moulded glass.

English cut-glass was developed through three distinct phases, dependent upon the metal itself and the manufacturing processes available:

1. Pre-1740. Edge cutting and scalloping; almost flat cutting disposed in geometric patterns; giant diamonds and triangles in low relief; shallow slices and faceting.

2. Late 1730s–1805. Similar types of cutting on a clearer and more refractive metal of thinner section.

3. 1790–1830. Elaborate cutting in deep relief on thick metal.

Because of the imperfect fusion of the lead oxide, glass until the 1730s possessed a metallic greyness preventing the perfect dispersal of prismatic light. This greyness varied in metal from different glasshouses. The dispersive power of this early glass was little if any greater than that of rock crystal. Cutting therefore was carried out in simple un-ostentatious motifs so that translucency was not impaired. Scalloping of rims was possibly the earliest form of cutting to ornament stock-lines of English table-glass. The tendency for this glass to fracture (Chapter 1) under grinding, because of haphazard methods of annealing, made deep scalloping unprofitable. Scallops of this early period were blunt rather than sharply bevelled, the edges being merely pared off at the sides. Such work was easily accomplished by grinders experienced in bevelling plate glass for mirrors and coaches. Zig-zag, saw-tooth, shallow arcs and other uniformly undulating rims and feet date from about 1705, and by the 1720s the arch and triangle pattern had become frequent. The term scalloped was current usage for this decoration. Lady Grisell Baillie in 1722 recorded a "high scoloped [sweetmeat] glass" and in 1727 "a scolloped glass cornered brim".

Small "German" facets might enrich the stems of drawn goblets from about 1715, thus embarking the glass-grinders on a new industrial craft. These early facets were flat-cut, that is, they were shallow diamond-shaped depressions ground into the surface of the glass. Faceting was not difficult, but skilful manipulation of the inefficiently an-nealed glass against the wheel was essential to grind into the glass a series of shapely scoops, and at the same time ensure that only the lightest pressure was brought to bear at any point where it might cause the glass to crack. This faceting, in which the length of the diamond was twice or three times the width, was produced by grinding upon the glass a series of closely placed concavities, their overlapping edges so arranged that they formed diamond shapes. Long hexagons were also cut. Occasionally knops are found cut with small flat-surfaced facets in the German style.

More ambitious cutting was soon ornamenting flint-glass table-ware. Attractive designs were cut into hollow-ware solely by grinding scoops, of varying outlines and depths, but always shallow. This was termed slicing or edge-fluting and was carried out with a V-shaped cutting wheel. The desired result was achieved by holding the glass at an incline against one side of the cutting edge, thus making an incision best defined as a lunar slice. Early slicing is recognized by the fact that it has been cut into the metal at a slight angle, with rounded edges. Heart-shaped snicks cut at intersections disguised the ugly sharp points. It is doubtful if this type of cutting was commercially profitable on flint-glass before the advent of double annealing in a tunnel leer (page 22). Some examples exist pronounced by experts to be earlier.

Cut motifs of this period are found in the following styles: flat or slightly concave slicing, occasionally cut at a very slight angle to the surface; small hollow diamond-shaped facets on knopped stems; triangular facets on bowls and other large articles; long hexagonal and diamond-shaped facets on stems; large flat diamond facets on hollow-ware; vertical rounded flutes, long and shallow, cut into hollow-ware bowls from about 1730, and, as the century advanced, becoming deeper, smaller and sharper; circuits of diamond or polygonal facets on feet.

So far glassmakers had been compelled to make their flint-glass ware sturdy of body because of limitations in working the metal (Chapter 1), but more easily worked glass became available from the mid-1730s. For decades old-type small-production glasshouses continued operating, but in general table-glass blanks were of a whiter, clearer metal. This glass could be blown to a thinner section and this, of course, immediately became fashionable. Shallow cutting, therefore, still continued. Greater toughness and increased dispersal power were added to these improvements by annealing in a tunnel leer.

At about this time Thomas Betts, a glass-cutter, "Ye King's Arms Glass-Shop, Opposite Pall-Mall, Charring Cross", issued a trade card[1] stating that he made and sold "all sorts of Curious Cut Glass such as Cruets, Castors, Salts, Lustres, Dessarts, Dishes, Plates, Punch Bowles, Cream Bowles . . . CHEAPER & BETTER than hitherto has been done". Betts's emphasis on price and quality is in

---

[1] Illustrated in *English Glass*, W. A. Thorpe, 1935.

line with the change that had occurred in glass-making and cutting.

Scalloping and faceting were in the height of fashion for a quarter of a century from the 1740s. T. Waller, in *A General Description of All Trades*, 1747, recorded that "the Glass Sellers are Masters also of the Art of scalloping and cutting diamonds on glass, which is now greatly in vogue". Shallow faceting did not impair the translucency of the glass, rather did it add a liquid beauty to the material, unknown in the deep and complicated cutting of the nineteenth century: appropriately designed and shaped the facets displayed all the colours of the spectrum. As one looks through a facet-cut goblet or decanter the cutting on the opposite side is reflected in the facets on the near side and the whole surface seems to be covered with a delightfully complicated pattern. The object of the cutter's art at this time was to beautify the glass with small, sparse decoration rather than to display the intricacies of his craft. Faceting was therefore simple and unostentatious. In 1773 the cutter charged half a crown a dozen for faceting wine-glass stems—then termed "Dutch diamond stems"—and the names of wines on decanters cost one shilling each.

Eight main types of shallow cutting were favourites between the late 1730s and 1805, although their decline in face of rivalry from relief-cutting began in about 1790. They were used in combination and with other less frequent patterns. These included:

(1) Large flat diamonds cut on hollow-ware.

(2) Borders composed of sprigs, sometimes known as the flat leaf or husk pattern: at first triple sprigs were cut with wide shallow units, followed by five-leaved sprigs, each unit cut deeper and sharper, the whole being symmetrical. Both types were used from the 1760s.

(3) Hollowed flutes usually encircling the base or neck of hollow-ware, and on stems. From the late 1760s they might be notched.

(4) Long diamonds in soft shallow relief, often termed lozenges; from 1750 these might be double-cut. A circuit of

these, cut in a single row and touching each other, might enrich a bowl or wine-glass.

(5) Simple festoon or swag and line cutting: often one or two incised zig-zag circuits, the angles of which might be capped.

(6) Geometrical motifs, sometimes termed vandyke or bull's-eye cutting, from the 1760s.

(7) Stem diamonds in various slightly hollow facet forms, such as parallelograms with angles approximating 120 degrees and 60 degrees; long diamonds which might be crested; polygonal facets such as long hexagons; scale patterns such as ornamented porcelain of the period, found also on decanter necks and sometimes encircling the base of an ogee bowl.

(8) Scalloping, more elaborate than formerly, in a short range of designs which encircled feet and loose nozzles of candlesticks, and the rims and feet of sweetmeat glasses, and ornamented epergnes and mantelshelf and table chandeliers. Castellated rims in various forms date from the early 1770s and a few years later the economy of design associated with the classical mood, so far a notable feature of the glass-cutter's art, began to be overshadowed by diamond-cutting in deep relief on weighty glass. Opinions differ widely as to the relative beauty of the early shallow cutting and the later bold, deeply incised cutting.

When Irish glasshouses began to be established on an extensive scale during the early 1780s they adopted the English methods of cutting glass in deep relief. Contrary to general belief they originated little of their own. There never was any purely "Irish style" in glass cutting, but their heyday happened to coincide with certain easily recognizable designs which now tend to be dubbed Irish without question by the average collector.

The finest and most brilliant of cut-glass was worked in metal prepared from the finest quality materials in piling pots (Chapter 1). Cullet was omitted, its presence adversely affecting clarity and flawlessness. According to Professor Turner as much as one-half of the pot of ordinary flint-glass would consist of cullet if it were available.

Improvements made in the annealing techniques in

about 1780 by George Ensall of Stourbridge, member of a glass-making family established there a century earlier, gave infinitely greater toughness to flint-glass and increased refractive power, making it an ideal medium for diamond-cutting in deep relief. Formerly, tunnel leer annealing had been haphazard. Ensall's improvements were used in conjunction with Josiah Wedgwood's newly invented pyrometer by which temperatures could be accurately gauged.

Considerable attention was now given to the control of draught, a long air tunnel passing below the furnace from the entrance of the leer to a tall chimney stack. The leer itself consisted of a pair of semicircular arches or ovens, 60 feet in length, and partly closed by iron doors. The glass entered at the furnace end and was discharged at the cool end. The further the tunnel receded from the furnace, the cooler the air, until eventually the glass entered an air-tight room. The iron doors were so arranged that the openings could be large or small as required, for it was important that as little cool air as possible should enter the oven: too much cool air would cause costly breakage in the leer. On the floors of the tunnels were placed iron pans in which the glass travelled by means of an endless chain.

Each of the arches operated at a different temperature range, the hotter being used to anneal ware intended for cutting, the cooler being for ordinary table-ware. The time taken for annealing the newly made glass varied from six to sixty hours. The hotter the glassware when it entered the leer the better: for this reason large ware such as decanters was reheated when finished, being held at the mouth of a pot heated by beechwood, called the "glory hole". Beside the mouth of each annealing arch were iron handles operating the chains which drew the glassware from one end of the arch to the other. The key of the receiving room at the cool end was in charge of an exciseman. Glass which passed unharmed through the leer was weighed for duty, twopence for every pound of flint-glass from 1815.

Glass-cutting was carried out at first on treadle-operated machines, the glass being held against the shaped rim of a cast iron wheel or disc mounted on a horizontal spindle. A mixture of sand and water forming an additional abrasive was fed in a constant stream from an overhead hopper. With the advent of deep relief cutting the machine was operated by a wheel-boy turning a driving wheel connected by a leather belt to a pulley on the machine. Cone pulleys began to be fitted in the 1790s, thus giving greater variation in speed and increasing flexibility of manipulation.

Steam-driven cutting machines date from the early years of the nineteenth century. The firm of Dixon, Maid Lane, Southwark, produced in 1807 the first steam engine designed specially for operating machine tools. This developed six horse-power and was introduced to the glass-cutting industry by William Wilson, 40 Blackfriars Road, London. Francis Buckley records the existence of a steam-driven glass-cutting mill in Bristol in 1810.

The action of the revolving cast iron and liquid abrasive against the much softer flint-glass ground into its surface lines or curves which were combined to form geometrical motifs, for the most part diamonds. After the incisions had been ground to the required depth the glass was held successively against a wheel of willow wood or blue stone, and a polishing wheel of felt or cork fed with fine abrasive putty powder. This was slow, laborious work, and a week of seventy-two hours could well be spent in cutting a single decanter with deep relief patterns.

Cutting wheel rims were shaped into three fundamental contours, with some fifty variants, combinations and modifications which cut all the motifs in general use:

(*a*) wheels with convex rims producing hollow cuts.

(*b*) pointed or V-shaped rim-edges making mitre or bevel cuts, usually at an angle of about sixty degrees: the double-mitre wheel was introduced with the steam mill.

(*c*) flat rim-edges producing panel cutting.

In cutting the glass the craftsman held the blank between himself and the stone, looking through the glass upon the rim of the wheel as it bit into the transparent material. His only aid was an outline design, brush painted in hair lines on the surface with a mixture of resin, red lead and turpentine, or brunswick black much diluted with turpentine. If the lines were drawn too thick, or the medium insuffi-

andole candlesticks with radiating flanges hung with lustres; in four examples these support
dle-sockets: (*l. to r.*) square foot, 1790s; square foot and notched stem, early 1800s; remainder,
0–20.

te 33
gency girandole candlestick with a section of the stem in ormolu; vase candlestick with square
t gadrooned beneath, with wide flange beneath the scalloped socket, early nineteenth century;
andole candlestick with vase-shaped body fluted and faceted and its revolving flange deeply
lloped and hung with six pendant lustres, 1790s.

Regency candelabra with diamond-cutting in deep relief, long icicle lustres and ormolu moun

Plate 34
Set of four early Regency double-cascade girandole candlesticks with socket and rim encircled wi
lustres extending to the revolving flange below.

ciently thinned, the cutting wheel would drag and blur the outline. Such was the dexterity acquired by glass-cutters that an operator would cut a thousand drinking-glasses with none materially differing in appearance from the rest.

The bulk of decoration cut on nineteenth-century flint-glass table-ware consisted of very deep diamonds covering the entire surface of the piece and accentuating the prismatic fire of the thoroughly annealed glass. These diamonds were of various types, named by glassmen of the period. These names have been recorded as annotations written on a collection of glass-makers' drawings made by the firm of Jones Brothers, Ludgate Hill. The two brothers were descendants of Inigo Jones and had been glass-sellers from the 1790s and cutters from about 1815. These drawings are in colour, and for the most part record glass commissioned by celebrities and foreign royalties and potentates.

DIAMONDS

(a) *Relief*, known also as raised diamonds, deep-cut diamonds, and plain diamonds. These date commercially from the 1780s. They are formed by sinking parallel mitre-cuts into the body of the glass with V-shaped wheels, these incisions being crossed at right angles by similar mitre-cuts. Where two pairs of mitres cross, a pyramidical projection or four-sided diamond is formed with a pointed apex. Such diamonds give the illusion of projecting from the surface.

(b) *Strawberry*. This style dates from about 1800 and first appeared in England. In cutting this pattern the parallel mitres are placed wider apart than for ordinary relief cutting. This produces diamonds with flat tables which in their turn are mitre-cut into sixteen lightly-cut relief or fine diamonds, each raised to a fine point. Less expensively, the flat table may be cut less deeply with criss-cross lines intended to simulate the fine diamond effect.

(c) *Chequered*. A large, flat-topped diamond made by mitre-cutting, with four minor diamonds cut on the flat table.

(d) *Cross-cut*. According to the Jones Brothers' drawings these were flat-topped diamonds or squares of large area,

10   145

each incised diagonally with a simple cross-cut or star. This is sometimes wrongly termed the hobnail pattern.

(*e*) *Hobnail*. Relief diamonds in which the tops are cut with tiny four-pointed stars in such a way that the four points fall across the four slanting faces of the diamond. These were expensive to cut and are comparatively rare.

(*f*) *Fine*. Very small, lightly cut relief diamonds with sharp panels, such as are found covering the entire field of an encircling band around hollow-ware.

FLUTING. Plain vertical fluting, slightly concave, came into popular use from about 1780, either alone or in association with diamond motifs. The crests might be notched until early in the nineteenth century. Pillared fluting or reeding—convex half-sections of cylindrical columns— was used in broad bands throughout the 1790s, but was abandoned because of its high cost. Comb-fluting is the term used for closely-spaced, thin, hollow flutes encircling the base of hollow-ware, such as finger bowls.

HERRING-BONE FRINGE OR BLAZES. This was a popular cut motif formed by lightly cut mitring in an alternation of crest and trough. The fringe could be upright or slanting and was usually cut in encircling bands. In some instances it was arranged in circular form around a printie, the design being known as a sunburst.

NOTCHING. A series of nicks cut intermittently into the sharp crests of hollow flutes with a V-shaped wheel. They were designed to catch and disperse a greater degree of prismatic light.

PRINTIES. This is the term applied by Westropp to the circular concavities ground into the surface of hollow-ware, such as around the rim of a bowl, or in two or three rows encircling a jug or decanter. Similar circular hollows were ground into English glass during the Roman occupation. A 10-inch cutting wheel and fragments of glass cut with circular concave hollows were found in a glass furnace of that period excavated at Warrington in 1899.

PRISMATIC CUTTING, sometimes termed step cutting. This was used with scintillating effect from the opening of the nineteenth century until about 1820 and again during the 1830s. This motif needs a fine-quality metal of thick section for its perfect display. The deep, simply cut, parallel grooves forming sharp horizontal prisms, are easily cut into curved surfaces. Prismatic cutting was seen at its best under gas-light, a feature contributing to its revival under William IV.

PRISMS, ALTERNATE. These are short, alternating mitre incisions cut counterwise, such as are found on the turned-over rims of fruit bowls.

SHELL BORDER, known also as escallop shell, pecten shell or fan-cut edge. This derived from the simple fan motif consisting of shallow grooves. In the nineteenth century this motif might be cut into the curves of escallops, each cut extending to the edge. Later the ends of the mitres were notched: the number of mitres cut into each shell was ten, eleven or twelve.

SPLIT. A small angular groove, in use from the early Georgian period.

SPRIG. This motif is of early Georgian origin and consists of three short incisions formally arranged in the form of a conventional arrow-head, the angle being much greater than a right angle. From about 1800 the angle was more acute, the cut deeper.

STAR. This is, obviously, one of the earliest cut motifs, consisting of six shallow nicks radiating from a common centre. The star gradually became more ambitious and geometrical patterns formed by eight, twelve, sixteen or twenty-four stars were popular and inexpensive to cut. More elaborate forms were also evolved, such as the Brunswick star found on expensive glass. In its simplest form this required twelve straight cuts making a twelve-pointed radiating star, the extremities of every sixth point joined in turn. As many as seventy-two mitre cuts have been noted in an elaborate star.

VESICA. This is a plain incised oval with pointed ends, often containing an eight-pointed star. Where the ovals join in a circuit sprigs are cut above and below. The vesica is associated chiefly with the productions of the Cork glasshouses.

Combinations of various diamond motifs were introduced into cutting designs to add interest to table-ware, with the addition of such self-explanatory motifs as arched pillars, rows of semicircles, basket weavings—the list is unending.

The early cutting often lacks the precise uniformity of the later relief cutting. In many eighteenth-century productions where the pattern was meant to be cut horizontally, the lines are slightly undulating and not quite parallel: there are likely to be many rifts in the metal, and edges may not be of uniform thickness. These irregularities continued until cone pulleys were fitted when speed could be controlled and constant. This made it easier for the operator to cut deep, symmetrical, sharp-angled mitres. Removal of the entire original surface of the glass immensely enhanced its prismatic qualities.

Collectors of cut glass look only for glass cut by hand from blown metal. The advent of the pressing machine (Chapter 14) enabled glass to be pressed with diamond and other cutting forms in shapes approximating those of the hand-cut. They were then finished merely by sharpening on the wheel instead of being laboriously ground into the surface. This gave all the effect of genuine hand-cutting with sharp, well-defined edges, but the brilliance is greater where the tool has been applied than in any part of the surface remaining uncut.

Plate 35

(*Top row*) Chequered diamonds; crosscut diamonds; large shallow diamonds.

(*Second row*) Strawberry diamonds; pillar flutes; hobnail cutting.

(*Third row*) Alternate prisms; printies; hollow facets.

(*Fourth row*) Vesica cutting; fan escallop edging.

(*Fifth row*) Slanting blazes; perpendicular blazes; prismatic or step-cutting.

Plate 36
(*Upper left*) Celery vase with fan-cut rim, bands of prismatic and hobnail cutting, bladed knop in stem star-cutting beneath the foot; height 7 inches; 1820s. (*Upper right*) Bulb glass with shallow diamond cutting, displaying the Derby blue tint; height 7 inches, about 1800. (*Lower left*) Sweetmeat bowl and cover, with shallow diamond-cutting, square foot, displaying the Derby blue tint; height 17¾ inches about 1800. (*Lower right*) Muffineer with foot, shallow cutting, silver mount; 7 inches; about 180

Chapter Thirteen

MOULDED AND PINCHED GLASS

MANY collectors are beginning to find a peculiar pleasure in glass designed to meet the needs of a far wider public than could ever afford the rich beauty of lavishly hand-cut work. Flint-glass in serviceable forms was enriched delightfully with moulded surface decoration. Much of this work is associated with the nineteenth century, but a representative collection may display a fascinating sequence covering two centuries of advancing techniques. This would extend from the late 1670s when George Ravenscroft was granted a patent for flint-glass (Chapter 1) to 1864 when William Leighton introduced a clear, lighter, less resonant lime-glass ideal for moulding and pressing, and much cheaper than flint-glass.

In Ravenscroft's price list of 1677 (Chapter 1) plain glass and ribbed glass were both entered at 3s. per lb.; purling and "glass nipt diamond wais" were 4s. per lb.; extraordinary ware enriched with applied trailing and prunts was 5s. per lb.

The surface decoration of flint-glass was accomplished by means of a hand-operated tool known as a part-size mould (Fig. 3). This consisted of a pair of link-hinged gunmetal half-moulds, each with an iron handle riveted to its outer surface. The moulds were sunk with matching intaglio patterns, such as a trellis design. A suitable gather of plastic glass was lifted into the mould which was at once closed, impressing the surface of the glass with the pattern in relief. The glass was then withdrawn from the mould, expanded by blowing and brought to its final form by hand manipulation. The blowing in no way distorted the moulded surface pattern, which was merely enlarged. Hence the term part-size mould. A great amount of surface moulding was carried out in this way during the eighteenth century: for example, collectors will find a long sequence of such work in sweet-meat glasses. Trade cards of the late eighteenth century show that there was still a considerable demand for part-size moulding.

Ornament, now known as purling, was adapted from the gadrooning so favoured by silversmiths of the period. Purling is the term given to a separate gather of glass applied so as to encircle the base of a piece of hollow-ware, forming a short outer case or layer known to Georgian glassmen as the pearl. The method used was to take this gather of glass and enclose the end of the hollow-ware while it was partially inflated. The whole was then blown into a shallow open mould cut with deep, vertically rounded flutes which afterwards might be manipulated into a swirled or wavy form, particularly during the second half of the eighteenth century. The purling was thick and heavy and the effect produced on the finished vessel was that of a holder receiving the body of the piece which usually remained plain.

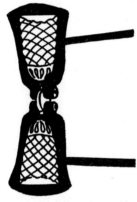

FIG. 9. Part-size mould with diamond pattern.

Single-piece, open-top earthenware moulds enclosed in iron bands were used for shaping the bodies of everyday serving bottles and some decanters: gunmetal moulds for this purpose were in general use by the 1750s. Single-piece moulds were smaller than the finished glass vessels as the shaped glass, when removed from the moulds, was expanded by further blowing. Glass shaped by this process may be recognized by a slightly pebbled surface where it contacted the mould. Such a mould, of course, has always to be made slightly greater in diameter at the top than at the base, so that the partially inflated glass may be withdrawn easily.

From the early 1760s the lower part of a decanter mould might be intaglio-cut with a circuit of slender flutes. The body of the blown-moulded piece was thus encircled by a series of flutes rising vertically from the base. After withdrawal from the mould a skilled glassman might twist the blow-pipe whilst inflating the metal, and so produce a writhen effect. The bowl of many an eighteenth-century drinking-glass was blown into a shallow gunmetal mould which gave it a vertical ribbing up to about half the height of the bowl.

Solid units for flint-glass table-ware, such as candlestick parts, certain drinking-glass stems, decanter stoppers and lustre drops, were often shaped by means of a hand-operated pincers device. The ends of the pincer arms were tipped with opposing gunmetal dies sunk with the required shape. A glass rod, its end heated until malleable, was laid between the dies and pinched into their shape. The pincers were then opened again and the glass removed and snapped off the rod. Pinching eventually became a specialized branch of the flint-glass industry. Pinchers might be employed within a glasshouse, but frequently operated their own small furnaces of the pre-Perrott type (Chapter 1), measuring no more than six feet in height. These were capable of working clandestinely from 1750 onwards and thus avoiding the excise duty. In this way they were in a position to supply their limited range of solid parts to the glasshouses at cut prices.

Pinching was noted as a separate branch of the glass trade as early as 1777, and the Birmingham *Directory* of 1780 lists eleven firms under this classification. It was from the hidden pinchers of Birmingham that the Stourbridge glassmen often obtained square feet with pedestal or domed insteps. These specialists continued in glasshouses until mid-Victorian times. Apsley Pellatt, the celebrated London glassmaker, illustrates appliances for pinching lustres and decanter stoppers in his book *Curiosities of Glassmaking*, 1849.

Flat-ware such as dessert and other dishes, ice plates, salt cellars, and other shallow table glass might be shaped with the aid of a hand-press when this was evolved in the early 1790s. As some indication of the results with this press, it may be noted that, for example, an oblong dish made by this press and measuring about ten inches in length weighs about six pounds. Two or three gatherings of metal were required. While viscous this glass, still on the glassworker's blow-pipe, was well rolled and its base flattened into a rough approximation of the outline required, such as a square or oval, upon the marver. The glassworker used a brass mould, previously heated and placed upon the ground, and into this he pressed his shaped glass. Pressure was obtained by "bumping" the glass into the mould. As he continued to inflate the gathers of glass on his rod only the free upper part could expand. This was called the blow-over, and the purpose of continuing to inflate it was to make it so thin that it exploded. A block of wood was then used to knock off this overplus, leaving the dish in the mould, from which it was removed for annealing. This method is noted in the trade price list of 1829, where it is mentioned in connection with dishes and rectangular salt-cellars.

It cannot be emphasized too strongly that the nineteenth century introduced a new era in table-glass. The key to this was the development of blown-moulded work, new techniques producing a wholly new range of shapes and decorations at prices that eventually fell within the range of the general public. Inevitably, then, the principal demand in blown-moulded table-glass was for the shapes and designs that would most nearly resemble the more costly, fashionable free-blown and hand-cut glass. Blown-moulded glass, surface-decorated with geometrical and curved motifs, was produced much more quickly than was possible by the old hand craftsmanship. Only in such a way could glassmen offer their products at reasonable prices while flint-glass was burdened by the high excise duty of $10\frac{1}{2}d.$ per lb. This tax was not reduced until 1835, and even then was still 6d. per lb. until the impost was abolished in 1845. It is surprising that so few early examples of the nineteenth-century techniques remain, for they were produced in considerable quantities.

Charles Chubsee, inventor of the two-piece open-and-shut mould in 1802, was a glassworker employed by Bradley, Ensall & Holt of Stourbridge. He could not, obviously, afford the £300 necessary to patent his invention, which was therefore open for any competitor to copy.

Chubsee's invention enabled the form of the vessel and elaborate, closely-spaced designs in relief to be applied to the outer surface of flint-glass table-ware in a few simple hand operations. The style of ornament was no longer restricted to the vertical ridges that could be withdrawn from a one-piece mould, but could include any amount of horizontal and slanting cuts copying the wide variety of diamonds and the like hand-cut in deep relief into the free-blown glass of the period.

The gunmetal mould was made the size required of the finished article, and the glass fully inflated in a single operation. The mould was divided vertically, one section consisting of a fixture to the base and the other being joined to the base by a hinge. The hinged section of the mould was kept shut by a removable pin. The purpose of the hinging was, of course, to enable the glassman's assistant to open the mould for removal of the shaped glass. The mould interior was sunk with the required ornamental pattern which, when used with glass prepared in the new furnaces, could display an over-complication of pattern at no extra cost.

A gathering of molten glass was taken on a blow-pipe, placed in the mould and inflated until it filled the interior. It was the duty of an assistant to keep the mould suitably hot and to open and shut it for the blower. Inflation forced the glass into the pattern on the mould and formed a clear, detailed impression. It is noteworthy that the blown glass remained the same thickness, whatever the shaping, so that a pattern in relief on the outer surface of the finished glass meant a corresponding series of hollows inside.

The inflation that forced the hot glass into the patterns of the mould also forced a little into the fine crevices between the mould sections. The resultant slight ridges may be detected. The hard gunmetal moulds did not wear appreciably and cannot, therefore, be regarded as the cause of the uneven impressions which adversely affected some early work. Faulty preparation of the mould and its unskilful use must be blamed for this common flaw.

An improved open-and-shut mould was evolved in about 1820. This was the three-piece mould with one fixed and

APSLEY PELLATT'S
ABRIDGED LIST OF
Net Cash Prices for the best Flint Glass Ware.

DECANTERS.

25 Strong quart Nelson shape decanters, cut all over, bold flutes and cut brim & stopper, P.M. each 10s6d. to 12 0

26 Do. three-ringed royal shape, cut on and between rings, turned out stop, P.M. each 10 0

Do. do. not cut on or between rings, nor turned out stopper, P.M. ea. 8s to 9 0

27 Fancy shapes, cut all over, eight flutes, spire stopper, &c. each, P.M. 16s. to 18 0

Do. six flutes only, each, P.M. 24s. to 27 0

DISHES.

31 Dishes, oblong, pillar moulded, scolloped edges, cut star.

5-in.	7-in.	9-in.	10-in.
3s. 6d.	6s. 6d.	11s.	13s. each.

32 Oval cup sprig, shell pattern,

5-in.	7-in.	9-in.	11-in.
7s. 6d.	9s. 6d.	16s.	19s. each.

36 Square shape pillar, moulded star,

5-in.	7-in	9-in.	10-in.
4s.	8s.	12s. 6d.	15s. each.

FINGER CUPS.

37 Fluted finger-cups, strong, about 14 oz. each 2 6

Do. plain flint, punted, per doz.... 18 0

Do. coloured, per doz.......18s. to 21 0

38 Ten-fluted round, very strong, each . 5 0

Eight-fluted do., each 8 0

39 Medicean shape, moulded pillar, pearl upper part, cut flat flutes, each .. 5 0

PICKLES

46 Pickles, half fluted for 3 in. holes, R.M ea. 4 6

47 Strong, moulded bottom, 3-in. hole, cut all over, flat flutes, R.M. each . 5 0

Best cut star do. for 3½-in. hole, PM ea. 7 6

Very strong and best cut, P.M. each 14 6

WATER JUGS

59 Quarts, neatly fluted and cut rings, each....................14s. to 18 0

60 Ewer shape, best cut handles, &c... 21 0

61 Silver do. scolloped edges, ex. lar. flutes 26 0

WATER BOTTLES

70 Moulded pillar body, cut neck, each . 3 0

71 Cut neck and star................. 3 0

72 Double fluted cut rings 3 6

73 Very strong pillar, moulded body, cut neck and rings 5 6

74 Grecian shape, fluted all over 7 0

TUMBLERS

	76	79	80	81	82	83	84	85	86	87
Tale 5s.										
Flint,	7s.	10s.	12s.	12s.	10s.	12s.	14s.	18s.	18s.	Doz.
	to	to	to	to	to	to	to	in	to	
	8s.	12s	14s.	15s.	13s.		13s.	21s.	21s.	30s do.

WINES

	88	89	90	91	92	93	94	95	96	97	98	99
	7s.	7s.	7s	7s.	8s.	11s.	12s.	14s.	15s.	18s.	21s.	90s.
	to	to	to	to	to							
	8s.	9s.	9s.	8s.	10s.							

* Glass Blowing, Cutting, and Engraving, may be inspected by Purchasers, at Mr. Pellatt's Extensive Flint Glass and Steam Cutting Works, in Holland Street, near Blackfriars' Bridge, any Tuesday, Wednesday, or Thursday.

Merchants and the Trade supplied on equitable Terms.

No Abatement from the above specified Ready Money Prices.

No Connexion with any other Establishment.

FIG. 10. An Apsley Pellatt price list, 1829.

two hinged sections held together by removable locking pins: four-piece moulds were sometimes used from about 1825. Each section was sunk with a pattern. Inflation of the glass within the mould tended to force the sections open at the joints, thus producing a corresponding number of fine ridges on the surface of the glass, or a slight break in the pattern. These mould-marks on blown-moulded glass are no more than fine surface swellings and in no way resembled the more sharply defined hair lines or threads on the machine-pressed glass made from 1833 onwards. The number of mould marks indicate the number of pieces forming the mould. By the late 1830s blown-moulded glass could be freed of the slight surface pebbling that had marred early moulded work and the full brightness of the flint-glass restored by fire-polishing, an innovation of the English glass pressers.

The process of fire-polishing on blown-moulded or pressed glass virtually obliterated tool and mould marks and produced a polished surface suggestive of free-blown glass. Designs containing diamonds, flutes, loops, and other geometric patterns acquired the clean, smooth edges of cut-glass.

The concave-convex effect of the inner and outer surfaces of blown-moulded flint-glass increased its typical brilliance. As explained above the inflation of the gather of molten metal within a full-sized mould that produced relief ornament on the outer surface of a vessel simultaneously made corresponding hollows on the inner surface. A smooth inner surface indicates that the glass was either free-blown or pressed, while a slightly rippled inner surface proves the glass to have been moulded for pattern only and then expanded by free-blowing.

The impression received on the surface of blown-moulded glass differs in general appearance from that of pressed glass. The decorative motifs on blown-moulded work tend to show soft, slightly rounded outlines, since their shaping depended merely on the pressure that the glassman could achieve with his blow-pipe. In contrast, the extreme pressure of machine work gave pressed glass a sharp, brittle definition.

Some blown-moulded glass-ware, such as decanters, salad bowls, condiment bottles, rummers and so on, had pinched feet made separately and welded to them. Square, round and canoe shapes were used, patterned on the underside and with their edges smoothed or notched. Target decanter stoppers and the heads of mushroom-shaped stoppers were shaped by similar hand-operated tools.

Patterns on blown-moulded glass may be roughly classed into three general groups: (1) Geometrical patterns constituted the earliest and largest group, the most common motifs being encircling bands variously composed of horizontal, vertical and diagonal ribbings; flutings; motifs composed of concave circles and ovals; diamond motifs; and diamond diapering in combination with ribbing and fluting. Nearly all hollow-ware displays one of these motifs. (2) Baroque decoration had been introduced to blown-moulded glass by 1825 and included elaborate designs composed of fanciful, delicate curves in high relief with the addition of honeysuckle flowers, hearts, shells, fans, trefoils and the guilloche motif. Gadrooning encircling the base of such hollow-ware is frequent. (3) Patterns based on Roman and Gothic arches, all in higher relief than the geometrical style, date from about 1840 onwards. They are found chiefly on decanters and other large hollow-ware. A spray of foliage is often displayed between each pair of arches and there may be a motif within each Gothic arch. There are, of course, many hybrid patterns.

Many pieces have plain bases with the punty marks ground away. Others are patterned in any of some three dozen simple designs which have been grouped into five classes, the units varying in number and size. The ray type is probably the most common, with at least five variations, long, medium, short, wide and narrow. Diamond-shaped indentations are almost as frequent, in some twenty variations. Ring bases are also found, as are combinations of rays and rings, and also circles of small printies or petal-shaped indentations.

Thick, heavy tumblers in metal of excellent quality were made in vast numbers. Even after a century and more of careless handling many remain unchipped, the only signs

Jpper left) Sweetmeat glass with band of large relief diamonds, wide fluting and deeply scalloped
n, early nineteenth century. (*Upper right*) Wine-glass, bowl with purled base, scalloped foot;
cond quarter of the nineteenth century, (*Lower left*) Shallow-cut butter dish with cover and stand;
rly nineteenth century. (*Lower right*) Fruit bowl, kettle-drum shape, with knopped stem and
und foot; early nineteenth century.

Sugar bowl with two fan-shaped handles, wavy rim, base encircled with flat cutting, and foot scar-c
beneath, about 1830; fruit stand with scalloped rim, each arch star-cut, plain foot and stem; sal
bowl with scalloped rim and cut with large relief diamonds.

Plate 38
Pair of blown-moulded toilet-water bottles, finished by cutting, the necks cut with flat facets, a
with ball finials to stoppers. (*Centre*) Stemmed fruit bowl, its turned-over rim cut with circuits
narrow alternating prisms, and the bowl with closely spaced circuits of shallow facets.

of wear being irregular masses of scratches beneath. Shapes followed those of cut-glass tumblers—for the most part short and broad. More than 250 patterns on blown-moulded tumblers were recorded by a writer in *The Queen* in 1902, when they were already considered desirable to collect. Their chief interest lies in the sharpness and fine detail of their design and in the brilliance of their metal: viewed in certain lights they might almost be made of silver.

Tumbler decoration is well suited to the vessel's size and shape and consists of flutings, facets, depressions and bosses in many forms and sizes. Early examples copied exactly the geometrical patterns found in contemporaneous cut-glass. By far the greater number, however, show decorations specifically designed to suit the new manufacturing method. The most elaborate are of North Country origin, round or pointed flutings being more frequent on tumblers made in Birmingham and Stourbridge. Apsley Pellatt illustrated ten types in his advertisement of 1839 at prices ranging from 3s. to 30s. a dozen.

Jugs in great variety have survived, ranging from two-quart capacity to miniatures. They were usually moulded for pattern and body shape in decanter moulds and finished by hand manipulation. Rims might be folded and given banded or threaded effects with incised lines. In some examples a foot was drawn from the body, thus slightly distorting the pattern.

Decanters in quart and pint sizes were made by the ton: half and quarter pint specimens are rare. The standard shape has a cylindrical body and a long neck with three rings, applied and tooled, the most frequent shapes being semi-circular, double round, single triangle and double flattened. After about 1835 the neck collar might be cut into the mould and formed as an integral part of the neck, a feature easily distinguished by inspection. Stoppers might be pinched or blown hollow, favourite finials being the mushroom, target, steeple and ball. Moulded decanters in green, blue, amber and red date from the late 1840s onwards.

Blown-moulded goblets, rummers, and wine-glasses with ovoid or bucket-shaped bowls are becoming increasingly scarce. Other blown-moulded glass worthy of the collector's interest includes celery vases, sugar bowls, mugs, compote bowls. There are also little glass hats shaped after the late Georgian and early Victorian beaver hats, the high crown usually tapering downward to a narrow brim turned up at the sides and down in front and back. They are usually smooth-surfaced, but an occasional example is to be found with a pattern impressed in the base. They were intended to hold toothpicks and range from about 2 inches to 2½ inches in height. They are found in clear flint-glass and in a variety of colours.

Salt-cellars are usually footed, often blown-moulded for pattern and finished by manipulation, the short stem being drawn from the body, and a foot attached. One collector accumulated more than two hundred differing examples in clear flint-glass and in colour. They are not, however, by any means common.

Christmas lights were blown-moulded in purple, green, blue, white and amber, and usually enriched with a close diamond-quilted relief surface. The little bowl, without stem or foot, was rimmed to take a wire for hanging in church or elsewhere. It was filled with oil into which a wick was fixed. Candles were used from the early 1860s.

A variant of the blown-moulded process by which domestic table-ware could be made cheaply was patented in 1835 by Thomas Green, who gave it the name of Roman pillar moulding because excavations in London at that time revealed some Roman glass made by the same process. The exterior surface of such ware was vertically corrugated, whilst the interior remained smooth. A part-size open-top mould was used, about one-third smaller than the required article, its interior sunk with deep, broad, rounded flutes or corrugations. A gathering of molten glass was taken in the usual way and when partially cool a second gather was taken over it. While the outer gather of glass was still molten the whole was forced into the mould and after withdrawal was inflated in the usual way. After shaping the vessel was fire-polished.

This patent was licensed to others. In the illustrated price list issued by Apsley Pellatt in 1839 several Roman pillar moulded pieces were illustrated: "finger bowls of Medician shape, the upper part hand-cut with flat flutes, 5/– each; water bottles with pillar moulded bodies and cut neck rings, 3/– each; dishes with scalloped edges and star-cut beneath 3/6 to 13/– each".

Blown-moulded ware is chiefly found in clear flint-glass: it was made in colour too, however, at one penny a pound extra and twopence a pound extra from 1833. The colours were chiefly blues, amethysts, purples and amber. A wide variety of delicate translucent colours was available from the late 1850s. This colourful ware consists chiefly of toilet table and desk equipment and mantelshelf ornaments.

Chapter Fourteen

PRESSED GLASS

THE story of early pressed glass in England is told here for the first time. The facts have been garnered from innumerable contemporaneous sources, technical and otherwise, and checked against existing specimens. The early press was a hand-operated lever machine capable of producing inexpensive glass-ware that at least superficially resembled cut-glass and was welcomed by those who could not afford to be over-critical. One point in its favour for the collector today is the fact that he will find only genuine specimens for, unlike blown-glass, it has not yet proved profitable for copying.

The glass-press was evolved in the United States of America during the late 1820s, adapted from devices associated with the English open-and-shut moulds. It met with no great success until in 1830 Deming Jarves patented a machine by which a handled article could be pressed with a single operation. This was described in *The Repertory of Patent Specifications*, London, 1831, as having "an excavation provided for the formation of handles. The plug or piston, which is to form the inside of the cup, is made to fit exactly into a rim which forms the top of the mould, so that when it is pressed down none of the molten glass can escape at the top, but will be forced into the cavities cut into it". Glass shaped by the blown-moulded process (Chapter 13) was thinner in section and the metal was of greater clarity than pressed ware, and hence, in England, was preferred until after the abolition of the excise tax.

The first glassman to install a pressing machine in England was W. H. P. Richardson of Wordsley, Stourbridge. This was in 1833, and it is believed that similar machines were

p) Two quart-size trade jugs intended for ale: (*Left*) engraved with two oval medallions of iron-
*r*king scenes flanking a monogram, with hop and barley motifs; (*right*) blown-moulded with comb-
ing and engraved with agricultural motifs. (*Centre, left*) Water jug, its lower half cut with large
*e*f diamonds: 1820s. (*Right*) Jug with ribbed neck engraved with Nelson and the *Victory*; height
inches. (*Bottom, left*) Ale tankard with lipped rim, engraved with hops and barley, purled base,
with coin dated 1785 in stem; height 5⅞ inches. (*Right*) Helmet-shaped tankard; 6¼ inches.

Plate 40

(*Top, left*) Tumbler, slightly waisted, engraved in diamond point, signed "Giles 1756", heig 5 inches. (*Top, right*) Wine-glass cooler with foot, 1840s. (*Centre, left*) Coaching glass with diamo cut stem, height 5 inches; early nineteenth century. (*Centre, right*) Tumbler with waisted bc engraved with portrait of Prince Charles Edward and the motto "Audentior Ibo"; height 4¾ inch (*Bottom, left*) Double-lipped wine-glass cooler; early nineteenth century. (*Bottom, right*) Sing lipped wine-glass cooler encircled with widely cut grooves and star-cut beneath; George IV peri introduced to Newcastle-upon-Tyne a few months later. Richardson marketed his pressed glass under the name of intagliated table-ware and was highly successful. Each of his machines was operated by a team of seven men, who produced glass at about the rate of ten glass-blowing teams. The low prices he was able to charge brought him a flood of orders, but the tax of sixpence a pound still kept flint-glass out of the majority of English homes. Pressing machines were not at all costly and, because of flaws in the patent laws, it was found possible to copy them freely in this country.

The molten glass was shaped in a gunmetal mould of two, three or four sections, a vertical plunger forming the hollow interior and forcing the exterior surface of the glass into every crevice sunk in the mould, thus producing an impress in relief. Each machine was operated by a gatherer, presser, melter and four boys. The mould necessarily required to be entirely stationary; the receiving die and plunger in perfect alignment, and fitted with air vents. The gathering of molten glass was not blown into the virtually red-hot mould as with blown-moulding, but dropped into it from the punty rod.

Precisely the correct amount of molten glass had to be taken up in the gather, for if the quantity was too small it could not be forced tightly into the mould, and this meant that the piece of glass-ware would fail to show the full effect of the impressed pattern; too much glass in the gather caused the press to raise thin fins at the mould seams. It was essential that mould and glass should be of harmonious temperatures, for otherwise tiny fragments of glass might be wrenched from the raised pattern on the pressed vessel, causing surface blemishes and uneven brilliance in the next piece to be pressed. This difficulty was not overcome until the early 1860s, and such defects are characteristic of pressed glass made before 1850. By then the punty rod had been replaced by a spring clip which was used to lift the shaped glass from its mould. The vessel was then fire-polished at the furnace mouth and annealed.

The lack of any trace of a punty mark on the base of this glass is one of the several features of pressed glass that distinguish it from blown-moulded work. On glass-ware made until the late 1840s, however, there is a mark of cutting shears on the base. The cutting shears to remove the molten gather from the punty were necessarily very sharp, with thin blades so that severing was instantaneous. Sometimes the shears would chill the glass and cause a tiny fracture—a very shallow, rough-edged fissure. It is most frequently found in the position where one would expect to find a punty mark on blown glass.

Decanters were pressed in a more complicated machine. The method was described in a journal of the period: "When a decanter or similar vessel is to be made, there are two moulds, side by side, with appropriate plungers above. In one mould the lower part of the decanter is formed: in the other the upper part and the neck. One of the moulds is fixed to a hinge in such a way that when the plungers of the two parts were withdrawn, one mould turned over upon the other and brought the edges into exact contact, when, by a slight pressure, they were made to adhere. The moulds were then opened and the decanter removed." The join is usually indicated by the presence of a faint encircling fin.

By 1840 there were workshops in London, Birmingham, and Newcastle-upon-Tyne specializing in the production of gunmetal moulds for glass presses. Designs might be created to commission or stock moulds sold or hired. A wooden model was first carved and a hand-finished master pattern prepared from it. From this any number of moulds could be cast in gunmetal. Upon the quality of this mould and its maintenance, as well as upon the skill of the pressing team, depended the final finish of the glass.

Several characteristics serve to distinguish early pressed glass from contemporaneous moulded work. Motifs in relief are more clearly defined than in blown-moulded glass; lines are mechanically correct, with a precision fully equalling that of cut-glass, although the actual patterns never achieve the sharp brilliance of cut work. There were, however, a number of imperfections, such as the granular texture of this glass which makes the edges of rims and bases tend to roughness. The pattern itself lacks the smoothness of blown-glass, but its slightly uneven inner surface is smooth. Many early examples have concentric ripple marks on their inner surfaces resulting from insufficient heat, the glass moving too sluggishly around the plunger. After fire-polishing, however, the glass displayed considerable brilliance.

Although both pressed and blown-moulded glass are patterned by the use of moulds, their only point of similarity is the presence of mould marks, which in themselves are unlike. These marks left by the tiny crevices between sections of the moulds are but one among several features that help the collector to distinguish between the two products.

It has been pointed out already that blown-moulded glass shows traces of joints between sections of the mould, but the pressure exerted to blow the glass into the pattern of the mould was slight compared with that of the metal plunger which forced the pressed glass into shape. The plunger's action even tended to force the sections of the mould apart and thus drive the molten glass into the crevices before cooling began. The result was that slight fins were visible on early pieces and distinct marks were unavoidable. These resemble sharp threads of glass applied to the piece after shaping and on early work are rough and of uneven thickness.

Another distinction is that on a piece of pressed glass these sharp mould marks are usually found in a continuous line from the rim to the foot. On a blown piece the stem and foot were usually added later and consequently show no mould marks. It must be recognized, however, that in this respect some pressed glass resembles the blown-moulded work but only when made during the early months of press-work when one-piece moulds were used.

If the inner and outer surfaces of a pressed vessel are closely inspected it will be seen that the outer surface is dull, and the inner surface even more decidedly dull: yet the glass displays brilliance created by light passing through the un-patterned surface to the faceted outer surface. By the mid-1840s it had been realized that the more numerous the outer facets and the smoother the inner surface, the more the glass would scintillate. For this reason pressed glass in which the ornamental motifs are set against a stippled background possesses a silvery metallic quality of a type peculiar to pressed glass.

The difference between the interior surfaces of pressed and blown-moulded glass is an important feature. Pressed glass is always plainly smooth inside, never following the exterior pattern. In blown-moulded glass depressions behind the relief motifs of the design can be felt distinctly on the inner surface. This uneven surface proved a disadvantage, making necked ware, such as decanters, difficult to clean. There is also a physical difference between the patterns found on the two types of glass. Blown-moulded pieces have a decided softness of pattern. There are no sharp angles at the meetings of different planes.

It was admitted at the time, however, that even the sharper patterns of pressed glass could not really make this ware comparable with hand-worked glass. The quality of the actual flint-glass used by the pressmen was usually second-rate because no process was known that would give the glass the finish that made hand-worked glass so desirable. Apsley Pellatt, in 1849, commented in a lecture to the Royal Institute that the glassmen's machines had not "realized the anticipations of manufacturers; for by the contact of the metal plunger with the glass, the latter lost much of the brilliant transparency so admired in cut glass; hence it is chiefly used for common and cheap articles. The process of re-warming and fire-polishing after the pressure has somewhat remedied this defect."

At the Prague Exhibition of 1836 local pressed glass with arabesque decoration was shown only as a curiosity, but the catalogue noted that American and French glassmen with presses tended to eclipse the manufacturers of blown-glass. So devastating became foreign competition in pressed glass that the export markets for English flint-glass were virtually lost after having enjoyed a monopoly for about 150 years. English glasshouses, hindered by the excise tax, were forced to let their fires go out for longer periods than had been customary. This competition in pressed glass finally resulted in the abolition of the excise tax, the alternative being to lose the remaining trade to foreigners.

As with blown-moulded glass, early decoration on pressed

glass was dictated by the geometric patterns of cut-glass. They were not exact imitations, but strawberry diamonds, ribbing, stars, swags and fan escalloped rims were used. Fine-cut diamonds were admirably suited to the pressing process, brilliance being enhanced by stippling. Wheat sheaves, hearts, oak leaves, flowers and fleurs-de-lis were notable among early pressed motifs. Oval printies, contemporaneously known as bulls'-eyes, were perhaps the most frequent decorative motif, continuing throughout the period. Simple to press, many attractive arrangements were evolved, particularly on hollow-ware.

Improvements in technique by 1840 made possible more elaborate designs using the lower relief favoured for such classical motifs as scrollwork, variants of the acanthus leaf and formalized honeysuckle flowers as well as floral and Gothic ornament. Even the eastern motif of the "Paisley shawl pattern" was widely used. Ornate designs were developed and reproduced on glass with skilful craftsmanship.

Glass designers of the period shared with furniture decorators in borrowing widely from various books of domestic ornament and in taking borders, medallions and floral compositions direct from magazines. Until 1845 pattern elements were well balanced. Then followed congestion and maldistribution of motifs. From 1850 the trend was towards even greater elaboration, with floral, leaf, fruit and other naturalistic motifs, and from about 1860 in higher relief than formerly. Patterns on pressed glass introduced at the 1851 exhibition included the arch and grape, pineapple, tulip, ivy, prunus, fern and horn of plenty.

Vertically ribbed ornament, with the convex units wider than the concavities, was popular with the pressmen during the 1850s and 1860s. The ribs could be sunk inexpensively into the moulds and were easily cleaned. This ribbing is usually close spaced, stopping short of the rim in hollow-ware, and may have sparsely spaced low relief motifs superimposed. Encircling wavy stems branching into simple flowers and foliage, ivy leaves, and fruiting vines were popular and have been noted on tumblers, celery vases, bowls and cream and water jugs.

Thousands of salt-cellars were pressed after the abolition of the salt tax in 1835. Because it had been taxed at thirty times its retail cost, salt had been a carefully preserved luxury for more than a century. Glassmen at once began to meet a new demand for salt-cellars, at first offering heavy flattened spherical blocks of plain flint-glass with depressions to contain the salt. Among the first objects to come from the pressing machines were rectangular salts, somewhat crudely decorated and still to be found today at negligible cost. The corners may be plain, in the form of pilasters, or vertically ribbed, while the rim shows alternate rounded and pointed scallops, and each end and side bears a relief motif. From about 1840 the corner pilasters might be extended downward to form feet, and the sides decorated with fields of tiny diamonds, stars, swags or baskets of flowers in low relief. More elaborately they might be patterned in arabesque scrollwork, and examples are to be found with the long sides pressed with scenes adapted from Dutch paintings.

Salt-cellars continued the oblong form, sometimes with clipped or round corners, scrolled end rims and scroll feet. Some may be noted raised on narrow, flaring base rims; others have twelve-pointed stars impressed beneath their bases. Oval and canoe-shaped salt-cellars were pressed from about 1845, usually with hexagonal stems and oval feet, star-impressed beneath. Coloured glass for salt-cellars had become popular by 1850 in various shades of blue, emerald and dark olive greens, ruby, amber, canary-yellow and opaque-white. By 1850 two or three colours might appear on a single salt-cellar.

Plates were among the early productions of the press. Proof of this is found in the fact that souvenir plates were issued upon the occasion of Queen Victoria's coronation in 1838: the design includes a central portrait of the Queen and a dated inscription. The majority of pressed plates—and they were in production for half a century—are in conventional designs. Backgrounds may be enriched with tiny hemispheres of crystal, giving a radiant effect, catalogued at the time of the 1851 exhibition as snake-skin, but known to collectors in the United States of America as lacy. A dewdrop effect was produeed by pressing slightly larger projections, chiefly on plate rims. Another and more massive effect was achieved by using printies. Serrations usually edge plate rims, a frequent type consisting of two points and a semicircle arranged alternately.

Cup plates have been collected enthusiastically in America for a long time. More than a thousand patterns have been collected there, including about sixty versions of the American eagle. The *Oxford English Dictionary* defines cup plates as "little flat saucers in which our grandmothers placed their tea-cups when they poured their tea into the deeper saucers to cool". This involved drinking from the saucer and was in the main a provincial custom dating from about 1820: tea-sets have been noted in blue Staffordshire bone china in which such plates were included. Cup plates in pressed glass were considered more attractive from the late 1830s. They measure from 3 to 3½ inches in diameter: an occasional 4-inch example will be found. In the majority of specimens the pressed decoration consists of a simple posy of flowers with a foliage rim, roses being frequent. Hearts grouped in the centre and encircling the rim were popular. An interesting, but now rare, series bear representations of sailing ships.

Towards the end of the cup-plate vogue an attractive series was made in colour. The range of hues seen in a single plate, due to the different thicknesses incidental to the design, give the piece a multitude of glistening tones of blue, amber, green, pink or red. Collectors sometimes misname cup-plates, labelling them honey plates, jam plates, tumbler plates or butter plates.

Tumblers, too, were among the first vessels to be pressed and, in a specially prepared faintly green bottle-glass, quickly became the standard drinking vessels in coaching houses, taverns and other public resorts, replacing the heavily leaded pewter mugs. They appear to have been made in three sizes, ¼ pint, ½ pint and 1 pint. The in-between sizes date from about 1850. Relief patterns for twenty years or so were mainly in designs adapted from hand-cut glass. Most frequently the vessel is circular with deep, wide flutes or hexagonal with flat sides, but many are plain surfaced with deep stars impressed beneath. Tumblers in translucent colours enriched the fashionable home during the 1850s and 1860s, often in a faint sparkling green, pale amethyst or blue.

Stemmed drinking-glasses were pressed from about 1840 onwards. These had ovoid or bucket bowls mounted on plain or knopped stems of many forms, and round or hexagonal feet. They were sold in several sizes: small to 4½ inches; half-gills to 6 inches; goblets and rummers over 6 inches. The pressed motifs on their bowls are in high relief, bands of diamonds and leaf ornament appearing in numerous designs. Diamond patterns were pressed beneath the feet, a characteristic feature taken from French cut-glass.

The toddy rummer is usually found with an ovoid bowl enveloped with ornament below a plain band encircling the rim; the barrel-shaped bowl is also found, and the bucket bowl on a plain stem. Feet were low-domed with diamonds or rays beneath. Wine services appear to date from the mid-1840s when goblets, wine-glasses, decanters, finger-bowls, wine-coolers and comports were made in matching patterns.

Early pressed candlesticks are rare. More frequent are those in three units welded together: a pressed stem, a hand-pinched foot and a hand-tooled socket resembling those in brass. The candlestick pressed in a single piece was more substantial and is to be found in an amazing variety of designs and sizes, indicating that vast numbers were made, as each set of moulds was costly.

The sporting dolphin was a candlestick stem that particularly appealed to early Victorians who kept up a continual demand for it until the 1860s. The dolphin's head rests on the candlestick foot, the body forming a vertical scroll supporting a candle-socket. Dolphins were also pressed as table-lamp standards and as stems for dessert bowls.

Another long and interesting series of candlesticks, to be found in clear glass and in colours, was inspired by the classical columns seen on late Georgian candlesticks in silver and Sheffield plate. Yet another style of pressed candlestick has a substantial baluster stem and a hexagonal socket and is supported on a square block of glass or rises from a succession of square steps numbering two to five. The candlestick with a petal socket and a matching stem knop was on the market in 1857, the socket occasionally being a separately attached unit in colour. Particularly attractive specimens may be found among the candlesticks pressed with intricate all-over patterns and supporting plain, deep free-blown sockets, their rims expanded into grease pans. These date no earlier than about 1850.

Tea-spoon holders are seldom recognized. In silver from the reign of Queen Anne they had been low, rectangular trays with rounded ends. Early in the nineteenth century it became acceptable for the spoons to be placed individually in the saucers. But a middle-class fashion of early Victorian days preferred a variant of the older custom and on such tea tables the spoons were offered in a glass spoon holder. This was a low, stemmed vessel, goblet-shaped, with a slightly flaring rim which might be gilded, or with a rim composed of six fan-motifs. The body was variously decorated, such as the popular design consisting of a band of strawberry diamonds with a narrow band of blazes above. The entire field of the bowl might be covered with small relief diamonds or a trellis design. Tea-spoon holders might be in coloured glass—green, blue and yellow have been noted, the two former sometimes with gilded transfer ornament, a feature patented in 1835.

Spill-holders resemble tea-spoon holders, but are rather deeper and have vertical sides and rims. As gas became more frequent as an illuminant, its exposed flame was found to be convenient for smokers and others. Thin strips of light wood or home-made rolled newspaper spills were used, and also acted as match-savers from the 1850s.

Egg-cups were pressed, some being double-ended to take large or small eggs: these are sometimes mistaken for double-ended spirit glasses. The majority, of course, are stemmed in the ordinary egg-cup style, usually with hexagonal stems and round feet. A series has been noted exactly resembling Wedgwood cream-coloured earthenware egg-cups: some of these are in coloured opaque glass.

Claret jugs, pickle jars, butter coolers, honey pots, sugar bowls, celery jars, beehives and covers, bowls and dishes were all pressed in glass, and from the late 1850s were in a wide range of transparent colours. Condiment sets were made, in a design consisting of mustard pot, salt and pepper shakers and oil and vinegar bottles.

Flint-glass was used exclusively for pressed work until William Leighton in 1864 discovered the value of using a glass prepared with soda and lime as a flux. This glass becomes molten rapidly at a lower temperature than the much more costly flint-glass: it also stiffens quickly on chilling. The result is that hollow-ware in this glass has a thicker section than was required with flint-glass. Although possessing the clarity of flint-glass it lacks toughness and comparatively few pieces appear to have survived. This glass is recognized by its light weight and its dull note: when flicked by the finger it entirely lacks the resonant tone of flint-glass.

Colourful pressed glass sold under the name of vitro-porcelain was made during the mid-Victorian period. This is now eagerly collected. To some collectors it is known as purple slag or marble glass, and to others as end-of-day ware. This is a cloudy, opaque mottled glass containing silicates obtained from steel-works. The makers were J. G. Sowerby of Gateshead, and the Kilner firm of Thornhill Lees, near Wakefield, Yorkshire. The waste or slag floating on the top of molten steel was normally tapped off into moulds and, when cold, was broken into chunks and thrown on to slag heaps. The first slag to be tapped resembled purple marbled glass. This was acquired by the glass-houses and, suitably tempered with flint-glass, was pressed into ornamental ware, chiefly vases and spill jars.

Its name end-of-day ware was derived from the fact that the slag was drawn off shortly before the steel was tapped at the end of the puddlers' shift. This so-called vitro-porcelain has a superficial resemblance to ornaments in blue Derbyshire spar—not to be confused with the radiant blue john. The press, of course, shaped it at a fraction of the cost involved in the production of hand-carved spar.

The Kilner firm impressed their productions with the mark of a griffin associated with Rockingham china. It was copied from the crest of the Earl Fitzwilliam who owned the estate upon which the Brameld brothers had operated their Rockingham china works until 1842. The Bramelds continued making bone china in London until about 1856, still using the griffin mark that had identified their productions from 1826. This suggests that the griffin-marked purple slag glass dates from the early 1860s. Tumblers, spill holders, pin trays, salt-cellars and comports have been noted bearing this mark. The comport design includes a scalloped flaring base, a scalloped beaded rim and relief ornament on the stem.

J. G. Sowerby began making superior vitro-porcelain in the late 1860s, in mottled blues, turquoises, opals, blue and green mixtures, and in malachite effects. Characteristically they were made with flat sides impressed with pictures in high relief such as Old King Cole, Jack and Jill, and other favourite nursery scenes and thus appears to be the first ornamental glass intended for children. There were also pilgrim-bottle vases. Salt-cellars and vases may be covered with diamonds in high relief. Some of this glass is found with encrusted decoration in a similar colour. Blue glass splashed with white enamel pressed with writhen grooves was made by Sowerby, who also issued pressed dishes in *blanc de lait*. Production continued until the 1880s. Sowerby's son emigrated to Canada where vitro-porcelain began to be made in lighter tints than the English.

Chapter Fifteen

GEORGIAN ENAMEL, BRISTOL-BLUE AND
RUBY-RED GLASS

GEORGIAN BRISTOL was celebrated for the splendid quality of its glass, particularly for its gorgeous blues, magnificent ruby-reds and a curious milky-white opaque glass somewhat resembling porcelain and painted in vivid colours.

"Milk-white glass and strong" were the instructions written by the London glass-seller John Greene when ordering consignments of opaque-white glass from the Venetian merchant Allesio Morelli during the 1660s. Greene made his requirements clear by attaching dimensioned drawings to his orders and many of these are now preserved in the British Museum. Several examples of opaque-white glass are thus recorded, including jars and bottles in shapes copied from the Chinese porcelain imported into London by the East India Company. None of this fragile glass is known to remain.

Although formulas for making such glass had been published in England as early as 1662, and again by Blancourt in 1699, its omission from the Glass Excise Act, 1745, proves that production, if any, was negligible during the first half of the eighteenth century. Germany, however, was sending England substantial consignments of decorated porringers, cream-jugs, vases, vinegar and oil cruets and other domestic ware in this material. Although somewhat resembling porcelain of the period and selling at less than half the price, this opaque-white glass was too fragile for lasting use.

The *Dictionary of Arts*, 1755, described a process evolved by de Réamur for making opaque-white glass, under the name of glass porcelain, defined as "the name given to a recent invention for imitating china ware with glass which may afterwards be painted or otherwise decorated". This may be compared with the opacified flint-glass mentioned by Thomas Dossie in 1758. This, he declared, was "made at a considerable work in London in great quantities and has been manufactured into a variety of different kinds of vessels". Dossie printed formulae and manufacturing processes. No information has yet come to light concerning the location of the glasshouse thus recorded.

Whether or not Bristol glassmen originated opaque-white glass, they probably introduced the tunnel leer (Chapter 1) to their factories at about this time and twice annealed this glass, thus toughening it to an extent previously impossible. The Bristol glassmen advertised their opaque-white glass as "enamel glass", the term which is recognized by collectors. The earliest advertisement so far noted in which enamel glass was specified appeared in the *Bristol Journal*, 1764, when Williams, Dunbar & Company established a glasshouse at Chepstow, announcing it as a "flint and enamel Glass Manufactory".

Josiah Perrin, a former Bristol glasshouse manager, established a glasshouse at Warrington, Lancashire, in 1766, and a year later announced in the *Liverpool Advertiser* that he had opened a warehouse in Liverpool for the sale, among other glass, of "White and Painted Enamel Glass". In the same year Jonas Phillips of Lynn advertised "compleat sets of neatly painted enamel jars, the Colours more beautiful than China". The New Glass Houses, Sunderland, advertised themselves as manufacturers of "White enamel glass" in 1769.

The enamel glass of Bristol and Warrington is dense in texture and has a very white tint. Hugh Owen found it comparable with the soft paste porcelains of Sèvres and Derby. The dense whiteness of its fabric was caused merely by the addition of tin oxide to a flint-glass formula. The tin oxide, however, made the glass exceptionally brittle, a fault not entirely overcome by double annealing. Against the light this enamel glass shows a creamy translucency, not unlike that of oriental hard paste porcelain. The surface feels smooth, and sometimes a very fine glaze is visible.

173

The lead content made this glass very soft, causing it to be scratched easily: such scratches eventually show as black scars.

The blown enamel glass of Bristol has a distinct punty mark on the base of each piece. The rod was usually cracked off very roughly, leaving a sharp scar. Around this it is sometimes possible to see twist lines, showing the rod to have been rotated while the glass was being shaped. An associated tendency frequently noted in blown enamel glass is a slightly striated surface.

This enamel glass, like most soft porcelains, has very little heat resistance: domestic hollow-ware which might be subjected to heat when in use is therefore very rare, and when found is of thick section. Otherwise the list of productions covers almost the whole range of the hollow-ware issued by the porcelain potters whose patterns were imitated. Outstanding are models after the Chinese, such as trumpet-mouthed beakers and pear-shaped or oviform covered vases, often in garnitures of five.

Scent bottles were plainly blown in numerous shapes. Often a specimen has flattened sides painted with posies and is fitted with a ground-glass stopper protected by a domed silver or gilded metal cover. Dated examples suggest that they were made during the late 1750s. By 1765 enamelled motifs included bright-plumaged birds, pastoral figures and diaper patterns in the manner of South Staffordshire painted enamels. So close is the resemblance that it may possibly be deduced that some of these, and some snuff-boxes, originated in the Glassborough glasshouse operating from 1761 no more than half a mile from the nearest Bilston painted enamel factory.

Collectors look for candlesticks and tapersticks with finely reeded stems rising from highly domed feet, their tall straight sockets fitted with spreading nozzles of heat-resistant South Staffordshire enamel rimmed with gilded brass, and for five-bottle cruet stands, their bodies decorated with floral sprays in colours and gilded inscriptions, fitted with appropriate covers in silver or heavily gilded brass. Jugs are to be found, too, and sugar basins, finger bowls and plates, wall flower-holders in spirally twisted cornucopia shapes, and salt-cellars in a design with three mask and scroll feet. There are small, long-necked bottles with deep foot-rings, too: these were intended for the display of specimen flowers on a dessert table.

The enamel glass of Bristol is notable for decoration painted in brilliant colours. Three methods of decoration were used: oil or varnish colours hardened by heat but not properly burned in; enamels muffle-fired and permanent; oil gilding fired at a low temperature.

Decorators were obviously experienced painters on ceramics and so far as is known they were free-lance artists operating studios and muffle furnaces in their own homes. One of these was Michael Edkins who settled in Bristol as a painter of earthenware in 1760: his ledgers from that date have been preserved. The earliest enamel glass he painted for sale was in 1762, and entries for such work continue until his death in 1787. In this quarter-century he painted, according to Hugh Owen, about 350 pieces of glass in opaque-white and blue. The number of so-called Michael Edkins pieces in the United States of America vastly exceeds this.

Over-elaboration with borders, bands and unnecessary ornament was consistently avoided. Flowers and foliage form the most frequent motifs and may be grouped into three classes: (a) the frankly imitative Chinese compositions, some floral, others introducing exotic birds and rockeries with tall, attenuated human figures; (b) sprigs and posies in the English naturalistic manner; (c) plump, brightly-coloured English birds, such as bullfinches and goldfinches perched on boughs—a style not noted on enamel glass from other glass centres.

Enamel glass displaying black transfer prints was made at Josiah Perrin's glasshouse at Warrington, and, no doubt, was decorated by Sadler & Green at nearby Liverpool. From about 1760 Sadler & Green carried on an extensive business in decorating porcelain and earthenware sent to them by the potters of Liverpool, North Staffordshire and Leeds. Some of the specimens noted, chiefly 12-inch vases, were over-painted in enamel colours and enclosed within frameworks of rococo scrollwork.

Reproductions of the enamel glass of Bristol have been

made: some may be detected by a faint trace of blue in their composition. Some old undecorated or poorly decorated enamel glass-ware has had its decoration removed and replaced with rich enamel colours in designs copied from those found on known pieces of enamel glass, often from museum specimens.

The Glass Excise Act of 1777 taxed enamel glass to the extent of $2\frac{1}{2}d$. per lb., making its production uneconomical in comparison with the vastly improved soft porcelain of the time. The glassmen retaliated by using glass made from a soda-lime-potash formula, opacified with arsenic or bone ash, and taxed at no more than $\frac{1}{2}d$. per lb.

Many collectors make the mistake of classifying enamel glass and soda-lime-potash glass without distinction. The latter glass, milk-white in reflected light, upon close inspection will be seen to have a creamy hue, sometimes with a hint of blue, particularly noticeable at the punty mark. If held to the light milk-white glass opacified with arsenic displays a fiery opalescence known to nineteenth-century glassmen as "sunset glow". This often has a tinge of bluish-green at the edges. Such glass was made at most English glass centres, at Sunderland, Stourbridge, Glassborough in Staffordshire, Birmingham, and in Lancashire and Yorkshire. Variations in quality, thickness of section and opacity are numerous. In early examples decoration and gilding might be unfired and these have worn away. Chemists' jars were popular in this glass, cylindrical, smooth-surfaced and labelled in gold. Vases of the 1820s decorated with bat-printed ornament have been noted.

Blown-moulded ware was made in this opaque-white glass, all of it apparently dating from about 1820 and often possessed of a fiery opalescence. Jugs were made with well-designed all-over patterns in relief, sugar bowls with large printies, and tiny smelling-bottles. This glass from about 1840 was considered suitable for the fonts and pedestals of oil-burning lamps.

The radiant, translucent deep blue glass associated with Bristol is eagerly acquired by collectors of eighteenth-century table-ware. This should not be confused with the

ristol white enamel glass vases painted with naturalistic flowers.

late 41

.namel glass: (*l. and r.*) pair of candlesticks with incised twist stems, painted in enamel colours, ristol, 1760–70; (*top*) flask decorated with black transfer prints painted over in coloured enamels, 760–70; (*centre*) tea-canister with enamel top to screw cap and decoration attributed to Michael .dkins.

Plate 42
Bristol-blue; (*Top*) Labelled decanters and sauce bottles. (*Centre, left*) Finger bowls marked I JACOB
BRISTOL in gold script. (*Centre, right*) Blown-moulded sugar bowl, early nineteenth century, (*Bottom,
left*) Loving cup with purled base and no strengthening disc, 1780s. (*Bottom, right*) Vase decorated
with all-over cutting; height 20 inches; early nineteenth century.

ordinary smalt blues of the nineteenth century. Unfortunately the name Bristol-blue has became a generic term applied to any dark blue translucent glass. The real Bristol-blue might not necessarily have been made in a Bristol glasshouse: it was customarily so named because the superfine smalt with which the flint-glass was coloured could be obtained only from a single merchant whose warehouse was in Bristol.

A vitreous form of cobalt oxide sold under the name of smalt and made in Saxony was used for colouring flint-glass. In 1681 *Grew's Museum* noted "a piece of smalt glass". The quality of smalt was progressively improved until when added to molten transparent glass it spread without variation of tint throughout the metal which, when vitrified, displayed a strong blue tint. This was the celebrated Bristol-blue. This fine smalt had been monopolized by Augustus III, Elector of Saxony, for use in the porcelain factory at Meissen. So precious was the smalt for fine decoration that its export was forbidden, although a less brilliant smalt was exported at £11 an ounce.

During the war waged by Frederick the Great against Saxony, the Prussians seized the Royal Saxon Smalt Works at Dresden, and stocks of fine smalt found their way to Bristol where, in about 1761, they were sold at the unprecedentedly low rate of fifteen shillings an ounce to glassmen and ceramic decorators. It is thought that the merchant distributing this smalt seized from Dresden was William Cookworthy, a wholesale druggist who later established the Plymouth and Bristol hard-paste porcelain factories. The glassmen used it to colour their glass an intense dark blue. When fresh supplies were needed in Stourbridge, Warrington, Sunderland or elsewhere, "Bristol-blue" was always demanded to distinguish it from ordinary smalt which produced a harsh dark blue. English smalt was available made from native cobalt, but unfortunately it tinged the glass with indigo, violet or purple in tints which could not be controlled.

"Parcels of fine smalt brought from Saxony has not long been available in England", wrote Thomas Dossie in his *Handmaid to the Arts*, 1764. "Its goodness consists of being dark, bright and cool although it always verges on the purple, but the less so the better." After emphasizing the exceptional hardness of the Saxon smalt, and the brilliance of its dark hue, he noted that it was used for many purposes for which common smalt was unsuitable.

Bristol-blue glass was made only in small quantities in piling pots measuring about 12 inches deep and 6 inches in diameter. These were covered and placed in the furnace upon the ordinary pots. It was discovered that the colour was vastly improved by retention in the furnace for a considerable time after vitrification, this making it harder, and freer from specks and microscopic bubbles. Production, of course, was necessarily limited, but continuous until about 1790, when supplies of Saxon smalt again failed.

Blue flint-glass had been made already in the form of vases, but when Bristol-blue appeared glass-sellers were faced with a demand for sets of mantel ornaments in this colour. Such handsome jars and beakers no doubt were considered inexpensive counterparts of the Derbyshire blue john chimneypiece ornaments then newly fashionable. Sugar bowls, cream pails and drinking goblets were also made in imitation of blue john. Goblets in several sizes soon appeared in the form of drinking rummers with drawn stems and plain round feet.

The ledgers of Michael Edkins record several entries regarding Bristol-blue glass, the earliest being on July 19, 1763, when he gilded "4 blue Jars and Beakers with mosaic borders" for two shillings, and a "1 Pint Blue Cannister with letters" for eightpence. Other articles in blue decorated by Edkins were tea-canisters, basins, hyacinth glasses, wall cornucopias and cans.

Decanters in Bristol-blue flint-glass were made, at first of the shouldered type with a spire-finialled stopper fitted into a slightly tapering unlipped mouth. With undecorated decanters the spires were smoothly round; otherwise they were cut into pyramid form. A label decanter might be ornamented in gold, the lettering enclosed in a scrollwork cartouche with grapes and vine leaves. A gilded chain added to the illusion that the label was hanging around the neck. Others were painted in oil colours which were mixed with a

desiccator so that they dried hard. Still others were enamelled with coloured frits, vitrified in a muffle. The form
of decanter thereafter followed those of flint-glass, but few
are to be found cut in deep relief. There was a fashionable
conceit for serving spirits from Bristol-blue decanters or
squares, usually in sets of three labelled in gold, for rum,
gin and brandy. These were accompanied by matching
drinking-glasses and a set of decanters has been noticed
with a large oval glass tray.

Finger bowls and wine-glass coolers from about 1780
to 1820 might be in blue glass, whilst the remainder of the
equipage was in cut flint-glass : this masking of accumulated
sediment continued until the 1850s with the addition of
green and ruby glass.

The Napoleonic Wars having blocked supplies of smalt
from the early 1790s, artificial ultramarine was invented,
reaching the glass industry in 1804. Its cost was low, but the
resulting glass was harshly purple-blue and is thus distinguished from the earlier Bristol-blue. Inexpensive blown-
moulded ware was made from this glass.

A third period of Bristol-blue dates from about 1820,
when Saxon smalt again became available to the glass trade.
This was now known as smalt-glass to distinguish it from
the synthetic production. The finest and most desirable,
displaying a royal purple tinge when held to the light, was
named king's blue after George IV had expressed admiration
of a spirit set made as a coronation gift in 1821. Purifying
treatments afterwards given to the cobalt oxide from which
the smalt was made removed copper, lead, iron, nickel and
so on. This so affected the resulting tint given to glass that
little, if any, king's-blue glass may be dated after about 1840.

Only second in popularity to blue among collectors of
coloured glass is the ruby-red tone. Even by the mid-
eighteenth century Stourbridge was celebrated for its
coloured glass, and Dr. Richard Pococke in June 1751
noted that it was "here coloured in the liquid, of all the
capital colours in their several shades and, if I mistake not, is
a secret which they have here". Coloured glass at this period
was being produced also in Bristol and in London, and ruby

and emerald glass were imported from Bohemia. Collectors may note particularly the patent granted in 1755 to Mayer Oppenheim the elder of London for making red glass. The specification shows that the colour was obtained by adding $\frac{1}{2}$ oz. of "a prepared solution of Dutch gold" to every pound of flint materials. The glass was heavily leaded and displayed a remarkable ruby hue, much less of a vermilion than the Bohemian. There was also, later, a cherry red. This red glass was usually ornamented with gilding, but usually this has long ago vanished from existing specimens, except for some embossed work.

A deep-hued, bright green glass also appears to have been made in Bristol and elsewhere from the mid-eighteenth century. In 1767 it was advertised by the Perrin firm of Warrington. In the early nineteenth century the Edinburgh and Leith Glass Company used it for roemers. Green and red glass in the early nineteenth century cost one penny a pound more than clear flint-glass.

There appears to have been no great demand for coloured glass during the period when cutting in deep relief was in high fashion. From about 1820, however, the number of colours available was increased. Colour is imparted to flint-glass by the addition of metallic oxides and when the whole mass is coloured it is termed pot metal, distinguishing it from surface-coloured glass where the colour is in the form of enamel. The Report of the Jury of the Great Exhibition, 1851, gives the following list of metallic oxides then in use by English glassmen: cobalt produces blue; manganese, violet; antimony, yellow; precipitate of cassius or gold produces pink; uranium an opaline-greenish colour; chromium, green; copper produces ruby or greenish-blue, according to the degree of oxidization; copper with iron produces ruby or green, according to the degree of oxidization of the copper; silver produces a pure and beautiful yellow. These colours, the basis of all early nineteenth-century glass colouring, could be modified or completely altered by different combinations of the metals, the degree of oxidization, the heat employed and the addition of vegetable carbonaceous matter.

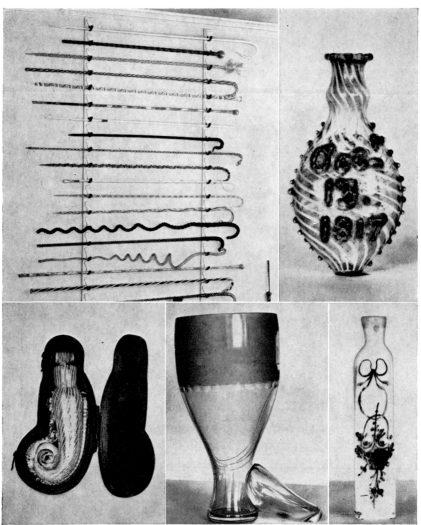

Plate 44
(*Upper left*) Glass walking-sticks. (*Upper right*) Scent bottle in clear glass with white opaque stripe dated Oct, 13, 1817, and with the initials I M in ruby trailed work. (*Lower l. to r.*) Scent bottle in clear glass with white opaque stripes and trailed ornament, in original shagreen case, height 3½ inches early nineteenth century; boot glass, cut and frosted, engraved A W, height 6½ inches, late eighteenth century; scent bottle in opaque white glass, painted with flowers, height 4½ inches, late eighteenth century.

Little coloured table glass was displayed at the Great Exhibition, and that mainly by Bacchus & Sons of Birmingham, and Molineaux & Webb of Manchester. Catalogue entries name the colours used as ruby, bright green, emerald green, purple, yellow. A directory entry of W. H. P. & J. Richardson of Wordsley in 1845 lists their productions as including "plain, gilt and richly cut glass of all colours". Later they introduced topaz and chrysolite.

Chapter Sixteen

NAILSEA GLASS

NAILSEA has given its name to some of the most light-hearted creations of the English glassman, and many collectors find pleasure in possessing a few of these playthings. The wide range of colourful trinkets and curios includes a multitude of gimmel, bellows and other flasks, smelling-bottles, rolling-pins, witch balls, paper-weights and door porters, walking-sticks, giant tobacco pipes and coaching-horns. Such glassware, opaque and translucent, and milk white, yellow, salmon pink, rose pink, green or any of numerous blues, is flamboyantly patterned with waves in contrasting hues, streaks, splotches or zig-zags: alternatively it may bear stripes and slender threads of colour in complex compositions reminiscent of Murano and Venice.

The late Georgian and early Victorian fripperies in gaudy glass were made not only at Nailsea near Bristol, but by the glassmen of Sunderland, Newcastle, Stourbridge, Warrington, Wrockwardine Wood in Shropshire, Alloa in Scotland, and elsewhere. So greatly alike are their productions in form and colour that collectors can do no more than group them all under a generic term, and for this purpose the glass centre, Nailsea, has been chosen. "Nailsea" glass may be grouped into five distinct types:

(1) A brownish-green bottle-glass garnished with encircling trails of white enamel, and flecking or mottling, 1790–1820.

(2) A light-green bottle-glass decorated with crackling or notched ornament in white enamel, 1800–20.

(3) Opaque coloured glass enriched with looped and mottled or flecked decoration, from about 1815.

(4) Latticinio ornament, white and pink in a pale green glass until 1845; then in clear flint-glass.

(5) Translucent coloured flint-glass decorated with contrasting tints, from 1845.

The Nailsea Glasshouse was founded in 1788 by John Robert Lucas, a British cider-master who found difficulty in obtaining bottles in the new cylindrical shape, and therefore established a bottle factory in a cider-making district at Nailsea Heath, nine miles south-west of Bristol. Here he produced bottles better designed for ease of transport than those made previously. The bottle's diameter was reduced to 3½ inches, its shoulder was higher and less pronounced, its finish smoother. His bottle-glass was of a paler hue than was formerly customary, having an attractive brownish-green tint, soon copied by other bottle-makers.

In 1792 Lucas came into contact with Edward Homer, member of a celebrated family of enamel painters in Wednesbury. Political unrest on the Continent was slowly killing the export trade in painted enamels of South Staffordshire and Birmingham. Homer, obviously, was highly knowledgeable regarding the behaviour under heat of metallic oxides used in enamel work, and it was his idea that attractive inexpensive domestic table-ware could be made from Lucas's bottle-glass. This was taxed at a much lower rate than flint-glass, which at that time was subject to an excise duty of 2½d. per lb., raised to 6d. per lb. in 1815. Homer reported that this bottle-glass could be decorated with quickly applied bands, spots and splashes of white enamel, using the tax-free compositions of the painted enamel trade. Thereupon, in 1793, Lucas, his brother-in-law William Chance, Edward Homer and a glassman named Coathupe formed a partnership to exploit the innovation. Success was immediate, for their domestic ware could be sold at prices considerably below those of glass produced elsewhere. Most of this hollow-ware was based on shapes blown in open-top moulds and then manipulated by hand tools (Chapter 13).

A second phase, dating probably from about 1800, consisted of domestic table-ware in green bottle-glass decorated by encircling necks and lips with white enamel trailing known as crackling or notched ornament, which might also be applied in vertical lines.

Edward Homer retired in 1807 and was succeeded as partner by his son, J. G. Homer, manager of the enamelling department. The firm was now vigorously flourishing with a capital of £60,000. When excise duty was increased in 1815 it was J. G. Homer who introduced the idea of colouring the pale green bottle-glass, making it a pot metal, and ornamenting it with loops of white, pink and blue. Already, in 1810, William Chance's son, Robert Lucas Chance, had been approved works manager of a new department specializing in the manufacture of sheet and crown glass. Under his influence prosperity continued, and the Nailsea Heath glasshouse eventually covered an area of five acres, with branches at Stanton Drew and Wick, and offices and warehouses in Nicholas Street, Bristol.

The ornamental glass was intended for the most part to attract the popular market. It was an inexpensive means of introducing radiant colour into what might otherwise be drab homes. The colours of Nailsea are thought by some authorities to be identifiable by a brilliant hue unapproached elsewhere, but there is no conclusive evidence in support of this theory, and the brilliant colours no doubt date to later than 1845. By 1820 the low-taxed Nailsea glass was being produced in many shades of blue, green, amber and red, and might be flecked, mottled or striped.

The Jury of the 1851 Great Exhibition, consisting entirely of authorities on glass, reported that in their opinion low-taxed bottle and crown glass had been made in suspiciously good quality for domestic ware during the late excise period. This strongly suggested that glassmen had effected the improvement through the use of materials unauthorized by law.

No fragments of coloured glass have been unearthed on the Nailsea Heath site and this has led to the suggestion that the coloured glass was made at one of the branch establishments. This may have been so, but as every fragment of glass was required for cullet (Chapter 1) it is very unlikely that the management would have tolerated the wastage of usable material upon which tax had already been paid.

Nailsea continued making coloured glass curios after the abolition of the glass excise tax in 1845. Records of the early 1860s show that an Irishman named Kelly was then mixing the pot metal for coloured glass, with William Maddock as foreman of the enamelling department. The Nailsea glasshouse closed in 1873, owing its creditors £30,000.

The flecking, mottling and encircling bands of white enamel on early Nailsea are found on jugs, mugs, jars, tumblers, rolling-pins and serving bottles, some of which bear seals and occasionally dates in relief. These are in a brownish-green bottle-glass, and the flecks appear to have been sprinkled haphazardly over the surface, varying in size from a pinhead to an inch or more across. These flecks, usually in a milky-white or bluish-white tint, feel rough to the finger and are in slight relief. Yellow and red speckled work is occasionally found—always a collector's prize. The speckles may cover the entire surface: in other instances they appear to have been sprinkled sparsely around the shoulders of bottle forms.

Inspection of the flecks will usually show them to be crazed, that is, covered with a network of thin, irregular lines crossing each other and resembling fine cracks. This crazing has taken place through the years and is due to innumerable changes in atmospheric conditions, the basic glass and the enamel contracting and expanding at different rates in response to these changes. Crazing is not observed on modern copies. Apart from these reproductions, it is improbable that this mottled effect on bottle-glass was made outside the Nailsea establishment.

Curved loopings or quillings, white or coloured, ornament the surfaces of many flasks in flattened baluster or pear shape, varying from about 5 to 9 inches in height. These were made in considerable numbers. For the most part they were sold as containers of toilet waters, but spirits and other liquors are known to have been sold in some. The quilling effect was cleverly accomplished by arranging coloured canes of glass, known as quills, around the inner surface of a mould shaped like a flower-pot. A gather of glass was taken on the blowing iron and pushed into the mould. The quills adhered to the hot glass which was immediately withdrawn from the mould and reheated at the glory hole. It was then inflated and tooled with the pincers to produce a hollow shape coloured with vertical stripes which were twisted into attractive curved patterns.

Collectors of Nailsea are always fascinated by the gimmel, or twin flask with two spouts. Two bottles were blown individually and fused together, usually with their necks pointing in opposite directions, but occasionally with them parallel. Gimmel flasks are included among the drawings which accompanied Greene's orders for Venetian glass in the 1660s. These were in soda-glass, some with pinched and trailed ornament. Their purpose at that time was to contain oil and vinegar. From about 1680 gimmels were made in flint-glass.

There is evidence that flint-glass gimmels fitted into saddle holsters, easily accessible for refreshment on a journey. The two bottles were strengthened with an ornamental strip passing between them. The sides of holster gimmels sometimes display signs of continual friction: their size approximates 8 inches by 3 inches.

A Nailsea gimmel is most usually found with pink and white spiral decoration, or white latticinio loops: a circular, crimped or petal foot may be added. It was generally sold containing toilet water, and a very early example might be inscribed with the name of the recipient, such as one example formerly in the Applewhaite-Abbott collection, inscribed "J. Lumley 1811".

Many flasks were made in the form of hand-bellows such as were formerly used at the dressing-table for powdering the hair. These are found in clear flint-glass garnished with notches, loops and trailed work, and in coloured Nailsea glass, such as blue with loops and trailed work in white enamel. These were a perfumer's speciality, sold containing toilet vinegars, waters and perfumes.

Giant bellows flasks measuring a foot or more in height, for the dressing-table or the mantelshelf, were made in the mid-nineteenth century. The flask itself in clear glass with translucent red and white loops and frilling is mounted vertically on a stemmed circular foot of clear or opaque-white glass. In some of these giants the bellows nozzle may be expanded into a deep saucer shape and crimped. These flasks were intended to be filled with perfumed water which slowly evaporated, pleasantly scenting the room in a day when ventilation was rarely considered essential. The front of the flask might be decorated with an applied motif such as Prince of Wales' feathers after the birth of the future Edward VII in 1841, a gilded monogram or an enamelled posy.

Jacob's ladders were pairs of colourful mantel ornaments, dating from the late 1840s, that had a great appeal to Victorians. Few of these delicate pieces have remained intact, but they are occasionally to be found in translucent blue, red, amethyst and clear glass. A Jacob's ladder consists of a delicate tapering open spiral of glass, like an elongated wire spring, some 9 inches tall and 2 inches across the top. This flimsy "ladder" twines around a central stem, equally slender, attached to it at the top and based on a highly domed foot with a folded rim.

Glass bells were made, decorative and with the pure resonant tone associated with flint-glass. They were originally made for carrying in the Glassworkers' Guild processions, annual events at Bristol and Newcastle. The *Newcastle Chronicle* describes the procession of glassworkers in 1823: "Each wore a hat decorated with a glass feather, a glass star sparkled at their breast, suspended from a chain or collar formed of drops of cut glass in variegated colours hung around the neck. Each man carried a staff, a cross-piece at the top displaying a specimen of his art: decanters, goblets, drinking-glasses, jugs, bowls, dishes. Some carried a glass bell which he rang lustily." Glass bells in colours were also made at Stourbridge and Warrington, and by John Davenport of Longport, Staffordshire, who for several years operated a glasshouse in connection with his celebrated pottery.

Colours are in numerous combinations, but clappers are invariably in fine clear flint-glass. Authentic bells, which measure from 9 to 18 inches in height, include the following colour combinations: blue tinted bell, spirally ribbed handle in pale yellow with opalescent triple-knopped finial; bell with pink strands on an opaque-white ground, with moulded opaque-white hand as a handle; bell with white stripes on a translucent red ground, opalescent blue handle; red bell with colour-twist spiral handle; green bell with opaque-white twist handle; opaque-white throughout and may be ribbed, or translucent white bell with clear handle. The glass bells still in production are often found masquerading as antiques.

Candlesticks of a form that, in flint-glass, is often wrongly attributed to the early Georgian period and even earlier, are included among Nailsea-type glass. These, in the full range of colours, are hollow throughout, from base to socket, and were shaped by hand-tools from short lengths of tube. One end of the tube was opened into a highly-domed spreading foot with a folded rim: the socket was also strengthened with a thick rim and ornamented with shallow ribbing which might be twisted. These candlesticks measure between 6 inches and a foot in height, the shorter sizes being more frequent. Hollow candlesticks were also made from tubes of latticinio work. The base might be trumpet-shaped, the stem widened into an expansive central knop, and the piece topped with an exceptionally deep socket.

Among the more massive objects in glass of the Nailsea type are coaching horns with widely expanded mouthpieces, measuring from 40 to 45 inches in length. These may be in blue or amber glass, in clear flint-glass, sometimes spirally ribbed, and in a pale yellow glass from the late 1840s. Those with the tube curved into three loops do not appear to have been reproduced.

Slender poignards were made with blades of translucent white glass, circular in section, enclosing spiral threads: the

rystallo ceramie by Apsley Pellat: (*Top*) Paper weights: (*l.*) portrait of George IV against a ground
f cross-cut diamonds; (*r.*) Frederick, Duke of York, against a ground of deep horizontal cutting.
Centre) Scent bottles moulded and cut with portraits: (*l.*) George III; (*r.*) Princess Charlotte.
Bottom) Toilet-water bottles: (*l.*) with panels framed by diamond cutting; (*r.*) with step-cut shoulder.

Plate 46

(*Top*) Glass rolling-pins; transparent green glass; dark green glass engraved with motifs and inscription dated 1843; black glass flecked with white. (*Centre*) Millefiori paperweights and dish. (*Bottom, left*) Vase of deep Bristol-blue lined with pale blue, decorated with storks, bamboo and rice plant with flowers and birds applied in white enamel, height 12 inches. (*Bottom, right*) Wine-glass with bowl and foot decorated with millefiori motifs.

guards are circular and in blue, the ribbed grip green, the pommel clear white. Others are adaptations of ceremonial dress swords with raspberry prunts on the hilt, and with the blade of triangular section with a broad red stripe on one side. These measure from 40 to 48 inches in length. Yet another type is in blue glass, with a square blade spirally fluted and the tip edged in red to simulate blood.

In the same group, intended primarily for wall decoration, may be included the glass mace. The hollow crown-shaped head is attached to a colourful spirally twisted staff. Among the early types are those in Bristol-blue decorated with applied enamel and gilding. In some there is a finial, but it is improbable that these date earlier than about 1850.

Riding crops measuring about 30 inches in length and containing broad white enamel bands are numbered among early Nailsea productions, but, like horns and swords, the majority seen will be of a more recent origin.

Fantastically shaped giant tobacco-pipes in colour were possibly at first intended to decorate tobacco shop windows illuminated at night by argand lamps. Soon they were in considerable demand as wall decorations for the home. Normally they measure between 10 and 25 inches overall, but a massive pipe recently seen in translucent red glass, with white loop decoration and a bobbin stem, measured 40 inches. This was accompanied by an example in Bristol-blue, with a white enamel bowl rim, and another of opaque-white rimmed with blue.

Other pipes, dating from the mid-1840s onwards, are translucent glass with heavy solid multi-knopped stems containing air-bubbles and slender mouth-pieces of equal length: the bowls of these copy the shapes of the newly introduced briar pipes. Mr. H. St. George Gray writing in the *Connoisseur*, 1911, proved that such pipes were actually made at Nailsea, quoting Eyres, one of the clerks, as saying: "A wagoner, from over Backwell Hill, must have heard of tobacco pipes, for he came into the works one day and asked of one of the teazers [stokers] if he thought he could find any 'cooriosity bacca pipes' among the cinders." Early

Nailsea pipes had small bowls and the solid stems were of coloured or opaque-white enamel twist.

Popular fairings in gaily-coloured glass were the walking-sticks, canes and shepherds' crooks made for parlour decoration, those with red, white and blue spirals being particularly numerous. Hollow canes with spherical or flattened knobs were made from drawn tubes of flint-glass and filled with "hundreds-and-thousands", then known as comfits. In a few instances the original comfits remain intact, arranged in 2-inch bands alternating in red, white and blue, the ferrule being plugged with a cork.

The Lennox-Boyd collection of walking-sticks includes some seventy examples in glass, the majority with U-shaped heads, some with crooks, others knobbed. Inspection of this collection shows that some are of pale green bottle-glass, with or without a mass of tiny air-bubbles, and others in clear and coloured flint-glass. Each differs in shape and colour arrangement. The glass rod itself may be twisted in relief, and either plain or with a ribbon of enamel within. One example has an incised twist handle and vertical incisions along the rod. The majority are enriched with coloured spiral threads in red, blue, green, amber or white, running their entire length. These interior threads of enamel often cause a very slight ridge on the surface of the glass. In still others the colour threads are spiralled around the surface of the sticks.

The earliest of these walking-sticks are tapered at the ferrule end: later specimens appear to have been simply rounded off in the glory hole. Those with shepherd's crook handles are merely sheared off with a cold iron, suggesting a common source. A ceremonial crook may have a ribbed handle and a writhen rod usually in clear glass with an amber core, or white latticinio with red and blue ribbons. Other colours are also found.

Glasshouses making coloured pot-glass usually featured at least a few gift souvenirs in such forms as have been described in this chapter and others discussed in the following chapter. This later series is easy to distinguish from the true Nailsea type. The firm of Coathupe & Co., Bristol, was awarded a gold medal at the 1851 exhibition for glass curtain poles and glass tubes. It is reasonable to assume that this offshoot from the original Nailsea partnership produced walking-sticks and other rod ornaments.

One is constantly confronted with the statement that many of the objects in glass of the Nailsea type now collected are friggers. This was a colloquial term for experimental or apprentice pieces made by the glassmen for their own amusement and profit. That friggers were made in considerable quantities cannot be substantiated. Glassmaking was a thoroughly commercial trade in which the burdensome excise duty made every pound of glass of value to the management. It would be extremely unlikely that works glassmen would be permitted to make more than an occasional frigger to take home, and these would not account for the quantities now available. It is true that some amazingly intricate pieces exist, but all noted have been in post-1845 pot-glass or have been twentieth-century productions.

Considerable numbers of "Nailsea" glass flasks, rolling-pins and so on still purport to come to light in districts surrounding old-time glasshouses. Nearly all these are fakes, their history bogus. As long ago as 1911 Mr. St. George Gray warned readers of the *Connoisseur* against imitations: "Fabrications of Nailsea glass specially prepared for the unwary collector are already on the market. Some of the most flagrant imitations offered for sale (perhaps more in the neighbourhood of Bristol than elsewhere) are copies of splashed Nailsea glass." Every type of article originally made is copied today and given bogus marks of wear by second-hand dealers.

Twentieth-century glass often mistaken for period Nailsea includes those interesting fox-hunting sets in which a huntsman riding a chestnut horse, and hounds, fox and trees are enclosed in a rectangular glass case. These were made between wars.

Chapter Seventeen

ROLLING-PINS, REFLECTING GLOBES AND WITCH BALLS

THE original purpose of "Bristol glass rollers" was for long a mystery. It has now been established that these bolster-like, hollow cylinders, knobbed at the ends and resembling rolling-pins, first made their appearance as salt-containers.

Salt taxes, continually rising from 1694 until 1829, made salt a costly commodity, and during that period it was illegal to sell salt except by weight. Dean Swift found salt expensive, for in his satirical *Directions to Servants* he bade them "Fold up the Table-cloth with the Salt in it, then Shake the Salt out into the Salt-cellar to use next day". During the Napoleonic Wars the English salt tax was thirty times the retail cost of the salt itself.

So valuable did salt become that it was no longer stored loose in capacious oak salt-boxes where it was liable to suffer from damp as well as becoming the servants' perquisite. Common salt was then sold in wide-necked bottles and in about 1790 the first glass rollers appeared. They were thick-walled and blown from the so-called black bottle-glass which, held to the light, displays a dark, muddy yellow-green tint. One end of the roller was stoppered, the glass being ground so that the contents would be kept air-tight. Both the closed end and the stopper were ball-knobbed so that the salt bottle might be hung horizontally in a dry place such as the chimney nook or corner cupboard under the eye of the housewife. Unlike a normal rolling-pin, this early type of roller tapered slightly from the centre to each end.

For many centuries the presence of consecrated salt in the

home had been considered potent protection against witch-craft. The new salt bottle immediately became a symbol of good luck, the credulous believing it to possess the power of holding any elements of ill-health which might gain access to the house. Each morning the roller would be wiped to remove such harmful elements and preserve good health for the family. Those who bought salt for its magic properties insisted upon Sunday salt, a large-grained flaky salt produced between Saturday and Monday when the fires at the salt-works were slackened. Such salt was considered to have been manufactured without the hand of man.

The cold glass tube, heavy with salt, was soon discovered by the less credulous to make an excellent pastry roller. Thereupon salt bottles were given parallel sides to serve their double purpose. The flint-glasshouses began to blow them with thinner walls, too, so that they were more capacious. By 1810 decorative salt bottles were being made in purple, blue, mottled and striped glass.

Once the idea of colourful ornament had been introduced, flint-glass rolling-pins in opaque-white glass became an obvious field for homely decoration in coloured enamels. These were used as colourful wall ornaments in farmhouse and cottage at a time when pictures were expensive. During the early 1820s rollers thus tended to lose their purely utilitarian purpose. Still retaining something of their old association, and regarded as lucky mascots, they proved acceptable gifts, but instead of salt their fillings were then chosen to suit the occasion. Some were filled with tea. The standard roller, 15 inches long by 2 inches in diameter, contained exactly one pound. This was given as a wedding present at a time when tea might cost as much as a guinea a pound.

Filled with comfits and suitably inscribed, rollers were presented by young men to their sweethearts as "fairings". Gilded, enamelled and painted, these rollers are inscribed with mottoes and good wishes, such as "To wish ye well", "Long may the sun shine on thee and thine", and "Good Luck attend thee". These glass rolling-pins were regarded entirely as lucky ornaments only to be taken down from the wall when pastry was ceremoniously prepared for a wedding feast. Such pastry was supposed to bring luck to all who ate it.

Decorated with seafaring subjects they were advertised as "Sailors' Charm, Glass Rolling-Pins for hanging in a Ship's Cabin, white, decorated in colours with ships, motto and inscription. 14¾ inches long". A great number were found in sailors' homes, presented as parting gifts before setting out on voyages that might prove long and hazardous. It was considered disastrous for a lucky roller to get broken and, among seafaring folk, there was the superstition that if this happened it signified the wrecking of the vessel carrying the giver. A roller of blue glass may display a finely-gilded schooner at one end, and at the other a mariner's compass and the words "Come box the compass". Between is a wreath of red roses with leaves enclosing a four-line verse, such as the following:

> "When far at sea—remember me
> And bear me in your mind.
> Let all the world say what they will
> Speak of me as you find."

Flint-glass rolling-pins were made at Nailsea, Sunderland, Stourbridge and Birmingham, and at Alloa in Scotland. To make one, a gathering of molten glass was taken from the furnace on one end of a blowing tube. The glassman blew this first into a sphere which he elongated by swinging it. He then shaped a solid knob at the further end, to which his assistant attached a punty iron. The blowing tube was detached and the glass tube held by the punty iron while its open end was warmed at the furnace mouth and a second knob formed. For a salt or tea container this was merely shaped for a stopper, but when the purely decorative rolling-pin came into fashion both ends might consist of matching solid knobs.

In the West Country they were called Bristol rollers because so many were made at Nailsea, of flecked black or greenish-black bottle-glass. The flecks were unevenly spaced and varied in size. Later these rollers might be striped, threaded or streaked in various tints. Opaque-white glass rollers decorated with enamel colours which were fixed by firing were made in large quantities, and so were those of Bristol blue. Nailsea examples are not always well shaped.

In the north of England glass rollers were made at Sunderland. Early decorations were in coloured enamels: later decoration was coarse, usually executed in oil colours lightly fired and of poor wearing quality. By 1845 transfer decoration was used. Pale bottle green and marbled red and white are Sunderland colours, and rollers may be inscribed " A Present from Shields" or elsewhere.

A Sunderland speciality of the 1840s is the rolling-pin ornamented with the sharpened end of a specially hardened tool, the design being portrayed in small, closely-spaced dots. Decorations include hounds chasing a hare, a paddle steamer, a farmer ploughing, the Sunderland Bridge and many others.

The Alloa Glassworks made rolling-pins of transfer-decorated opaque-white glass. Wrockwardine in Shropshire made them in striped glass of two or more colours. Tens of thousands came from the Birmingham–Stourbridge area, often plainly coloured amber, green, purple or blue.

The final chapter in the roller's story was a return to a purely utilitarian status as a rolling-pin. Following the repeal of the glass tax in 1845, solid rolling-pins of heavily leaded flint-glass were produced in various plain colours and still with knobs at their ends. Birmingham examples were shown at the Great Exhibition made by Bacchus & Co., and Nailsea is known to have been making them as late as 1865.

Reproductions of the early decorated types have been made in many thousands since 1910, and they continue to appear in so-called Bristol-blue, lavishly gilded with nautical subjects and other homely decoration.

Glass spheres lustred to resemble shining silver have enlivened dark rooms since Elizabethan days. Such a globe can mirror a whole room in miniature with the vividness of a Dutch painting, and it is significant that they are shown in countless numbers of these pictures. It is probable that the popular name witch ball is a romantic corruption of the more obvious term watch ball. Early examples found in England were Continental products in fragile soda-glass, but from about 1690 English work appeared in tough, clear flint-glass. The hollow interiors were silvered with a preparation composed of two parts bismuth, one part lead, one part pure tin and four parts mercury. The lead, tin and bismuth were melted together and the mercury added when the mixture was almost cold. A gentle heat was sufficient to melt this amalgam which was then poured into the sphere by means of a paper funnel reaching almost to the bottom. By slowly rotating the ball the liquid amalgam was spread in a thin film over the glass, to which it adhered; surplus amalgam was then poured out. The health of the operators carrying out this work suffered severely through the inhalation of mercury fumes.

In these early balls there was considerable distortion in the reflections. Not until 1843 was a method discovered of coating the interior surface with real silver without the use of mercury. The process was never popular, however, owing to its high cost. Reflecting globes made in this way may be recognized by their faintly yellow tint. An improved method was invented in 1848, of which *The Magazine of Art*, 1852, reported "so great is their power of reflection that the entire details of a large apartment are caught upon them with surprising minuteness and clearness of definition and in amusing perspective". Such glass balls were made in a wide range of metallic hues and in sizes varying from 3 to 30 inches.

Dampness from the atmosphere damaged most lustred globes produced before the mid-century. In 1848, however, another method was devised. Two globes were blown, one within the other, the space between the two being filled with silver solution inserted through a hole in the base. When the interior was satisfactorily coated with silver it was emptied and the opening almost invisibly sealed with a blow-lamp. Tarnish due to the atmosphere was thus prevented and the brilliancy of the glass preserved (see page 225).

From late in the seventeenth century the glass-makers blew short-necked spherical bottles of clear flint-glass, their shape inspired by the silvered balls, but intended as containers for holy water. Such a bottle was hung in the living-room or elsewhere as protection against the malign influence of evil spirits. Eventually, like the glass rolling-pin, it became an emblem of good luck that the credulous handled with respect and wiped each morning to guard them from ill-health. Large numbers of these flasks were made of thick dark bottle-glass.

Late in the eighteenth century spherical bottles of green and blue glass were made for this purpose, sometimes inscribed with scriptural texts in gold. Early in the nineteenth century Nailsea made coloured balls in a variety of tints, such as green, crimson, gold and deep blue. Soon these might be enlivened with various forms of decoration: some are spotted; some show either opaque-white or air-thread spirals (very rare) in the thickness of the glass. Yet another type has four or more loops of coloured glass festooning the surface of the ball.

The Pottery Gazette, 1942, described the method by which these looped balls were made: "The worker would first blow a smallish sphere of glass and his assistant would then wrap around it a thread of softened glass of a different colour, encircling the ball a number of times, spacing the spiral as he went along. With his tool the maker would drag the threads at four equidistant points around the ball, thus forming four sets of loops. He would then re-heat the whole at the pot mouth and blow the article to its finished size when the glass was sufficiently softened and the applied threads had merged somewhat into the body of the sphere."

Spirally-threaded balls were made by a similar method, the threads of plastic glass being applied singly to the globe longitudinally, while the glassman slowly rotated his iron. Extra emphasis could be given to the twist if the globe was reheated, and the design might be enclosed within an outer layer of clear or transparent coloured glass.

A later type was decorated with transfer pictures applied to the interior surface. As a background to these the interior was coated white to make the glass opaque, marbled with various vivid colours. Such balls were blown in various sizes. Many were made without any opening: these were intended as jug covers, but were somewhat inadequate to keep out insects and dust. These colourful balls were made from about 1780 until 1865.

Chapter Eighteen

CRYSTALLO CERAMIE

TINY decorative objects wholly encased in solid blocks of clear flint-glass had an immense appeal to the easily mystified public of the early nineteenth century. Among these small treasures for desk and dressing-table one of the most notable was the splendid *crystallo ceramie*. This work was a speciality of Apsley Pellatt between 1819 and about 1835, and was continued by other glassmen in profusion but of graceless quality between 1845 and 1865, when the little articles were advertised as medallion inlays. Collectors usually refer to both groups as sulphides, incrusted glass or crystal cameos. Georgian specimens display real beauty in the restrained simplicity of the small bas-relief portrait or coat of arms made of a specially prepared china clay: beneath the refractive brilliance of the incrusting flint-glass it assumes the glowing loveliness of silver.

Distinction was given to the crystal cameo by the celebrated London glassmaker Apsley Pellatt (1791–1863), who used the exceptional refractive power of his notably lustrous flint-glass to envelop the simple bas-relief portrait in a mellow radiance. In 1819 Pellatt was granted a patent (No. 4424) protecting for fourteen years his process of glass incrustation under the name of *crystallo ceramie*. The patent cost him about £300—worth at least £3,000 in present-day values—and he issued these lovely crystals from his father's London glasshouse in Holland Street, Southwark. In the following year, Mary Rollason, the firm's Birmingham agent, was advertising "ornamental incrustations, called *Crystallo Ceramie*, which bids fair to form an era in the art of glass-making. By the improved process, ornaments of any description, Arms, Crests, Cyphers, Portraits, Landscapes of any variety of colour, may be introduced into the glass so as to become perfectly unperishable ".

Many of these bas-reliefs were embedded in paperweights, but others enriched a wide range of table-ware and jewellery, such as decanters and stoppers, goblets, tumblers, mugs, sugar-basins for tea-caddy sets, knife rests, ice plates, ornamental plaques, toilet water and scent bottles, pendants, ear-rings, finger rings, seals and girandole stems. Most commonly the cameo bas-relief was a profile portrait of a contemporary celebrity.

Queen Mary made a small collection of this glass displaying royal portraits. These, now at Buckingham Palace, include George III, Queen Charlotte, George IV, Princess Charlotte, her fiancé Prince Leopold of Belgium, Frederick Duke of York, Queen Victoria and Prince Albert. Collectors will also find portraits of Alexander I of Russia, Louis XVIII of France, Washington, Wellington, Napoleon, Blücher and innumerable others. Most of these profiles were copied direct from medals, insignia or coins: occasionally the signature of the medallist appears in letters so minute as to be decipherable only with the aid of a glass.

Profile portraits were made to the commission of sitters now unknown. A wax model carved by one of the many wax portraitists then in business was supplied to the glasshouse, in a size nearly one-fifth larger than the completed sulphide. Any number of copies could be ordered, but not fewer than ten. A set of twelve matching tumblers, elaborately and deeply cut, has been noted, each with a portrait on one side and a coat of arms on the reverse.

The embedding of ceramic ornament in glass was a Bohemian invention of the mid-eighteenth century. There was little demand for this work, however, because the glass entirely lacked the flawless brilliance of Pellatt's metal, and because the unequal contraction of the glass and its enclosed cameo whilst cooling distorted the portrait.

Pellatt gave the name of sulphide to the cast bas-relief, which was composed of fine white china clay and supersilicate of potash. Care in the selection and grinding of these materials to flour-like fineness was essential to ensure that the sulphide would not fracture under the heat of the molten flint-glass. The sulphide was cast in a plaster of paris mould prepared from the coin, medal or carved wax portrait, and lightly fired until hard enough to be removed from the mould. After cooling slowly the features and finer lines were accentuated with delicate tools and the sulphide was ready for embedding in glass.

Apsley Pellatt used a superbly clear and brilliant flint-glass made in small piling pots (Chapter 1), using Australian sand free from oxide of iron and other impurities which might tint flint-glass, and oxide of lead free from Derbyshire blue (Chapter 1). The sulphide, heated to cherry redness in a small muffle, was enclosed within a molten mass of glass. Every speck and air-bubble had been carefully removed from the glass with a pair of shears, by a process described by Pellatt in the specification of his patent, and again in his book *Curiosities of Glassmaking*, 1849.

An elongated bubble was formed with a blow-pipe. The end distant from the pipe was cut open and the red-hot sulphide deftly inserted with the aid of small pincers. "The outer edges are then collapsed and welded together by pressure at a red heat, so that the figure is in the centre of the hollow glass pocket. The workman next applies his mouth to the end of the tube, while re-warming the glass at the other extremity. But instead of blowing, he exhales the air, thus perfecting the collapse by atmospheric pressure, and causing the glass and sulphide to become one homogeneous mass." More glass was then gathered around the sulphide-glass mass and it was tooled to the desired shape. When hollow-ware was decorated the red-hot sulphide was more conveniently laid upon the shaped outer surface of the vessel raised to approximately the same temperature at the glory hole. A blob of plastic glass spread evenly over and around the sulphide fused it invisibly with the rest of the glass, entrapped air-bubbles being forced out. The sulphide thus appeared to be embedded in a single thickness of glass. This work required skilful care in annealing to avoid distortion of the sulphide. The high cost was mainly due to the expense of preparing the ultra-fine glass which at that time could be made only in very small pots, and to the large percentage of sulphides damaged during the process of incrustation or distorted during annealing.

Coloured sulphides such as crests and flowers are extremely rare. They were modelled in refractory material and painted with metallic oxide colours before being encased in flint-glass. In some instances a white bas-relief might be superimposed upon a coloured opaque base.

Pellatt was also responsible for a series of sulphides enclosed in pressed glass by a method protected by his patent of 1831. These were chiefly used as plaques and for decorating sugar basins. Their silvery glow is dull in comparison with the earlier series. The sulphide, made exactly as before, was inserted by means of a slide cut in the mould in which the glass was being shaped. The piece was then reheated and re-pressed.

Sulphides applied to the surface of hollow-ware were usually framed with well-designed cutting in deep relief to mask the slight thickening of the glass. The plain oval containing the sulphide was so curved that it magnified the cutting seen through the vessel. Frequently a radial star was cut beneath the base of a footed article, often carried over the rim to the upper surface of the foot. This produced serrated edges, alternate serrations being decorated with strawberry cutting. Similar cutting might ornament bottle stoppers. Deeply-cut vertical furrows with fields of strawberry cutting are also characteristic. To enhance refractive light the backs of plaques, medallions and flat disc paperweights were cut with star radii or crossing lines. Medallion rims might be faceted or cut in elaborate scallops or points. On rare occasions an example is discovered marked "Pellatt & Co".

Only when the minute size of some specimens of *crystallo ceramie* is taken into consideration, such as ring mountings and other jewellery, can the remarkable delicacy of this work be appreciated fully. Pendants containing portraits made to the commission of sitters now unknown were ordered for presentation purposes, sometimes as many as half a gross at a time, each enclosed in a morocco case. Many a pendant is oval or circular, its beauty enhanced with diamond-faceted knife-edges, but otherwise entirely plain with a gilded silver or heavily gilded bronze pendant ring at the top. Portraits of ladies are sometimes found in heart-shaped crystals.

Cut-glass flagons for scent and small bottles for aromatic vinegar set with sulphides were fashionable conceits for the handbag throughout the reign of George IV. They were provided with plain ground-in stoppers covered with silver or silver-gilt screw-on caps. The majority are flat and may be heart-shaped. One or both sides might be enriched with sulphides framed in heavily-cut ornament. The sides might be pillar cut, deeply serrated or diamond cut. In some instances a sulphide is set in a panel of relief diamonds and the back cut in horizontal grooves or diamond cutting. Portraits of members of the royal family were always popular on such bottles, and a few classical figures have been noted. A posy of garden flowers may ornament one side of a scent bottle. A frequent combination consists of a woman praying at a Gothic shrine with a troubadour on the reverse.

Toilet-water bottles for the dressing-table may be square or almost globular. In the square type one face displays a sulphide, the opposite face frequently being cut with large relief diamonds, the shoulders encircled with step-cutting. The ground-in stopper usually has a mushroom finial and the base is ground flat or star cut. The body of the nearly globular bottle is divided into three wide panels alternating with three narrow ones, the sulphide portrait or coat of arms appearing on a wide panel, while the narrow panels are cut with three diamonds.

Paperweights, the Georgians preferred the term "letter-weights" and the early Victorians "press-papers", may be flat plaques measuring between 3 and 6 inches in diameter, or rectangular, the edges framed with elaborate scallops and points. To enhance refraction and illuminate the sulphides the backs were cut with star radii, cross lines and facets, or with cross-cut or strawberry diamonds. Another attractive type is circular with the portrait against a ground of close-cut rays, the rim ground to a bevel. Favourite sulphides for these were members of the royal family, in particular a profile bust of George IV in coronation robes and wearing the Garter. The king is also found modelled to resemble a

Roman Caesar. Another paperweight design consists of a flat circular or square base which may be stepped, supporting a vertical tapering plaque, its upper edge serrated, containing a sulphide seen against a ground of deep horizontal cutting. In 1849 Pellatt described these as suitable for press-papers or chimney ornaments.

Ice-plates measuring about 6 inches in diameter and star-cut beneath were illustrated in Pellatt's first book, *Memoir on the Origin, Progress and Improvement of Glass Manufacture*, 1821 where he recorded that "sets of these have been executed in varied fancy or classical subjects, also with arms and crests". Bas-reliefs of Christ and the Madonna were made, set in benitiers, reliquaries and candlesticks intended for devotional use.

The success of Pellatt's *crystallo ceramie* was such that it encouraged other workers in cut glass to set aromatic vinegar bottles with medallions in the fine earthenware known as jasper ware, usually blue with the profile in white. These, of course, were on the surface of the glass and enclosed in frames of double gilded brass cemented into position.

The repeal of the excise duty created a demand for decorative flint-glass among those previously unable to afford the luxury. *Crystallo ceramie*, which had declined in popularity from about 1828, again became popular, particularly paperweights containing portraits of celebrities, but now made less expensively by a simpler method than Pellatt's. Because they were embedded in flint-glass of no better than standard quality, their silvery sheen was less brilliant than that of the early series. The composition of sulphides remained unaltered, but they were less meticulously finished.

The process for making these cheap crystal cameos, issued in varying qualities until about 1865, was published during 1850 in a report on china decoration. "Prepare a copper mould, whose size and depth depends upon the size and thickness of the cameo to be incrusted. The first workman pours in molten glass from his dipper; a second levels the surface with his copper palette knife and puts in the cameo, face downward; a third workman pours more molten glass on the back of the cameo which is thus held between two layers of glass; the man with the palette knife gently presses the mass in the mould. An apprentice carries the hot mould in a pair of tongs to the glory hole where two minutes heating is usually sufficient to set the glass, no matter what size the object." The ground layer of glass might be coloured, either amber, ruby or black.

A variant was issued in about 1850 and continued in demand for about ten years. In this the embedded sulphide takes the form of a small trinket modelled in the round and brightly decorated with metallic oxide paints, the colours set by stoving at high temperature before being embedded in the plastic glass.

Exquisite crystal cameo paperweights, door handles, decanter stoppers and flower vases, of a quality comparable with those of Apsley Pellatt, were made for a few years from about 1875 by John Ford & Company, Edinburgh. More than seventy different sulphides from this source have been listed. Sulphide portraits of Queen Victoria were embedded in cube paperweights on the occasion of the 1887 Jubilee. The majority of these sulphides are slightly flawed.

A series of paperweights, which at first glance may appear to be crystal cameos, were made during the 1850s, when they were catalogued as medallion paperweights. These are flat, circular or hexagonal blocks of flint-glass which whilst plastic have been impressed beneath with deep, intaglio portraits. After annealing and cooling the weights were clouded by dipping into hydrofluoric acid. Grinding removed this clouding from the smooth surfaces which were then highly polished. The portrait remained clouded and when viewed from above greatly resembles a silvery sulphide enclosed within clear crystal.

The cloudy finish might also be left as decoration to the edges. The finest paperweights of this type were made by William Kidd, 12 Poland Street, London. Others with elaborately cut borders were made by the firms of Lloyd & Summerfield, and F. & C. Osler, both of Birmingham. The long series of portraits include royalty and all the leading ecclesiastical, military, naval, scientific, political and stage celebrities of the period.

Chapter Nineteen

MILLEFIORI WORK AND OTHER ASSOCIATED PAPERWEIGHTS

GLASS paperweights radiant with brilliantly coloured florets, like flowers in a Victorian posy, are spectacularly successful revivals of early Victoriana. The most exquisite of these with their cunningly devised circles and spirals, wheels and florets of brilliant unfadable colours were made in France during the late 1840s. It is seldom realized, however, that hundreds of thousands in a quality little inferior were made in England at Stourbridge, Birmingham, London and Bristol.

The decorative motifs in these little weights were themselves fashioned in glass, coloured, opaque-white, silver and striped. These were then embedded in clear, solid, weighty flint-glass of fine quality, dome-shaped and polished to magnify and enhance their brilliance. These have come to be known as millefiori work—the Italian "glass of a thousand flowers". So appealing did such paperweights prove that millefiori work was extended to a considerable range of minor glass-ware, from bottles to buttons. At the same time, heavily leaded flint-glass was so obviously ideal for paperweights and the larger weights used as door porters, that such weights are to be found encasing a number of other ornamental motifs but bearing a general resemblance to the millefiori work. Colourful birds and butterflies, snakes, fruits and geometrical designs are to be noted among such wares. Only a little further removed are the flowers modelled in the round, or presented in silhouette, and the earliest designs of all that were no more than cascades of air bubbles, coolly green and remarkably effective.

A typical millefiori weight consists of a flat base of clear or latticinio glass on which a pattern is arranged with an assortment of many-coloured florets, wheels, spirals and occasionally more elaborate shapes, thinly sliced from multi-coloured rods of glass. This meticulously neat and indivi-dual design is enlarged and intensified by the solid mass of flint-glass over and around it. All types of millefiori glass-work are based on the fact that flint-glass can be built up layer by layer and yet appear a clear homogeneous mass, in which the fragments of coloured glass appear to be suspended.

Colourful glass paperweights were probably first made in England by W. H. P. & J. Richardson of Wordsley, near Stourbridge, who produced enamelled and cased glass immediately after the abolition of the glass tax in 1845. The first to make fine millefiori work was Apsley Pellatt, who introduced into his London glasshouse two Frenchmen already experienced in this work. In 1849, when Pellatt issued his slender volume on *Curiosities of Glassmaking*, he displayed a colour plate captioned: "A specimen of modern French Mille-Fiori Glass—formerly made by the ancients and the Venetians: it consists of slices of the ends of canes of various colours, inclosed in white transparent glass." Elsewhere in his book Pellatt wrote: "Millefiori Glass consists of a great variety of ends of fancy-coloured tubes, cut sectionally, at right angles with the filligree cane, to form small lozenges or tablets; and these, when placed side by side, and massed together by transparent Glass, have the appearance of an innumerable series of flowers or rosettes."

English makers of millefiori work included also George Bacchus & Sons, Dartmouth Street, Birmingham, whose "millefiori letter-weights" were exhibited at the Society of Arts in 1848; J. G. Green, London, who had an example of his work illustrated in colour by Sir M. Digby Wyatt in *Industrial Arts of the Nineteenth Century*, 1852; James Powell & Sons, White Friars Glasshouse, London; Davis, Great-head & Green, Stourbridge; Thomas Hawkes & Company, Dudley; Harris, Rice & Son, Islington Glassworks. The Jury responsible for inspecting "the glass mosaic, mille-fiori and Venetian glass paper-weights" at the Great Exhibi-tion of 1851 reported that "the mille-fiori style of work adopted for making *presse-papiers* and other ornaments and sold in their hundreds of thousands, has become a very important branch of glass manufacture". Earlier in the same year the *Birmingham Journal*, 1851, had already "millefiori which is now in use as letter weights, an elegant ornament made here only within the last two or three years," and added that "our workmen have quite mastered the mysteries of manufacture".

English millefiori paperweights may be classified into four chronological groups, according to their methods of manufacture:

1. Venetian balls, 1845–57;
2. Venetian star-work or early millefiori, 1846–50;
3. Fine-quality millefiori, 1848–60;
4. Late millefiori, 1870–85.

The Venetian balls may be shaped as spheres, cubes, ovoids or rhomboids. They display no more than a crude suggestion of the millefiori effects, their colourful interiors being composed of scraps of filigree enamel haphazardly conglomerated together. This mass of colour was inserted into an elongated bubble of transparent flint-glass blown by the glassworker with his blow-pipe. The end of the bubble away from the pipe was cut across and the core quickly inserted with the aid of pincers. The cut was then reheated and closed by welding. More glass was gathered round this and hand-tooled to the shape and size desired for the paperweight. Those with flat sides were cut and polished. Such weights, dating from 1845 to 1847 and even later, are now very rare. They seldom measure more than 3 inches across.

Venetian balls were soon superseded by the earliest true millefiori work, then known as Venetian star-work and dating from 1846 to about 1850. It was in Venetian star-work, a name given by Apsley Pellatt, that English glassmen first introduced the little florets and multicoloured circles cut as thin slices from long rods of variously prepared glass canes. The construction of such canes was a craft in its own right, each cane containing the same built-up concentric pattern of variously arranged clear and coloured glass, opaque and transparent, throughout its length.

Collectors have grouped paperweights of this period into three classes: large or magnum, measuring more than 3¼ inches in diameter; medium or normal, measuring between 3¼ inches and 2 inches in diameter; and small or miniature, with a diameter of less than 2 inches. They have also been classed in accordance with decorative details: (*a*) the compact or close millefiori; (*b*) patterned millefiori with florets arranged geometrically; (*c*) scattered millefiori with florets spaced at regular intervals over a latticinio or other ground.

To make a Venetian star-work paperweight two layers of clear glass were shaped into a hollow dome by blowing, and thin slices cut from the rods were introduced through an opening at the top, and arranged inside it, "in geometric patterns, regular design, or haphazardly", accurate placement so far being a difficult feat. The dome was then reheated at the furnace mouth, and air was expelled from the hot glass so that the outer layer of flint-glass closed tightly over the decorative slices within. This homogeneous mass was then enclosed in a thick covering of clear glass which fused imperceptibly over the rest.

The collector of today, however, recognizes the styles that succeeded Venetian star-work as more typical millefiori work. The dome is entirely of fine flint-glass, and the carefully arranged bed of kaleidoscopic colour restricted to the flat base. Tiny transverse slices cut from the glass canes were arranged on a cushion of glass and clear molten glass poured over them and shaped. When polished, this dome magnified and enhanced the beauty of the design.

Cane-making was a complicated, time-taking operation, possible only because of the extreme ductility of glass. The materials from which the canes were made melted at a higher temperature than the flint-glass which subsequently enveloped them. This obviated the dangers of distortion and running colours, such as may be observed in some very early examples.

Each cane, whether simple or complex, was formed by encircling a central core of glass with concentric layers of glass in various colours which were plated on to it. Most simply, a gather of glass on the end of a punty rod was rolled on a flat surface to make it cylindrical and some 6 inches long, dipped into glass of another colour and rolled again. Ruby red, green and blue glass might be combined with opaque-white in successive platings. Should a wavy outline to one colour be required, this was tool-shaped on the outer surface of the plated cylinder, the following layer restoring the cylinder to a rounded pencil shape which repeated dippings built up to a diameter of nearly 3 inches.

This short cylinder, consisting of several thick layers of varicoloured glass, was then reheated and a second punty rod attached to the opposite end. Two men, each holding one of the punty irons, moved rapidly backwards from each other over a wooden track, elongating the glass rod suspended between them. To prevent sagging and distortion the irons were kept continually rotated, and to assure uniform elongation a boy walked quickly alongside fanning the glass. The cane, lengthened until it was less than one-twelfth of its former diameter, was cut when cold into slices one-quarter of an inch thick, these being whetted off with a steel file. Every one of these slices displayed unaltered, but in miniature, the design created by the plating process. No annealing was necessary.

Innumerable patterns were produced by varying this basic method. For instance, if the original core, after its first plating, were inserted into a perpendicularly ribbed mould, this corrugated its surface. This might then be plated with opaque-white and rolled into cylindrical form again, producing a cogwheel design in the centre of the finished slice.

For greater elaboration, a cylinder might be set in a mould whose inner walls were lined with thin rods, crystal alternating with colour. These would adhere to the hot cylinder, surrounding it with coloured stripes. A final plating of opaque-white would convert this once again into a cylinder ready for drawing. The rims of slices cut from such a cane appear to be encircled with coloured dots, for the intervening clear glass is indistinguishable from its background.

Cross-sections of cane may include central microscopic

silhouette images of profile portraits, horses, dogs, goats, deer, rabbits, elephants, monkeys, flowers, trefoils and other devices. Although these are relatively scarce in English paperweights they were simple to make. An open cylindrical mould with the inside shaped to the required design was cast in gunmetal and the cavity filled with molten black glass. This was lifted from the mould by means of the punty rod, dipped into pot metal of a contrasting colour, such as white, scarlet or vivid purple, and then rolled into cylindrical form. Additional platings of coloured glass were then applied, forming an elaborate framework for the silhouette. This again might be enlivened by a circle of colourful rods.

Slices cut from the canes were sorted into sectioned trays, similar to those used by printers for hand-set type, and were lifted out with tweezers for incorporating into the pattern. Each was heated at the lamp and, when sufficiently plastic, was placed upon the disc of flint-glass that formed the basis of what were known in the trade first as Victorian flower clusters and later as set-ups. The paperweight-makers' lamp was an apparatus consisting of a pair of blowlamp flames directed towards each other. This lamp was also used for reheating set-ups, and for reheating and modelling ornamental motifs used in hand modelling. The beauty of the finished weight naturally depended on the skill of the women at this work who, with slight rearrangements of the same range of canes, were able to produce a seemingly unlimited variety of patterns.

The cushion of glass mosaic was now ready for its clear-glass base and magnifying dome. The base was shaped first. The set-up was laid, pattern downward, on a brass plate, heated, and topped with a conical ring. This shaped the molten flint-glass dropped into it. The weight was then taken up by its newly-acquired base on a punty iron and dipped into more clear glass to form the dome. Whilst plastic this was tooled to shape by the glassmaker at his chair whilst the punty rod was rotated on its sloping metal arms. Internal cracks were avoided by ensuring that all parts of the weight were kept at the same temperature during assembly.

These paperweights were made in several shapes, such

as hemispheres, cones, ovoids and the ever-popular mushroom or bun-shape. Bases were variously treated. The punty mark was ground off and the whole base might be made concave before being polished, so as to present a diminished version of the millefiori mosaic, in contrast to the magnification achieved by the dome above. Or a star might be cut into the base, small in very early work, but later extending to the perimeter. The flash star, dating from the time of the Great Exhibition of 1851, consists of two stars cut one within the other. Alternatively the base might be ground perfectly flat and criss-crossed with lines cut at right angles to prevent it slipping on the desk. In later work less satisfactory pressing was substituted for cutting. Some of the cheaper paperweights and most of the heavier, larger weights designed as door-porters were fire-polished.

Fascinating effects were achieved by introducing opaque coloured "overlays" on the surface of the clear glass dome. The millefiori set-up was built in the usual way but before being polished the weight was given a thick overlay of opaque-white enamel followed by an outer casing of one or two coats of coloured pot metal. Wonderful effects were produced by grinding the surface of the paperweight to form shallow circular or oval concavities, each about the size of half a crown and usually arranged at the apex, and equally spaced at five positions around the sides. These, when polished, revealed clear crystal windows through which the colourful millefiori could be viewed against a shining white background. The colours most frequently encasing overlay paperweights are turquoise, dark blue, rose Dubarry, pink and emerald green. The windows may be edged with radiating flutes.

The background against which the millefiori design was arranged, known as the cushion, may be either transparent, opaque-white, pale or dark blue, green or amber. On elaborate work the cushion may contain opaque-white or blue and white Venetian latticinio, full of twists and curls. This latticinio background consisted of a criss-cross mesh network formed by fine threads of coloured glass, usually in a spiral effect. Variations in latticinio design are endless: some one hundred and twenty patterns were included in one individual collection. This type of filigree is seen to exquisite effect in the coraline paperweight, wherein slices of millefiori and fragments of spiral filigree appear to be held in suspension above a cushion of latticinio.

Venetian latticinio cushions are also an effective foil for the colourful glass motifs hand-modelled in the round into birds, posies, clusters of fruit, butterflies and moths, and other paperweight ornaments, including the rare snakes and lizards. These were made by the firm of Bacchus in Birmingham and possibly elsewhere. The modelling of these central units was delicate work. In the case of single objects the glass-worker gathered a lump of plastic glass on his punty rod and dexterously modelled it with tools. But the more complicated work, costly in time, was modelled entirely at the lamp. Each petal, leaf and stem or other motif was separately shaped from a piece of specially prepared glass and the parts skilfully assembled. The illusion of reality was heightened by impressing leaves with vein marks, small instruments being specially designed for the purpose. Tiny apples and pears and other fruit were squeezed into shape from solid pieces of glass. Sometimes such decorations are separated from the cushion by a thin sheet of crystal, giving the motif the appearance of floating on air. The set-up, complete with its cushion, was then "capped", that is, enclosed within its magnifying dome of crystal.

Several flint-glasshouses at this time possessed specialist departments in colour work, making coloured, cased and enamelled glass. Their factory facilities and the technical skill available urged them to mass-produce individual units —canes, latticinio and other ornaments—selling them to other glasshouses who made the actual set-ups and converted them into paperweights and a variety of other glass objects. These units, known to the trade as "paperweight goods", enabled any capable glassworker to assemble acceptable millefiori work, and were also exported.

In their final phase Victorian millefiori paperweights were made in a hit-or-miss style, and frequently the women assemblers copied designs from numbered diagrams placed before them. The coloured slices were of rather greater diameter than formerly, and therefore not so numerous.

A note on French millefiori paperweights may not be out of place here. They were made during the late 1840s at Baccarat and St. Louis in the Vosges Mountains and in the old city of Clichy, a suburb of Paris. A vein of outstandingly pure white sand extends from the Vosges to Fontainebleau. Consequently these three glasshouses, specialists in making glass for optical purposes, produced a crown glass celebrated for its purity and brilliance, free from striae, bubbles and other defects. English glassmen found it impossible to compete against this superb, but expensive, glass.

Of these three glasshouses, La Compagnie des Cristalleries de Baccarat produced the most meticulously set, perfectly balanced paperweights of the millefiori type. Many of those made between 1845 and 1849 were signed with the letter B and dated. In this connection it is interesting to note that a millefiori paperweight bought on Brighton Pier in 1848 for half a crown contains the letter B, but without a date. It appears reasonable to ascribe this, and others similarly marked, not to Baccarat but to the Birmingham firm of Bacchus. The firm was at that time exhibiting such weights in the house of the Society of Arts.

The signed and dated paperweights of Baccarat were the work of two men, father and son, named Battestini, later changed to Batest. These glassmen, experts in colour work, went to Baccarat from Venice in about 1815 and remained there until the elder Batest's death in 1850. The father was immensely proud of the fine millefiori work he began making in about 1844 and, after perfecting the technique, he insisted on signing his paperweights with the initial of his surname and the date. At the same time he incorporated tiny silhouettes of animals, birds and fish into a few of his canes. The son gave a further identifying touch to his own productions by including a silhouette elephant in each paperweight. Study of a series of these dated paperweights shows that by 1849 the younger man was exceeding even the fine craftsmanship of his father.

Baccarat signatures vary with the size of the paperweight. In miniatures the date is so tiny that only a keen eye will detect it. Dates range from 1845 to 1849, the latter being rare: B in conjunction with either of the dates 1845 or 1849 is very rare indeed in a genuine specimen. Paperweights patterned geometrically with florets are found only in the medium size: all others are to be met with in three sizes. In weights of this class with solid backgrounds the B and date occupy a circular area, the upper layer of cane apparently removed to accommodate the tiny date panel. In paperweights with lacy backgrounds the date panels are inserted without disturbing the decorative detail. St. Louis and Clichy, believing the B stood for Bacarrat, similarly marked their finest paperweights with the initials of their firms and the date.

The original St. Louis glasshouse still operates, but only as a branch of the Baccarat establishment. One series of St. Louis paperweights is to be distinguished by the presence of a cane containing tiny dancing figures in silhouette. Details otherwise closely resemble those of Baccarat. A type not known to have been made elsewhere is the St. Louis crown with alternate transparent and opaque spirals radiating from a central coloured floret. Fine quality St. Louis paperweights were usually marked with the initials S. L., and a date is sometimes included: 1847 is rare, 1848 frequent, suggesting increased output from that year.

The Clichy glasshouse was founded in 1840 and closed thirty years later. A characteristic of Clichy paperweights is the presence of the factory symbol, a pink and white rose, incorporated somewhere in the pattern. A purple rose and an open purple flower are features exclusive to Clichy. Some of the Clichy paperweights are signed with a C in black, green or red in the centre of a cane: rare examples bear the name "Clichy" in fine letters.

In addition to paperweights a variety of glass objects may contain colourful millefiori decoration, including small tazzas for wax wafers, shot glasses for holding writing quills, inkpots and scent bottles with floral mosaics in stoppers and bases, curtain-pole ends with knobs as large as pineapples, exquisitely faceted with shallow diamond-cutting, door knobs, bell pulls, tumblers with millefiori designs in the base.

There was a demand also for puzzle bottles apparently filled with water in which the mosaic seemed to be lying loosely. It would be suggested that the water be poured out and the ornaments examined. This was, of course, impossible as there was only a teaspoonful of water in a small cavity at the top, the rest of the bottle being solid glass.

Egg shapes of solid glass containing coloured canes sliced diagonally and thrown in haphazardly were known as ladies' hand coolers. They were devised when costume was voluminous and at the same time cool hands were essential to gentility. Hand-kissing was then a fashionable salute, the lady holding the glass in the palm of the hand until the moment of the ceremony, when it was dexterously transferred to the other hand. More frequently and prosaically, however, these egg shapes served as stocking darners.

Glass buttons containing colourful millefiori work were fashionable dress accessories for men and women between about 1846 and about 1860. Few appear to remain: consequently complete sets are valuable, such as a fancy waistcoat set. As in the early Venetian ball, the core of the early type of button consists of pieces of coloured filigree enamel glass conglomerated irregularly. This "Venetian ball" button has a wire-loop shank with both ends inserted into the glass. Both spherical and ovoid buttons were made during the mid-1850s with this decoration at their bases under coverings of clear flint-glass which were sometimes flattened.

Next came the true millefiori type, requiring exceptionally delicate workmanship. These buttons are ball-shaped and early examples have heavy wire-loop shanks. Decoration may be near the base of the button, in the centre, or near the top. Between 1850 and 1855 such buttons might be faceted: later the upper surface might be lightly impressed with a simple motif. A wire-loop shank with a shank plate was usual on such a button from about 1852; shortly afterwards came the square or four-way shank. Shoe buttons in several sizes were made of millefiori scraps without a final coating of glass. A later Victorian button consisted of a central core covered with metal foil. This was dipped into fine crystal glass. Millefiori buttons were imported from Czechoslovakia and Japan between 1925 and 1939: colour is much brighter and harder than in their early Victorian counterparts.

Paperweights were also imported with crowns slightly higher than English paperweights of similar diameter. In many instances set-ups were not cut evenly, with the result that some canes project slightly below the design: when viewed from the side this uneven effect is conspicuous. The glass is hard and brilliant and in some instances displays a slight trace of yellow. Millefiori paperweights are now being made in England by at least three firms, one series containing a cane signed PY, the initials of Paul Ysard of Perth.

Flower motifs were always favourites with the makers of glass paperweights, the persuasive millefiori work by no means being the first or only style. Less flatly meticulous and often notably graceful flowers were poised in taller, heavier weights, often large enough to serve as door porters. The earliest of these, in high-crowned, egg-shaped weights, appeared before 1830, containing fountain-sprays of flowers in the silvery style of early sulphides (Chapter 18), with tiny air-bubbles like dew drops on their leaves, and the general colouring a subdued watery-green.

Probably the very first were the somewhat more crudely finished specimens decorated with elongated bubbles and known in the West Country as dumps. Such a weight was made by gathering a ball of viscous glass on a punty iron, allowing it to cool somewhat, and then piercing it deeply to form small conical depressions at regular intervals. When this core was embedded within a second gathering of hot glass the air enclosed in the depressions expanded, forming air-bubbles of various shapes and sizes. Further depressions were made and the process repeated several times. The bubbles were elongated by swinging the dump on the end of the punty iron. The centre of the flattened base in this type of dump was left concave, showing the rough scar caused by breaking the punty iron from the finished piece: the more finely finished dumps were ground flat beneath.

Glass dumps were made at Bristol and Nailsea from about 1828, and at Birmingham and Castleford a few years later. Although it is difficult to distinguish between the green bottle-glass of Bristol and Nailsea during this period it is generally conceded that the brighter pieces were made at Bristol, the softer hues at Nailsea. The coarse bottle-greens were made in Birmingham. Soft transparent greens coloured with metallic oxide date from 1845 onwards and are in flint-glass.

An early Nailsea type, later made at Birmingham, Stourbridge and Newcastle, contains a filmy, silvery flower-pot supporting flowers of the same composition "growing" in two or three tiers, with tiny bubbles like dew on the petals. The motif was arranged to suggest a fountain spraying up from the base, the general colouring being a subdued watery-green. The flower-pot was made by gathering and shaping a small quantity of molten glass on the punty iron and then swiftly dipping it into a mixture of white clay and water, which gave it a silvered, crizzled appearance. This core of glass was then reheated at the furnace mouth and more molten glass gathered and shaped around it. When the second gathering of metal had cooled slightly, it was pierced at three points by a sharpened apple-wood stick that had been dipped into the clay mixture. At regular intervals around these depressions single spots of water were dropped on the glass surface, forming silvery petals. More molten glass was gathered over this and the process repeated two or three times.

The cascades of pear-shaped bubbles which form the decoration on other glass door-porters were made by piercing the red-hot glass to any desired depth with a cold steel instrument, sharply pointed, and quickly withdrawing it. The layer of glass which collected over each indentation completed the formation of a pear-shaped air-bubble.

Door-porters of flint-glass date from the late 1840s onwards. These were heavily leaded and usually have a smoky hue. At this time Birmingham and Stourbridge began making giant specimens enlivened with tiny air-bubbles fountaining up from the centre base and cascading down the sides. Millefiori door-porters were also made.

When coloured glass motifs dominated paperweight design a new style of flower spray was devised. This fountained up from a Venetian ball base consisting of fragments of multicoloured opal glass, or from a conical "vase", the up-sweeping stalks of streaked opal glass supporting enamel flowers—ruby, blue, purple, green and yellow. Such sprays were made at the blowlamp with enamels capable of resisting the heat required to melt the flint-glass that enclosed them. The base and spray were placed in the centre of an iron ring and a gathering of molten flint-glass poured over them and tooled into a tall dome. In the course of this process, tiny bubbles of air were trapped around the flower petals. These silvery air-bubbles are viewed at their best when shielded with the hands from all side lighting: they then appear as ghost petals of the flowers themselves.

The coloured mound occupies only half the area of the paperweight base, and the spray is similarly proportioned. Yet the spray appears to fill the entire interior of the glass. In Victorian paperweights of this type colours have a mellow quality: modern reproductions are garishly tinted and lack the silvery air-bubbles.

Of these weights, too, inexpensive variants were made during the 1850s. Instead of the modelled flower spray the decorative motif was a simple flat silhouette, such as a butterfly or bird executed in metal foil, vividly coloured and patterned with spangles.

Infinitely more appealing among early Victorian glass paperweights was the design in which movement of the weight magically produced a snow-storm within the crystal dome. Fortunate indeed today is the owner of such a weight with the chemistry of its drifting storm still in working order. Copies are now being sold, but they lack the delicate craftsmanship of those created a century ago.

Chapter Twenty

CASED AND OVERLAY, FLASHED, STAINED, SPUN,
MOTHER-OF-PEARL AND SILVERED GLASS

THOSE who toured the Continent in the early nineteenth
century enthusiastically adorned their dining-tables and
dressing-rooms on their return with specimens of colourful
Bohemian work known as cased or overlay glass. Those
tall, slim decanters and wine-glasses, eau-de-cologne bottles
and powder boxes, in two-colour effects, were not made in
England until 1845. The colour combinations then developed included ruby and white, green and white, blue and
white, red and gold, blue and gold, and green and gold, cut
with large thumb-prints and other devices.

Casing was a decorative technique that had been practised
by the glassmen of ancient Rome. Layers of different
coloured glass were laid over a basis of clear glass and cut
obliquely to produce patterns composed of rainbow stripes
bordering clear, highly-polished, light-reflecting flint-glass.
The Bohemian soda-glass did not possess the quality of
dispersing light that contributed largely to the success of
the English flint-glass. Immediately the excise tax was
abolished in 1845 English glassmen became formidable
competitors with their higher quality materials. Perfect
regularity of surface in the concentric layers of colour was
quickly achieved, and as many as five layers might be
applied, compared with two in Bohemian work. A great
stimulus to the new decoration was provided by the 1851
exhibition, resulting in a considerable vogue which lasted
until the mid-1860s. Bohemian cased glass remained cheaper
than English, but its quality was inferior. In 1847 there
were 160 glasshouses in Bohemia compared with 40 in
Murano and about the same number in England.

Glassmen engaged in cased glass manufacture needed to be exceptionally skilful and to work with unusual speed. A casing of white enamel glass was prepared by inflating a gather, knocking off the knot that formed at the end, and spreading the sides to form a cup-like shell. This was placed in a gunmetal mould of corresponding shape, and a gather of clear flint-glass gently blown into it. The white shell adhered to the colourless transparent glass and was withdrawn with it from the mould. The whole was then reheated to complete the fusion of the two layers. Other colours were applied over this in a similar manner. The mass thus formed was reheated and tooled into its final shape. After the glass had been annealed the glass-cutter ground through the overlying casings so that parts of each colour were revealed and incorporated into a design. This was achieved by grinding off parts of the outer layers with a convex stone wheel and by cutting through to the flint-glass. The opaque-white overlays were of considerable thickness requiring lengthy cutting to penetrate to the flint-glass. The final surface, partly coloured and partly clear, was brilliantly finished with a polishing mixture of tripoli, putty and oil.

The colouring matter in the pot metal used for casings consisted of various metallic oxides which were combined with suitable fluxes so that they fused at progressively lower temperatures than the flint-glass base. The glassmen employed in this work needed to possess exact knowledge of the effect of great heat upon the metallic oxides used.

The interplay of the colourful outer layers with the opaque-white inner layer and the scintillating flint-glass basis was usually considered sufficiently decorative, particularly when faceted or cut with geometrical patterns. Sometimes, however, further enrichment was added. This might take the form of engraving and deep cutting in a variety of shapes. Vine leaves and grapes constituted favourite decorative motifs on the surfaces of decanters, drinking-glass bowls and wine-glass coolers.

Vases are uncommon, and may be regarded as a class of their own. Their colours are always clear and intense, and their cutting sharp and geometrically accurate. A series of superb vases came from the Birmingham firm of Bacchus in the 1850s. These have urn-shaped bodies with rolled-over rims, baluster stems and double-domed feet scalloped at the edges. These display motifs in deep ruby and wreaths of green ivy upon a casing of white enamel. The same firm also issued the rare cased glass vase in the form of a colourful goblet, the bowl serving as a calyx to the flower-shaped container, tall and narrow, rising from its centre.

Lucky is the collector who discovers an example of the black cased vases made by Rice, Harris & Son, Birmingham. These are richly cut with scrolls and strapwork, revealing the off-white overlay and enriched with gilding. This firm also issued a style of covered goblet with an exceptionally tall finial cased in ruby and white. This is cut with three shields, one displaying the arms of England and the other two bearing the monograms of Queen Victoria and Prince Albert.

Collectors will find a wide range of decanters with casings of three different colours. The lightest cutting through the coloured surface layer of such a vessel may bring a bloom to a bunch of grapes; the next layer of colour may appear in the shapes of vine leaves, whilst deeply cut flutings encircling the lower body, shoulders and neck may penetrate to the basic layer of clear flint-glass. Some long-necked decanters with plain glass bodies, which may be engraved, have cased necks and stoppers.

Drinking-glasses in cased glass usually have stems in solid colour, contrasting with the bowl decoration. The feet are usually greater in diameter than the bowl rims. The scar left by the punty rod was always eliminated by grinding, but traces may be detected with the finger. Contemporaneous Bohemian examples have thin foot rims, whereas in flint-glass these are invariably thick.

Cased glass may be further enhanced with applied ornament, such as enamelling in colours and gilding or silvering. The brush-applied enamels were composed of metallic oxides selected to fuse at a lower temperature than would melt the outer casing. Favourite colours from about 1857 were ruby, oriental blue, mazarine blue, turquoise, black, rose and apple green. From 1857 an opaline-green was produced from uranium by the firm of Lloyd & Summerfield, Birmingham, using the first gas-regenerating furnace built by Siemen.

Gilding was carried out with pure gold applied as a smooth brown paste containing fine gold dust amalgamated with mercury and rubbed up with fat oil. This was applied with a pencil brush. The glass was later fired at a low temperature, thus freeing the mercury and fixing the pure gold. This firing left the gold with a matt surface. A brilliant, lasting lustre was secured by polishing with a bloodstone.

Cased glass might also be decorated by the less expensive process of acid-etching. This was first carried out on English cased glass by Henry Richardson of Wordsley in the late 1850s: it had long been practised in Bohemia. The glass was dipped into melted wax. Standard patterns were inscribed and scraped into this film by means of a series of sharp and blunt needles. The glass was then dipped into hydrofluoric acid which ate into the unprotected glass, thus producing the design. Such pieces are less desirable than hand-cut glass. Etched ornament is easily distinguished from engraving by its thin shallow lines: designs, too, are clumsier than hand engravings on cased glass.

Cased flint-glass, not yet classed as antique, is already difficult to acquire. If of fine quality it is always weighty with deeply cut decoration, not merely shallow depressions. Emphasis was placed on brilliance of colour associated with delicacy of workmanship. Coarse-cut shallow ornament does not fall within the collector's province. All too often such examples are Czechoslovakian productions which were imported in large quantities from 1923 to 1938 and again more recently. Much of this is sold to the unwary as Regency glass. The majority of bowls, often on pedestal stems, and the shouldered decanters with mushroom stoppers are from this source.

A less costly style of coloured flint-glass dating to the same period is flashed glass. This was made in a range of articles following the same shapes as the work in cased or overlay glass, and by the uninitiated it is often classed as the more costly, highly-skilled work. Flashed glass was, in fact, a means of economizing on the enamel overlay and on the quantity of coloured glass used. A gathering of clear flint-glass was inflated, allowed to cool slightly, and then dipped into molten coloured glass, known as pot metal, and quickly withdrawn. Thus the clear glass acquired a film of colour. It was then reheated, blown and tooled into shape, annealed and in some instances cut into the various styles described for cased glass.

When the glass is flashed yellow, the appearance of gold is very successfully imitated: deeper shades give bronze effects. By flashing with thin layers of various colours, and grinding the latter away in devices, an endless variety of harmonizing and contrasting effects could be obtained. One maker described these flashed combinations as "composed with due attention to chromatic harmony and proportion, and in adapting the vessels themselves to objects of ornament or use, a proper regard to purity of form is observed".

Stained table-glass made its appearance in about 1850 and was extensively used, representing another step in the endless attempt to decrease costs. The staining compound was brush-applied to annealed flint-glass which was then fired in a muffle-kiln. Chemical changes occurred which produced the colour and fixed it to the clear glass. Pressed and blown-moulded glass forms could be stained, whilst it was impossible to case them. Ruby stain was the most popular, but bright green had a considerable vogue. Designs were applied with the aid of stencils.

Clear and pale ruby glass very closely wound with delicately tinted glass threads constituted a mid-Victorian delight. At first the thread was spun by hand on a revolving wheel. Then in the mid-1860s Benjamin Richardson of Stourbridge patented a threading glass machine which made it possible for glass table-ware and vases to be ornamented in this way, "old gold" proving an immense success.

Mother-of-pearl glass, which is sometimes collected, was perfected in about 1880 by Thomas Webb of Stourbridge.

This purely ornamental glass was produced by blowing a core of white opaque glass in a pattern mould. Whilst the glass was still hot the outer surface was dipped into transparent coloured pot metal. A transparent crystal casing was applied over this. After annealing, the piece was placed in a tank where acid vapour acted on the surface and produced a satin-like finish. Several colour combinations might be applied on a single piece: an example recently noted was shaded from a pale orange to a reddish hue at the top, the whole displaying iridescence. The majority of specimens in this glass, however, have a milk-white lining and a coloured coating.

Silvered glassware scintillating with rainbow colours fascinated Victorians of the 1850s. For a brief five years this ornamental glass had a fashionable vogue, followed by a decade of second-rate productions sold in small provincial shops and at fairs. The finest of this glass was made by the London firm of Hale Thompson, using the Drayton process of silvering glass patented in 1848. Instead of a reflecting surface of mercury a much less costly silver solution was used. Thompson produced an extensive range of glass vessels such as comports, butter coolers, sugar basins, mustard pots, salt-cellars, vases, goblets, inkstands and so on. These were sold in their plain mirror form to decorators who cut, enamelled or gilded them. John Mellish exhibited a selection at the Great Exhibition of 1851, when the "new manufacturing art" attracted considerable notice.

Silvered glassware was blown double, one glass within the other, leaving a space between them that could be filled with Drayton's solution through a hole left in the base for that purpose. After silvering, the remaining solution was poured out and the opening hermetically sealed. The *Magazine of Art*, 1851, described the process:

"All tarnish from the action of the atmosphere, and wear from continued use, is prevented, and the brilliancy of the glass is preserved as long as the article remains whole; thus uniting the ordinary advantages of glass with the apparent solidity of silver, and forms the nearest resemblance to silver workmanship that can be attained.

"When the glass is cut, the brilliancy of the effect is heightened and the soft floating character of the lights is broken into countless scintillations. On the other hand, by grinding the glass surface, the reflection is dispersed, and the appearance of frosted silver and the delicate lustre of the pearl are produced. With coloured glass a wide scale of metallic hues is obtained. These dazzling tints may be compared to the plumage of the humming-birds and the wing-cases of tropical beetles. Indeed, there is not one of the gorgeous metallic tints with which the insect and feathered kingdoms are adorned, that may not be closely copied by this process." (See Chapter 17.) A century of exposure to the light has caused a yellowing of the silver in the inferior examples.

INDEX

(Plates are indicated by italic figures.)

Hartshorne, Albert, *Old English Glasses*, 27, 53, 55, 74
Hats, toothpick, moulded, 158
Hawkes, Thomas, 207
Heal, Sir Ambrose, 21, 37, 48, 105
Hearts, ornament, 167
Herringbone fringe, *see* Cutting
Henry VIII, 14, 88, 121
Higgins, Cecil, Museum, Bedford, *41*
Highmore, Joseph, 74
Hiring of banquet plates, 88
Hobnail cutting, *see* Cutting
Hogarth, William, conversation piece, 72
  "Tartuffe's Banquet", 48
Hollow knops, *see* Knops
Hollow stems, *see* Stems
Holly Hall Glasshouse, Dudley, 75, 106, 137
Homer, Edward, 183–4
Homer, J. G., 184
Honeycomb moulding, 130
Honeypots, pressed, 170
  and see Beehives
Hop and barley motif, *see* Engraving
Horizontal cutting, *see* Cutting
Houghton, John, 93
Howard Household Book, 88
Hughes, G. Bernard, *English, Scottish and Irish Table Glass*, 29, 40
Hunting horns, opal glass, *43*

Ice-cream glasses, 85
Ice plates, 88, 200, 204
Icicle drops, 116, 134, 135
Illuminaries, mantel chandelier, 116, 117, 118, 119, 120
Images in millefiori work, 211, 213
Imported glass, Bohemian, 180, 222
  Czechoslovakian, 216–17, 223
  French, 214–15
  Japanese, 216–17
  Venetian, 14, 29, 55, 172, 186
Impressed fluting, *13*
Ince and Mayhew, 117
Incised twist, *see* Stems
Indian club decanters, 106

Ingilby, Sir William, inventory, 91
Inkstands, silvered, 225
Inner surfaces of vessels indicative of manufacturing processes, 155
"Intagliated table-ware", 161
Invalid cups, 89
Iridescence on mother-of-pearl glass, 225
Irish glass, 134
  glasshouses, 142
  lustres, 119–20
  quality, 120
  and see Cork glass; Waterford glass
"Irish style" in glass cutting, 142
Islington Glass Works, 207

Jacob, John, trade card, *16*
Jacob's ladders, 187
Jacobite glasses, 7, *10*, *12*, 17, *20*, *40*
Jacobs, I., Bristol mark, *42*
James Stewart (Old Pretender), *12*
Japanese millefiori work, 216–17
Jars, chemists', 176
  Nailsea, 185
  pressed, 170
Jarves, Deming, 160
Jarvis, J. & A., 104
Jasperware, 204
Jelly glasses, 81, *2*
Johnson, Jerom, 86, 126
  trade card, 103
Jones brothers, glass sellers and cutters, 145
Jug covers, 198
Jugs, ale, *39*
  claret, 170
  cream, 165
  moulded, 157
  Nailsea, 185
  opaque-white glass, 176
  pressed, 165, 170
  water, 165, *39*

Keeling, John, 106
"Kentish fire", 71

SELECTED BIBLIOGRAPHY

Bate, Percy. *English Table Glass*. 1905.
Buckley, Francis. *History of Old English Glass*. 1925.
Buckley, Wilfred. *The Art of Glass*. 1939.
Arthur Churchill Ltd. *History in Glass*. 1937.
Downey, Alan. *The Story of Waterford Glass*. 1952.
Elville, E. M. *English Tableglass*. 1951.
—— *English and Irish Cut Glass, 1750–1950*. 1952.
—— *Paper-weights and Other Glass Curiosities*. 1954.
Fleming, Arnold. *Scottish and Jacobite Glass*. 1938.
Francis, Grant R. *Old English Drinking Glasses*. 1926.
Guttery, D. G. *From Broad-Glass to Cut Crystal*. 1956.
Haden, H. J. *Notes on the Stourbridge Glass Trade*. 1949.
Hartshorne, Albert. *Old English Glasses*. 1897.
Haynes, A. B. *Glass Through the Ages*. 1948.
Honey, W. B. *Glass*. 1946.
Hughes, G. Bernard. *English, Scottish and Irish Table Glass*. 1956.
Percival, Maciver. *The Glass Collector*. 1918.
Powell, H. J. *Glassmaking in England*. 1923.
Thorpe, W. A. *English and Irish Glass*. 1927.
—— *A History of English and Irish Glass*. 2 vols. 1929.
—— *English Glass*. 1935.
Westropp, M. S. D. *Irish Glass*. 1920.
Wine Trade Loan Exhibition of Drinking Vessels Catalogue (edited by André Simon). 1933.
Young, S. *The History of the Worshipful Company of Glass-Sellers of London*. 1913.